Blood Debts:

What Do Putin and Xi Owe Their Victims?

BLOOD DEBTS

What Do Putin and Xi Owe Their Victims?

WALTER C. CLEMENS, JR.

Westphalia Press
An Imprint of the Policy Studies Organization
Washington, DC
2023

BLOOD DEBTS: WHAT DO PUTIN AND XI OWE THEIR VICTIMS?

All Rights Reserved © 2023 by Policy Studies Organization

Westphalia Press
An imprint of Policy Studies Organization
1367 Connecticut Avenue NW
Washington, D.C. 20036
info@ipsonet.org

ISBN: 978-1-63391-930-3

Daniel Gutierrez-Sandoval, Executive Director
PSO and Westphalia Press

Updated material and comments on this edition can be found at the Westphalia Press website:
www.westphaliapress.org

For

The Children and Their Parents Who Have Suffered

Under These Power-mad Monsters

CONTENTS

INTRODUCTION: HOW CLOSE TO WORLD WAR III? ix

1. A RUSSIAN GENERAL AND A CHINESE DIPLOMAT PREDICT EVERYTHING 1

2. IMPERIAL REVIVALISM IS OLDER THAN PUTIN 9

3. WAS NATO TO BLAME? 31

4. RUSSIAN VALUES IN A "RUSSIAN WORLD" 49

5. PUTIN LAYS WASTE TO RUSSIA AS WELL AS UKRAINE 65

6. ARE RUSSIANS AGAIN "DIZZY WITH SUCCESS"? ARE CHINESE? 89

7. WHAT DO PUTIN AND XI OWE THEIR VICTIMS? 99

8. CAN—SHOULD—PUTIN AND XI REMAIN IN POWER? 133

9. TRIANGULAR DIPLOMACY IN THE AGE OF PUTIN, XI, AND BIDEN 147

10. CONFRONTING EVIL 167

11. WE VERSUS US: TOTALITARIAN TRENDS IN RUSSIA, CHINA, AND THE USA 191

12. REQUIEM FOR RUSSIA? FOR YIN AND YANG? A PERSONAL NOTE WITH ACKNOWLEDGMENTS 217

ABOUT THE AUTHOR 227

INDEX 229

INTRODUCTION: HOW CLOSE TO WORLD WAR III?

Our age faces multiple challenges. The most pervasive are those of the anthropocene epoch as humans change earth more than all natural forces combined. Human activities help rivers to flood and to disappear; harvests to bloom and to shrink; life spans to lengthen and be cut short; insects to multiply even as whales and elephants risk extinction. Entire civilizations have disappeared or are now disappearing. Among the traits being lost are some of the most attractive facets of Russia and China—the spirited uplift of Tchaikovsky and the harmonic balancing of Yin and Yang.

Starting around 2014, Vladimir Putin's Russia and Xi Jinping's China have led a global trend toward top-down, authoritarian rule and away from humane development and self-government. Putin and Xi have brutalized their own subjects and their neighbors and endangered all humanity. This book initiates a reckoning of what the dictatorships in Moscow and Beijing owe to their victims. It also outlines the factors that permit the West to enjoy peace and prosperity and asks whether such forces could ever reshape Russia and/or China. Unless their politics are transformed, they will not pay their debts.

Even as humans work to save whales and elephants, we need to avoid wars that could end all life. In just one year, Putin's war on Ukraine has cut short the lives of over 100,000 Ukrainians and 100,000 Russians, wounded even more, and forced millions of Ukrainians to flee their homes and try to live elsewhere. The leaders of Russia and China have done great harm to their own peoples as well as to others near and far. Their crimes against humanity create huge debts—at least $2 trillion from Russia to Ukraine. Their aggressive policies also endanger the United States, seen as their Number One enemy, and other nations—from Poland to Tibet to Vietnam. The policies of Vladimir Putin and Xi Jinping pose a danger of a global nuclear Armageddon. They pressure the United States and its partners to spend billions on defense—a serious drain on budgets and societal well-being.

Why consider all this? It may help us think about the dangers noted by the 2021 Nobel Peace Laureate Dmitry Muratov as he talked to the BBC in Moscow in March 2023.[1] Editor-in-chief of the outlawed *Nezavisimaya [Independent]Gazeta,* Muratov worried that nobody can know if, or when, Putin will push a nuclear button. The Russian *prezident* that same month announced plans to station tactical nuclear weapons in Belarus. One of Putin's closest aides, Nikolai Patrushev, warned that Russia had a "modern unique weapon capable of destroying any enemy, including the United States." Bluff or bluster? Muratov observed that Russian "state propaganda is preparing people to think that nuclear war isn't a bad thing." On TV channels "nuclear war and nuclear weapons are promoted as if they're advertising pet food." They announce: "We've got this missile, that missile, another kind of missile. They talk about targeting Britain and France; about sparking a nuclear tsunami that washes away America."[2]

Yet state propaganda also portrays Russia as a country of peace, unfairly threatened by Ukraine and the West. Many Russians believe it. "People in Russia have been irradiated by propaganda," Muratov explains: "Propaganda is a type of radiation. Everyone is susceptible to it, not just Russians. In Russia, propaganda is twelve TV channels, tens of thousands of newspapers, social media like VK [the Russian version of Facebook] that serves completely the state ideology."

Similar concerns have been voiced by Utah Senator Mitt Romney. He warned in 2022 that Russia's foreign minister and its ambassador to the United States signaled that a Russian debacle in Ukraine could lead to a nuclear strike. By warning that Russia sees a "serious" risk of nuclear escalation and by declaring "there are few rules left," Russian officials rattle the ultimate saber. Russia's desperate and frustrated dictator Vladimir Putin claimed he has weapons Russia's opponents do not and that he will "use

---

[1] Muratov shared the prize with journalist Maria Ressa in the Philippines "for their efforts to safeguard freedom of expression, which is a precondition for democracy and lasting peace."

[2] Interviewed by Steve Rosenberg, 3/30/23 at https://www.bbc.com/news/world-europe-65119595

them, if needed." Romney said Americans need to imagine the unimaginable—how they would respond militarily and economically to such a seismic shift in the global politics.[3]

Retired Brigadier General Kevin Ryan, now a Russian expert at Harvard, predicts that as Russia's conventional forces falter, Putin will attack Ukraine with tactical nuclear weapons. The Russian president has warned the West and indoctrinated the Russian public to prepare for this contingency.[4]

For years, Putin looked like a calculating rational actor. By invading Ukraine, however, the Russian president showed he is capable of self-defeating blunders. If he loses in Ukraine, he not only will have failed to achieve his ambition to reverse what he sees as the "greatest geopolitical catastrophe" of the 20th century—the collapse of the Soviet empire—but he will also have diminished Russia as a great power and reinvigorated its adversaries. It is possible that Putin could face significant internal challenges to his leadership. In such a circumstance, he might convince himself that the United States and the West *are* the reason he invaded Ukraine and that the propaganda he has deployed to justify this immoral invasion was true from the beginning.

Is there any hope? Russia's "younger generation is wonderful," replies Muratov. "It's well-educated. Nearly a million Russians have left the country. Many of those who've stayed are categorically against what is happening in Ukraine . . . As soon as the propaganda stops, this generation—and everyone else with common sense—will speak out."

But will the mass brainwashing ever stop? Muratov is cautious: "Twenty-one thousand administrative and criminal cases have been opened against Russians who've protested. The opposition is in jail. Media outlets have been shut down. Many activists, civilians and journalists have been labelled foreign agents." Does Putin have a support base? "Yes, an enormous one. But these are elderly people

---

[3] Mitt Romney, "We Must Prepare for Putin's Worst Weapons," *The New York Times*, May 23, 2022.

[4] "Why Putin Will Use Nuclear Weapons in Ukraine," *Russia Matters*, 5/17/23 at https://www.russiamatters.org/analysis/why-putin-will-use-nuclear-weapons-ukraine

who see Putin as their own grandson, as someone who will protect them and who brings them their pension every month and wishes them Happy New Year each year. These people believe their actual grandchildren should go and fight and die."[5]

How best respond to these issues? Some observers caution against provoking Russia—and thus avoid a possible Russian nuclear strike. Some politicians say we should restrain Ukraine from routing the Russian military; limit the weapons we provide; hold back on intelligence; and pressure President Volodymyr Zelenskyy to settle. Against such arguments, Romney and many other policy analysts urge free nations to continue supporting Ukrainians' defense of their country. Failing to continue backing Ukraine would be like paying the cannibal to eat us last. If Russia or any other nuclear power can invade and subjugate other nations with near impunity, then Ukraine would be only the first of such conquests. (Some Russian officials say that, after Ukraine, Russia must "denazify" Poland, Estonia, Latvia, Lithuania, Moldova, and Kazakhstan.[6]) Eventually America's allies and friends such as Taiwan would be devoured by brazen, authoritarian nuclear powers, drastically altering the world order.

In the second half of 2022 it appeared that the Kremlin's offensive had stalled, and the Ukrainian armed forces could be poised to drive back and even defeat Russia. French President Emmanuel Macron and some other Europeans used this situation to call for a negotiated end to the war. Professor Alexander J. Motyl at Rutgers University observed that the intentions of the would-be mediators could be laudable but their chances of success zero. Why? Kyiv had no claims on Russian territory, but wants to survive as a nation and as a state. By contrast, Putin wanted to destroy Ukraine as a nation and as a state and to seize all—or at least large parts—of Ukraine's territory. Both sides could take a breather to regroup but a stable, long-lasting peace would require Russia to accept Ukraine's

---

5 Muratov auctioned off his Nobel medal for more than $1 million in 2022 to raise money for Ukrainian child refugees.

6 Vladimir Vinokurov, "The Local Roots of European Nazism," *Nezavisimoe Voennoe Obozrenie* [*Independent Military Review*] (April 21, 2022). Vinokurov is a professor at the Diplomatic Academy of the Russian Foreign Ministry.

existence as both a nation and a state. For this to happen, the Putin regime needed to be defeated in Ukraine.[7]

Speaking as the Republican nominee for president in 2012, Romney warned that Russia, with more nuclear weapons than any country, was the most serious geopolitical adversary to the United States, but that China poses a much larger economic and political long-term challenge. More than a decade later, China's armed forces are girding to fight and defeat U.S. forces in Asia.

Granted that the United States and other Western governments have seriously mistreated their own peoples and those in many other countries, they must now cope with aggression and threats of aggression by Russia and China.

As noted here in Chapter 10, the leaders of all states pledged in 2005 to protect their own and, indeed, all peoples. Someday there should be a reckoning for the harm—the crimes—that Russian and Chinese leaders have inflicted on their own peoples and others. The rough estimates here suggest that Russia owes Ukraine at least $2 trillion for lives and property destroyed since 2014. The Chinese leadership also owes immense debts to its subjects—to Han Chinese as well as to Tibetans, Uyghurs, Mongolians, and other minorities. Passing over the abuses by long past imperial regimes, the physical and cultural genocides committed by Mao Zedong and most of his successors also amount to crimes against humanity. Even if there is no global war, Moscow and Beijing compel the free world to pay out billions for defense and deterrence, monies diverted from more constructive uses.

To evaluate these issues, consider why it is that Western democracies have never fought each other while Russia (Soviet and post-Soviet) has invaded its allies (East Germany, Hungary, Czechoslovakia) and neighbors (Afghanistan, Moldova, Chechnya, Georgia, Ukraine), and threatened the world with nuclear weapons?

---

7   At the least, Ukraine would have to drive out Russian forces from the territories occupied after February 24, 2022. Ideally, Russia would also be expelled from Crimea and the Donbas. Alexander J. Motyl, "Is a durable peace between Ukraine and Russia possible?" *The Hill*, May 26, 2022, at https://thehill.com/opinion/national-security/3500625-is-a-durable-peace-between-ukraine-and-russia-possible/

Consider also that while Communist Chinese have not launched a full-scale war, as in Ukraine, Beijing has used armed force and its threat to compel submission by ethnic minorities. China's rulers have repressed and jailed freedom-living people across China, including those still in Hong Kong. They have fought with Vietnam and with Indian and Soviet border troops. China's forces actively menace Taiwan and all nations bordering the South China Sea, risking a collision with the United States.

Why the "liberal peace" among westernized nations? Part of the answer is that *all Western democracies (including Japan South Korea, and Taiwan) have met the five essential conditions for "perpetual peace" set out by Immanuel Kant in 1795.*[8] *Neither Russia nor China nor any other Communist or post-Communist state has done so.*

The five conditions—detailed here in Chapter 10—are representative government, a federal association with like-minded nations, respect for international law, a spirit of trade, and a common, enlightened culture. Their combined effect—their synegy—leads nations never to fight each other and to settle their disputes without war.

The only way to get Russia and China to make good on their debts to their own peoples and others would be to have a new regime in Moscow and Beijing. Like Germany and Japan after 1945, Russia and China need to start afresh. They need to join the nations that have enjoyed liberal peace and slowly growing prosperity since 1945. They need to enjoy representative government committed to law-abiding cooperation with other nations. For shorthand this is called a "Western" or "liberal" way of life. At bottom, however, it is a *humane* kind of life—optimal for coping with the challenges and opportunities of global interdependence.

What happened to the spirit of Russia's Silver Age and to the milieu that gave humanity the symphonies and operas of Glinka, Mussorgsky, Tchaikovsky and Rimsky-Korsakov? Their works are still played—often by Russian masters with superb technical skills.

---

8   His *On Perpetual Peace--Zum ewigen Frieden*—was written in Königsberg, now Kaliningrad, not far from Riga, where Muratov and other Russian émigré journalists moved in 2022-2023.

But where is the deep creativity that spawned *Swan Lake* and *Boris Godunov*? When I look at the Metropolitan Opera's productions of *Prince Igor* or *Eugene Onegin*, I weep for the culture that spawned them but is no more. And where is the mingling of Confucian wisdom and Taoist harmony that underlay China's culture for centuries? Many Chinese still dance the fox-trot and tai-chi at sunrise, but their leaders are working steadily to augment their own power and China's for zero-sum struggle. The force of China's hard power undermines its quest for soft power.

What happened to Russia and China? Their top leaders have lived by the all-crushing maxim of Vladimir Lenin and Iosif Stalin: *kto kovo*—who will do in whom?

The policies of Xi Jinping and Vladimir Putin—overreach at home and abroad--have stirred alarm and resistance in the West and some other parts of the world. Xi's rule has been personalistic but overreach developed under his more collectivist predecessor, Hu Jintao (2002-2012).[9] The debts of China and Russia to their victims have grown, while the strains on their own eternal friendship have deepened, thanks to the Ukraine war and the Prigozhin-Wagner mutiny in June 2023.

---

9   Susan L. Shirk, *Overreach: How China Derailed Its Peaceful Rise* (New York: Oxford University Press, 2023); see also Shree Jain and Sukalpa Chakrabarti, "The Yin and Yang of China's Power: How the Force of Chinese Hard Power Limts the Quest and Effect of its Soft Power," *Asian Perspective* 47, I (Winter 2023): 145-166.

CHAPTER 1
A RUSSIAN GENERAL AND A CHINESE DIPLOMAT PREDICT EVERYTHING

One month before Russian forces invaded Ukraine on February 24, 2022, a retired Russian general, Leonid Grigoryevich Ivashov, head of the All-Russian Officers' Assembly, condemned the imminent war and spelled out its likely consequences. His analysis proved quite accurate; it anticipated many of this book's findings.

On January 31, General Ivashov posted a statement by the Assembly on its website.[1] It began: "Today humanity expects war—which means the inevitable loss of life, wide-scale destruction, the, suffering of large masses of people, an end to daily habits of life, and to the life support systems of states and peoples. A major war is a huge tragedy—a serious crime for which someone is responsible." The scale of the coming war, Ivashov warned, was evident in the number and combat formations of troops formed by the parties—more than one hundred thousand servicemen on each side. Russia, leaving naked its eastern borders, was moving units that faced China and Japan westwards to the borders of Ukraine.

Apparently speaking for other retired officers, Ivashov called on President Vladimir Putin to step down. War against Ukraine, the general wrote, would be an unnecessary and criminal act that will harm the Russian people and their country.

Ivashov was no pacifist. Compelled by Putin to retire in 2001, Ivashov for years served as president of Russia's Academy of Geopolitical Studies. He also contributed to a book on geopolitics that called for Russia to defeat the United States and retake control of Eurasia using every kind of combat. In 2022, however, his manifesto declared: "For the first time in history. Russia is at the center of this impending catastrophe. Before, Russia and the USSR fought

---

[1] Reposted in *Sovetskaya Rossiya*, February 1, 2022. *Sovetskaya Rossiya* kept its name after the dissolution of the Soviet Union but presently presents itself as a left-leaning but independent newspaper.

only just wars—when there was no other way to protect its vital interests." Ivashov seemed to forget his own role in putting down Czechoslovak reformers in 1968 and in sending paratroopers into Kosovo in 1999. He also supported Russia's military intervention in Syria—necessary, he told Russia's Channel One TV viewers in October 2016, to prevent construction of a Qatar-Turkey pipeline that would bring disaster to Gazprom and the Russian Federation's budget.[2]

What threatens Russia today? Ivashov said that the country is on the brink of dying—mainly for internal reasons. "All important spheres including demographic are degrading. The rate of extinction is breaking world records. Degradation is systemic. As in every complex system, the failure of any one element can lead to the collapse of the entire network."

Why did Russia provoke [*provotsirovaniia*] tensions to rise to war? "The frenzy whipped up around Ukraine is artificial and mercenary [*korystnyi*] for some internal forces," Ivashov said, implying some forms of corruption and military-industrial collusion. Ivashov stated that the real danger for Russia was not NATO or the West, but "the unviability of the state model, the complete incapacity and lack of professionalism of the system of power and administration, the passivity and disorganization of society." Under these conditions "no country survives for long." Putin risks "the final destruction of Russian statehood and the extermination of the indigenous population of the country."

Yes, there are also external threats, but they were "not now critical and do not directly threaten Russian statehood or vital interests. Strategic stability is being maintained; nuclear weapons are under reliable control; NATO forces are not building up or showing threatening activity."

As Ivashov anticipated, the West stood by Ukraine. The United States and other NATO members funneled huge quantities of military equipment—anti-tank rockets, battle tanks, howitzers, medium-range missiles, and anti-aircraft defenses—to Ukrainians.

---

2 On March 23, 2022, Ukrainian President Volodymyr Zelenskyy praised Qatar as a reliable supplier of gas and urged it to step up exports to reduce Europe's dependence on Russia.

1. A Russian General and a Chinese Diplomat Predict Everything

At the same time, Washington and its allies held back longer-range weapons more likely to produce a direct engagement with Russia. Still, Russian losses of men and materiel were staggering—more than 200,000 dead and wounded in a year, plus so many warplanes that Russian pilots became gun-shy. The erstwhile superpower sought weapons and ammunition from Iran and North Korea as well as a reluctant China.

Ivashov defended Ukraine's right to individual and collective self-defense, as stipulated by UN Charter Article 51. "As a result of the collapse of the USSR, in which Russian President Boris Yeltsin took a decisive part, Ukraine became an independent state, a member of the United Nations." The professor of geopolitics seemed unaware that Ukraine and Belarus became founding members of the United Nations in 1945, long before the Soviet breakup, thanks to Stalin's insistence and a revision of the Soviet Constitution.

The Kremlin on February 28, 2022, recognized the independence of the Donetsk and Luhansk republics bordering the Russian Federation, but had not yet done so when Ivashov posted his statement, which claimed that Moscow regarded these territories as integral parts of Ukraine. Ivashov noted that neither the UN nor the Organization for Security and Cooperation in Europe backed Kremlin claims that Ukraine has perpetrated genocide in these areas.

The fact that most of the international community refused to recognize Russia's acquisition of Crimea and Sevastopol, said Ivashov, demonstrated the failure of Russian policy. He added that "ultimatums and threats of force to compel others to like [*poliubit'*] Russia is senseless and dangerous." To have Ukraine remain a friendly neighbor, Ivashov wrote, Russia needed to show the attractiveness of the Russian model.

Ivashov asserted that the use of military force against Ukraine will jeopardize Russian statehood and forever make Russians and Ukrainians mortal enemies. Tens of thousands of young men on each side will die, worsening the future demographics in our dying countries [less than 0.2% population growth in both Russia and Ukraine]. Russian troops will face not only Ukrainian soldiers, among whom will be many Russian lads, but also military personnel and equipment from many NATO countries. Oversimplifying reality, the retired general and professor warned that NATO members will be obliged to declare war on Russia. Adding another fantasy, Ivashov wrote that Turkish president Erdogan will dispatch two field armies and ships to liberate Crimea and Sevastopol and possibly invade the Caucasus. (Instead, Erdogan mediated some issues and let Turkey increase its trade with Russia.)

Ivashov correctly predicted other results of the Ukraine war. "Russia will definitely be included in the category of countries that threaten peace and international security, will be subject to the heaviest sanctions, will turn into a pariah of the world community.... Russia's president and the government, the Ministry of Defense cannot fail to understand such consequences, they are not so stupid."

The officers' statement ended by demanding that the President of the Russian Federation reject the "criminal policy of provoking a war in which Russia would find itself alone against the united forces of the West." The officers demanded the president resign according to Article 3 of the 1993 Russian Constitution. Its provisions, however, are vague and contradictory. Article 3 provides that "the people of the Russian Federation shall exercise their power directly, and also through organs of state power and local self-government. The referendum and free elections shall be the supreme direct manifestation of the power of the people. No one may arrogate to oneself power in the Russian Federation."

Ivashov appealed to all military personnel whether in the reserve or retired and to all Russian citizens to support the demands of the All-Russian Officers' Assembly, actively to oppose war and war propaganda, and to prevent an internal civil conflict with the use of military force.

How influential the views of the retired general and the officers' assembly are remains unknown. Kremlin censors did not take down Ivashov's online statement or stop him from making the same points again and again in interviews accessible on You Tube.[3] Speaking by phone to *The New York Times* in December 2022, Ivashov said that that his warnings in January echoed what he heard from

---

3 See the many citations on the Russian Wikipedia under Ivashov, Leonid, e.g., Леонид Ивашов и Общероссийское офицерское собрание.

1. A Russian General and a Chinese Diplomat Predict Everything

nervous military officials at that time; some told him that victory in that situation would be impossible, but their superiors averred that war would be "like a walk in the park." The reality, Ivashov said, was that ten months of war had proved "even more tragic" than predicted. Nimble Ukrainian generals and soldiers outmaneuvered a much larger, more lethal foe, backed—over time—by ever more powerful weapons from NATO countries.

"Never in its history has Russia made such stupid decisions," the general declared. "Alas, stupidity has triumphed—stupidity, greed, a kind of vengefulness, and even a kind of malice."[4]

Did the failure of Russian censors to muzzle Ivashov mean the Kremlin wanted to not offend some influentials or that it chose not to bother with an insignificant faction? In any case, there seemed to be some overlap between the views of hardline nationalists and with liberal idealists inside Russia and foreign critics such as the U.S. president and most members of the UN General Assembly.

On May 16, 2022, the military analyst and retired colonel Mikhail Khodaryenok confirmed what General Ivashov had foreseen before the invasion began. Khodaryenok stated on the Russian TV talk show "Sixty Minutes" that the Ukraine situation for Russia will clearly get worse.... We are in total geopolitical isolation...the situation is not normal."[5] A few days later, however, he reversed these views—also on Russian TV.

Kremlin censorship intensified as the fighting wore on, but one TV broadcaster held up a sign on air: "No More War."

A Chinese Diplomat Also Denounces Putin's War

The somber views of General Ivashov were echoed a few months later by a senior Chinese diplomat who had served as China's ambassador to Ukraine and to several former Soviet republics in Central Asia such as Uzbekistan. Ambassador Gao Yusheng, a 75-year-old career diplomat, explained why Russia was losing the war in Ukraine and the effect this could have on world affairs.

---

4 "Putin's War," *The New York Times*, December 18, 2022.
5 BBC, May 16, 2022. and *The New York Times,* May 17, 2922.

Gao delivered a scathing indictment of Putin's war during an internal webinar in May 2022 hosted by the government-affiliated China International Finance 30 Forum and the Chinese Academy of Social Sciences. It is unclear whether Gao intended for his remarks to be made public, but *Phoenix News Media*, a partially state-owned television network, published an edited transcript of his remarks on May 10, 2022—"with revisions from the ambassador himself." But his words were taken down within hours.[6]

Gao complained that Putin relied on fabricated history to restore Russia's alleged glory. Gao faulted the Putin regime for "considering the former Soviet Union as its "exclusive sphere of influence" and "violating the independence, sovereignty and territorial integrity of other former Soviet states"—an orientation that poses "the greatest threat to peace, security, and stability in Eurasia."

Gao contended that Russia's coming defeat was already clear. Painting a grim picture of Russia's deep economic and political catastrophe in the aftermath of the war, Gao argued the country had been in a "continuous, historical process of decline" since the demise of the Soviet Union. "The so-called revitalization of Russia under Putin's reign is based on a false premise. Russia's decline is evident in all areas." All this had "a significant negative impact on the Russian military and its combat capabilities," he said.

According to Gao, the odds were stacked so heavily against Putin that "it's only a matter of time before Russia is fully defeated." The so-called revival or revitalization of Russia under Putin's leadership was false—it simply did not exist. Russia's decline was evident in its economic, military, technological, political, and social spheres, all of which undermined the Russian military and its war effort. Russia could not support a high-tech war costing millions of dollars a day. Every day the war dragged on was a heavy burden for Russia.

Unlike other Chinese diplomats who condemned the United States for orchestrating the war from behind the scenes, Gao

---

6   Lizzie C. Lee [Ph.D in Economics, M.I,T.], "A Former Chinese Ambassador's Trenchant Comments on Ukraine War Attract Notice," 5/12/22 at https://thediplomat.com/2022/05/a-former-chinese-ambassadors-trenchant-comments-on-ukraine-war-attract-notice/

1. A Russian General and a Chinese Diplomat Predict Everything

expressed a more nuanced view of the U.S. role in the war. He acknowledged Washington's goal of "weakening and isolating" Russia, but predicted a post-war global order renewal in favor of the West. "The U.S. will vigorously push for substantive reforms of the United Nations and other international organizations, or even start new ones if such reforms find roadblocks," according to Gao's published statement. In either case, said Gao, ideological lines will be drawn.

"Gao is one of the handful of senior Chinese diplomats with extensive real expertise. Unfortunately, they are required to carefully tread the official line when in office, and they can only voice their views more candidly after retirement," said Pin Ho, founder and CEO of the New-York based Mirror Media Group.

Gao's opinions may not have much influence on PRC policy but could reflect the views of other well-informed Chinese including some researchers at the Chinese Academy of Social Sciences (CASS), an important think-tank for the Party and government. The CASS had invited Gao to speak at an internal event; possibly knowing his views when they invited him.

While international pressures pushed Beijing to fine-tune its public narrative to slightly distance itself from the Russian narrative, the majority of Chinese foreign policy and security experts were sympathetic to Russian perspectives, according to Tong Zhao, a senior fellow at the Carnegie Endowment's Tsinghua Center for Global Policy in Beijing. As China braces itself for a world in greater chaos, Xi Jinping increasingly focused on "filling the gap to win the hearts and minds of the Global South," as evidenced by his Global Security Initiative which aimed to "uphold the idea of indivisible security," according to Zhao.

As the war in Ukraine dragged on, what happened to life within Russia and China? Nothing very positive, as we see in the next chapters.

CHAPTER 2
IMPERIAL REVIVALISM IS OLDER THAN PUTIN

Russia's *prezident* has offered three justifications for invading Ukraine—none of which stands up to factual scrutiny. First, Putin asserts there is no Ukraine apart from Russia. Therefore, what claims to be an independent country should be reintegrated with Mother Russia. Second, what claims to be Ukraine is ruled by Nazis intent on wiping out the country's Russian speakers, whom Moscow must protect. Third, these Ukrainian Nazis are backed by the aggressive NATO alliance headed by the United States. In return for Moscow's allowing East Germany to unite with West Germany, NATO leaders promised not to expand into lands of the former Soviet alliance, the Warsaw Treaty Organization. But NATO now borders Russia and plans to include not only Ukraine but also Georgia—virtually encircling Russia. NATO has broken its word and poses an active threat to Russian security. Justifications two and three are addressed in the next chapter. Here we examine the assertion that shared origins dictate unity.

Ukraine = Russia?

Vladimir Putin contends that Ukraine and its people are part of Russia.[1] He wants to reunite Ukrainians with their homeland—just as Hitler acted to bring German-speakers in Austria and Sudetenland *heim ins Reich*—"home" in his Third Reich. Explaining his annexation of Crimea in March 2014, Putin told the State Duma: "We are one people. Kiev is the mother of Russian cities. Ancient Rus' is our common source, and we cannot live without each other. Crimea is our common historical legacy.... And this strategic territory should be part of a strong and stable sovereignty, which today can only be Russian."

---
1 Vladimir Putin, "On the Historical Unity of Russians and Ukrainians," 7/12/21 at http://en.kremlin.ru/events/president/news/66181

Historian Timothy Snyder observed, "As we see in the ruins of Ukrainian cities and in the Russian practice of mass killing, rape, and deportation, the claim that a nation does not exist is the rhetorical preparation for destroying it—genocide."[2]

Is "Civilization" the Answer?

Ukraine and Russia are one, says Putin, because they share the same civilization of Orthodox Christianity imported from Byzantium in 988 and sustained by Muscovy, the "Third Rome," after Byzantium fell to Muslim Turks in 1453. Putin's view resembles that set out by monks in Kyiv's Monastery of the Caves in 1674. Fearing attacks by Ottomans and pressures by Catholic Poles to retake Kyiv, the monks published the *Synthesis,* a history textbook presenting Kyiv as the first capital of the Muscovite tsars and Muscovite Orthodoxy—a city that could not be abandoned to infidels or to Catholics. The monks called for the unity of Muscovy with the Cossack Hetmanate. Russian empire builders in the 17th century did not yet think about national affinities but the myth of Kyivan origins got more resonance in later times, including the Putin era.[3] The facts remained the same, but their interpretations evolved.

The idea that "civilization" is key to understanding world affairs is a gross oversimplification. British historian Arnold Toynbee traced the rise and fall of twenty-one major civilizations from ancient times to the mid-20th century. American political scientist Samuel Huntington identified six or seven civilizations interacting—often clashing—with each other in the late 20th century. Ukraine, Huntington wrote, is "cleft" between its Catholic/Uniate west and its Orthodox east. In 2011, Niall Ferguson published *Civilization: The West and the Rest.* These authors are correct that civilization—defined by Huntington as the broadest form of cultural identity—provides much of the *context* for state behavior, but it is seldom decisive compared to *identity*—how governments and

---

2 Timothy Snyder, "The War in Ukraine Is a Colonial War," *The New Yorker*, April 28, 2022.

3 Serhii Plokhy, *The Gates of Europe: A History of Ukraine*, Rev. ed. (New York: Basic Books, 2021), p.121.

peoples *perceive* their values and interests.[4]

Stalin and other observers have tried to describe the objective factors that make a nation and inspire nationalism, such as geography. But this quest cannot succeed because reality is subjective. If people feel they are a nation, they can be.[5] Great Britain and its American colonies shared a great deal of the same culture and language, but their values and perceived interests diverged in the mid-18th century. Step by step, they found themselves at war—from 1775 to 1783 and again in 1812–1815. Unlike the United States, Canadians did not revolt against the homeland—in part because their religious views aligned better with the established Church of England or with Catholic France.

Johann Sebastian Bach, Immanuel Kant, Ludwig van Beethoven, and Johann Wolfgang von Goethe were shaped by the same civilization as Adolph Hitler, Hermann Göring, and Heinrich Himmler. If "civilization" can spawn such diverse outcomes, what does it explain?

A similar question emerges if we consider Taiwan and mainland China. Elites in Taipei and Beijing use the same language. Both regimes now claim to honor Confucian and other shared values. Both polities have grown richer from their economic interactions. Still, they hover on the brink of war because most Taiwanese want to do their own thing—like Americans in the 1770s.

Xi Jinping claims that today's China inherits a four-thousand-year-old civilization. Xi's mythology ignores the centuries when Chinese kingdoms fought one another; when China was ruled by Mongols; and, in more recent centuries, by Manchurians. When the Manchus faded, Nationalists and Communists waged a long civil war that could reignite at any time. Divergent readings of "civilization," like religion, can spur conflict as well as unity.

---

4 Bruno Maçães, "The Return of Civilizations," *Noēma* 3 (Fall 2022): 13-20; also, my "Clashes of Civilizations and Interests in Central Asia," *Journal of Conflict Studies* 17, 1 (Spring 1997): 156-58, and "Interests Clash but Civilizations Can Cooperate," *International Herald Tribune*, January 7, 1997.

5 See the chapter "Nationalism and World Order" in my *Dynamics of International Relations: Conflict and Mutual Gain in an Era of Global Interdependence*, 2d edition (Lanham MD: Rowman & Littlefield, 2004).

As we see in a later chapter, Vladimir Putin claims that the historic convergence of values among the various peoples of Russia has produced a "Russian world" in which they cooperate. But many Russians—not to speak of Ukrainians, Tatars, Chechens, Buryats, Chuvash, and Circassians—reject Putin's vision of a "Russian world."

Ukrainian Fitness: Insights from Complexity Science. Unlike the views of Huntington and Putin on civilization, complexity science (developed at the Santa Fe Institute) helps us understand the ebb and flow of events in Rus' from the Viking age to the present. Complexity science defines societal fitness as the ability to respond effectively to complex challenges and opportunities. Interdependent actors can collaborate for mutual gain, go head-to-head, or pull each other down—like crabs in a basket. High levels of societal fitness seldom result from top-down direction[6] or from the opposite extreme—random anarchy. It emerges from self-organization within a framework of shared values, laws, and customs—as in today's European Union or yesterday's "United" States.

Self-organized fitness failed to develop in the anarchic polities of Kyivan Rus'. The Viking princes had multiple incentives to collaborate for self-organized fitness but ignored opportunities and reasons to do so. Narrow-minded self-seeking persisted in the top-down politics of Russia under the tsars, the Soviets, and Vladimir Putin, where the rule has been *sauve qui peut*—each for him/herself.

Departing from Soviet behavior, in the late 1980s self-organized fitness emerged in the popular fronts of the three Baltic republics and in Ukraine. It has been the source of Ukrainian vitality in the on-going resistance to Russia's invasions.[7]

---

6 Singapore is a partial exception.

7 For details, see my *The Baltic Transformed: Complexity Theory and European Security*, Foreword by Jack F. Matlock, Jr. (Lanham, Md.: Rowman & Littlefield, 2001); "Complexity Theory as a Tool for Understanding and Coping with Ethnic Conflict and Development Issues in Post-Soviet Eurasia," in *Complexity in World Politics: Concepts and Methods of a New Paradigm*, ed. Neil E. Harrison (Albany, N.Y.: State University of New York Press, 2006), pp. 73-93; also Clemens, *Complexity Science and World Affairs (*New York: SUNY Press, 2013). For another application and a current bibliography, see Adam Day and Charles T. Hunt, "A Perturbed Peace: Applying Complexity Theory to UN

2. Imperial Revivalism Is Older Than Putin

Self-seeking in Rus' and Later. Whatever the traditional roots of today's Ukraine and Russia, these bonds mean little compared to the values and perceived interests of leaders, elites, and publics in each country. Indeed, their perceived interests have often conflicted for more than 1,000 years. Today's Ukraine and Russia originated in Novgorod and Kyiv, small settlements turned into towns by Vikings in the 9th and 10th centuries. These adventurers, mainly from Sweden, founded the House of Rurik, the dynasty that ruled the East Slavic lands for more seven hundred years—from 862 until 1598. The Vikings traded slaves—many of them Slavs—and other goods in Constantinople as well as in Muslim realms reached via the Volga.

The Byzantines often referred to these aggressive Scandinavians as *Rus'*—a term that may have derived from the Finnish word for Swedes—*Ruotsi*. The origin of the word Viking is unclear, but the Old Norse word *víkingr* meant "pirate" or "raider." The Vikings are also called Varangians in English and *varyagi* in Russian. Across Europe, as in the lands of the Eastern Slavs, the Vikings first plundered; then traded; and then merged with the locals, giving up their language and pagan gods.[8]

The Vikings were highly competitive. Rival princes struggled to ascend the pecking order from remote places like Vitebsk and Pereyaslavl to the pinnacle principality, Kyiv--called "Mother of all the Russias." Kyiv was established centuries before Moscow. Kyiv was long seen as the center of political as well as religious power in the lands of Rus'.

For centuries the Rus' were threatened by Turkic-speaking nomads from Central Asia. However, the Varyagi princes seldom collaborated with one another to resist the invaders When Cumans (also known as Polovtsy) encroached in the 12th century, Prince Igor in Novgorod-Seversky fought to resist them, but got little support from other Rus' princes. Indeed, some allied with the Cumans. Parts

---

Peacekeeping," *International Peacekeeping*, December 2022 at https://doi.org /10.1080/13533312.2022.2158457. Day and Hunt argue that polities can self-organize via feedback loops and other adaptive activity. Self-organization means such systems are highly resistant to attempts to change behavior via top-down or input-output approaches.

8 Bertil Almgren et al., *The Viking* (New York: Barnes & Noble, 1971).

of this story are chronicled in in *The Lay of Igor's Host* and Borodin's opera *Prince Igor*. Indeed, some princes fought *with* Cumans against other rival princes, many of whom fought each other to gain hegemony in Kyiv. Many Russians see the *Lay* as a monument of Rus' civilization, but Kazakh writer Olzhas Suleimenov in *Az i Ya* showed that it reflected many Turkic influences.[9]

A Millennium of Colonialism

The presidents of today's Russia and Ukraine take their first names—Vladimir and Volodymyr—from the first grand prince of Kyiv, Volodymyr the Great, also known as Saint Volodymyr, because he officially brought Christianity from Constantinople to what became Kyivan Rus'. This first Volodymyr imported Viking warriors from today's Sweden to establish his dominion in Kyiv and surrounding areas. "Saint" Volodymyr acquired a new wife as well as a state religion from Byzantium and, soon after, the Cyrillic alphabet to render Christian texts into what we call Church or Old Slavonic. Whatever his sainthood, one medieval chronicler called Volodymyr *fornicatur maximus*.[10]

After Russia, Ukraine is now the seventh most populous country in Europe—thanks to emigration, less than Poland in numbers. After Russia, it still occupies the largest territory in Europe. But Ukraine did not exist in its current form until 1991. In ancient times, Scythians and Sarmations occupied the Pontic steppe, followed by Goths and Huns. But Slavs lived in today's Ukraine and Russia for several centuries before the arrival of the first *varyagi*. They were agriculturalists rather than fighters and bowed to Viking rule. They paid tribute to Viking Kyiv each year but usually lived in peace.

---

9 The book *Az i Ya* published in 1975 by Kazakh author Olzhas Suleimenov threatened the roots of Russian pride by noting the Turkic influences in the *Lay* and by de-mythologizing Prince Igor. Suleimenov wrote that Igor "was ruled not by patriotic feelings, but by exorbitant ambition." He was greedy and dishonest as well as ignorant in military affairs. Banned in 1976 by Communist authorities, *Az i Ya* was rehabilitated at a time of glasnost in 1989. Suleimenov (born 1936) gave me a copy when I escorted him around Boston in 1990.

10 Nina Khrushcheva and Jeffrey Taylor, *In Putin's Footsteps: Searching for the Soul of an Empire Across Russia's Eleven Time Zones* (New York: St. Martin's, 2019), p. 45.

2. Imperial Revivalism Is Older Than Putin

Within a few generations, Slavs assimilated the Scandinavians. The name of Prince Volodymyr is Slavic for "Power of the World." All his sons had Slavic names. They and other Viking offspring lorded it over principalities across the vast expanse of Rus'—what is now Belarus, Ukraine, and European Russia.

Kyiv fell to Mongol invaders in 1240. In the north, however, Aleksandr Nevskii, Prince of Novgorod, maintained peace with the Mongols. Secure to the east, in 1242 he faced west and defeated Teutonic Knights in a battle near Pskov on the ice of Lake Peipus.[11] Later he claimed the title Grand Prince of Kyiv.

Nevskii died when his fourth son, Daniel, was just two years old, But the child was named prince of Muscovy, then a small settlement near Vladimir and Suzdal'. Under Daniel, Muscovy superseded and then absorbed the Vladimir-Suzdal' principality to become the dominant political unit in northeastern Russia.

The term *Rus'* described all the lands that had once been under Kyiv's sway. The rulers of Muscovy fused the concept of Rus' land with the idea of their own Rurikid dynasty. For them, Rus' meant not only all the lands under Muscovy's control but also other parts of the Kyivan heritage that awaited acquisition in the future. Even after Kyiv was sacked, its magnetic luster remained. Nevskii and, after him, other rulers of Moscow claimed to be grand princes of Kyiv.

The Byzantine Orthodox Church recognized the Metropolitan of Kyiv and All Rus'. After the Mongol conquest, the Kyiv metropolitan moved to Moscow. Byzantium recognized a second Rus' metropolitnate in Galicia. In Byzantine Greek it was called *Mikrā Rosiia*—inner or Little Rus'; the more distant Muscovite jurisdiction became *Megalē Rosiia*—outer or Great Rus'.

These distinctions were maintained as Muscovy expanded. Beginning in the 14th century, Muscovite rulers styled themselves grand princes, then tsars, of all Rus' (*vseia Rusii*), and after the mid-seventeenth century their title was reformulated as tsar of all Great, Little, and White Rus' (*vseia Velikiia i Malyia i Belyia Rusii*). During the first half of the 18th century, the term *Rus'* became *Rossiya* when Tsar Peter I transformed the tsardom of Muscovy into the

---

11 In Russian, *Chudskoe Ozero*; in Estonian, *Peipsi Järv*.

Russian Empire (*Rossiskaia Imperiia*). The term *Rossiskaya* refers to anything or anyone including non-Russians with the Russian empire while *Russkii* is reserved for anything or anyone specifically "Russian."[12] Someone born of Russian parents in Moscow is *russkii*; someone born of non-Russian parents in Chechnya is *rossiyanin*. Today's Russian Federation is the *Rossiskaya Federatsiia*.

What is now Ukraine was contested in the north by Swedes and Russia; in the south by Central Asian nomads, Ottomans, and Crimean Tatars; in the west by Lithuania, Poland, and then by their joint Commonwealth.[13] In the midst of this turmoil was the Host of Zaporozhian Cossacks settled just beyond a large set of rapids on the Dnipro River. Having escaped serfdom in the north, these freedom-lovers elected their own hetman and employed their fighting skills against Tatars, Ottomans, Poles, and Russians. Hard-pressed by Catholic Poles in the mid-17th century, in 1654 Hetman Bohdan Khmelnitsky and Cossack officers recognized the sovereignty of Moscow. In 1667, however, a truce between Muscovy and Warsaw divided Ukrainian lands along the Dnipro, producing a Cossack uprising against both powers. Cossack leaders broadened their horizon to the entire hetmanate, which they called Ukraine. Fearing attacks by Ottomans and Poles, as noted earlier, Kyivan monks in 1674 published a history textbook extolling the unity of Muscovy and the hetmanate. In 1685, however, Kyiv lost its metropolitinate to Muscovy.

Upset by what he saw as Russian violations of Cossack rights, Hetman Ivan Mazepa in 1708-1709 joined the forces of Sweden's Charles XII in fighting Peter the Great, and suffered a major defeat at Poltava. In 1795, the Zaporozhian Cossacks were wiped out as

---

12 Similarly, Welsh, Scots, and some Irish, as well as Englanders, are citizens of the United Kingdom.

13 The Lithuanians claimed for themselves and conquered what they described as the Rus' lands from Polatsk and Smolensk in the north, to Volhynia and Turaû-Pinsk in the center, to Kyiv, Chernihiv, Pereyaslavt, and beyond in the south. For their part, the Poles designated Galicia, their mid-14th-century acquisition, as the Rus' land or Rus' palatinate. By the late 16th century, Rus' meant all the Orthodox faithful and the lands they inhabited in the Belarusan and Ukrainian palatinates of the Polish-Lithuanian Commonwealth. Most Ukrainians kept their Orthodox Christianity but many in the west became Uniate Roman Catholic with the Byzantine rite.

2. Imperial Revivalism Is Older Than Putin

Catherine the Great conquered southern Ukraine and Crimea.[14] By 1795, all of Ukraine, Poland, and Lithuania was partitioned into the empires of Russia, Austria-Hungary, and Prussia. The Habsburgs took Galicia; Russia got Right-Bank Ukraine and Volhynia.

Tsarist officials sought to atrophy local cultures. As Putin's history essay acknowledges, Tsarist Russia tried to Russify Ukraine and in 1863 and 1876 banned publications in Ukrainian—moves that Putin says were provoked by nationalist agitation in parts of Poland also ruled by Russia.[15]

Not just the Tsarist government but some Russian literary greats—Pushkin, Lermontov, Tyutchev, Gogol, and Dostoevsky—helped shape, transport, and ingrain Russia's imperial ideology and nationalist worldview. When Gogol—Ukrainian by birth—switched his identity to a Russian imperial one, he spent much of his talent to prove that all things Ukrainian are obsolete and, more importantly, cruel. In Gogol's telling, they need the Russian empire so they can become civilized. As Volodymyr Yermolenko makes clear, at the same time that European orientalism was developing an image of African and Asian societies as having no history worth telling, Russian literature was constructing an image of the Caucasus and Ukraine as societies whose violent histories deserved to be forgotten. To this day, these authors and their works are telling Russians that there is nothing to respect in the lands occupied by Russian soldiers. When Pushkin depicted Ukrainian Cossacks as bloody and cruel, this was just the 19th-century version of today's propaganda narrative about Ukrainians as alleged Nazis whose historical fate is death and submission.[16]

Xi Jinping also put culture in his crosshairs. The Chinese government has worked to stamp out Uyghur cultural and national identity, aiming to quell a restive region and preserve territorial

---

14 Crimea was part of Russia from 1783, when the Tsarist Empire annexed it a decade after defeating Ottoman forces in the Battle of Kozludzha. See Mark Kramer's introduction to https://www.wilsoncenter.org/publication/why-did-russia-give-away-crimea-sixty-years-ago

15 On these events, see Plokhy, *Gates*, pp. 155-158.

16 Volodymyr Yermolenko, "From Pushkin to Putin: Russian Literature's Imperial Ideology," *Foreign Policy*, 6/25/22 at https://foreignpolicy.com/2022/06/25/russia-ukraine-war-literature-classics-it

hegemony. Alongside the mass detention of Uyghur citizens in reeducation camps, which seek to instill Chinese national dogma and pride, Beijing has targeted Uyghur writers, scholars, and artists.[17]

Culture has been criminalized, As in Soviet Ukraine, those writing about minority traditions, values, and communities are charged with stoking ethnic hatred or advocating separatism. Beijing's long-standing campaign of "Sinicization" in Tibet likewise seeks to extinguish the region's language and religion, including by forcing children into Chinese boarding schools.

In Hong Kong, too, China labored to snuff out the embers of democracy with an aggressive assault on the island's culture. Beijing tries to replace Cantonese language with Mandarin through mandated instruction in schools. Hong Kong's arts institutions, publishers, and universities—all proud emblems of the territory's vibrant, cosmopolitan culture—are all coming under Beijing's tightening grip, with paintings and sculptures being removed from public view and academic and press freedom withering. In 2022, authorities arrested a 90-year-old Roman Catholic cardinal, a singer, and a scholar on charges of colluding with foreign forces to endanger China's national security.

Starting in the 17th and 18th centuries, Moscow treated Ukraine as a virtual colony, siphoning off its raw materials and grain to the central power. Yet the territory, a breadbasket for the world, endeavored to maintain its own language and culture. Widely called the father of Ukrainian literature, Taras Shevchenko (1814–1861) was born to a family of serfs but, thanks to his landlord, was educated in St. Petersburg. He wrote nine novellas in Russian, but was convicted in 1847 of promoting the independence of Ukraine by writing poems in the Ukrainian language and ridiculing members of the Russian Imperial House. His poem Testament (1845) still resonates in 2022–2023:

> *When I die, then make my grave*
> *High on an ancient mound,*
> *In my own beloved Ukraine,*

---

17 Suzanne Nossel, "How to Help Ukraine Fight Cultural Erasure," *Foreign Policy,* 5/18/22 at https://foreignpolicy.com/2022/05/16/ukraine-russia-fight-cultural-erasure/

2. Imperial Revivalism Is Older Than Putin

In steppeland without bound:
Whence one may see wide-skirted wheatland,
Dnipro's steep-cliffed shore…

When from Ukraine the Dnipro bears
Into the deep blue sea

The blood of foes … then will I leave
These hills and fertile fields—.[18]

Other well-known writers born in Ukraine include many who published mainly in other languages—Nikolai Gogol in Russian, Sholem Aleichem in Yiddish, Joseph Conrad in English; and—in more recent times—Mikhail Bulgakov, Ilya Ehrenburg, Anna Akhmatova, Mikhail Sholokov, and Svetlana Alexievich—all in Russian.

Soviet Ukraine Before Independence

Ukrainians have no reason to esteem Tsarist or Soviet rule. The Red Army of Lenin and Trotsky crushed efforts to form an independent Ukraine from the remains of the Tsarist Russian Empire. Having studied in Vienna and written about the national question in 1912, Stalin sought a way to incorporate national strivings within the framework of Soviet power and Communist revolution. A Ukrainian Soviet Republic joined Soviet Republics from Russia, Byelorussia, and Transcaucasia in December 1922 to form the Soviet Union. Over two decades, Stalin added a dozen other "union-republics" to the USSR.[19] Smaller units called autonomous republics and oblasts became part of the Russian Socialist Federative Soviet Republic. Several Soviet constitutions gave the "union-republics" the right to freely secede from the union. Communists, of course, were told to work for unity. Ukraine did not again declare its independence until 1991.

---

18 Translations by Vera Rich and by John Weir in 1961.

19 Trying to improve ties with Helsinki, Khrushchev in 1956 demoted the Karelian-Finnish Union-Republic, created in 1940, to Karelian Autonomous Soviet Socialist Republic within the Russian Republic. In November 1991. the last days of the USSR, the Karelian ASSR became simply the Republic of Karelia within the Russian Federation.

To finance industrialization and feed industrial workers, Stalin collectivized agriculture and animal husbandry.[20] In the early 1930s, he orchestrated a famine that killed millions of Ukrainians and Kazakhs—a number that matched or exceeded the millions of Jews who perished in Hitler's Holocaust.

Ukrainians did not forget. Some Cossacks and Ukrainians fought against Stalin's USSR in World War II. Entire units of these fighters later surrendered to British and U.S. forces but were forcibly repatriated to Soviet authorities and near-certain death after the war. Ukrainian guerrillas fought Soviet rule until the early 1950s.[21]

Crimea did not become an East-West issue until 2014. The Big Three Yalta Conference took place there in February 1945. Stalin arranged that the U.S. president reside in what had been the vacation residence of Tsar Nicholas[22]—the same palace where Germans celebrated their advance into Crimea in 1942. After the Red Army drove out the Germans, Stalin in 1944 deported more than 200,000 Tatars and other minorities from Crimea to remote regions of the USSR, where half of them died from hunger and other hardships. Since some Tatars collaborated with the Germans or deserted from the Red Army, Stalin punished all of them.[23]

In 1944–1945 Stalin arranged that Ukraine and Belarus, along with the USSR, would have seats in the UN General Asembly. This was only fair, Soviet diplomats argued, to partially offset the many votes controlled by London and Washington via the British Empire and U.S. dominion over Latin America.

After 1945 Ukrainian Communist Party boss Nikita Khrushchev repressed moves toward Ukrainian autonomy and presided over another famine. Khrushchev returned to Moscow in 1949 as part of Stalin's inner circle. After Stalin's death in 1953, Khrushchev struggled for supreme power in Moscow against Soviet

---

20 Faced with collectivization, peasants butchered two-thirds off their livestock.

21 *Enemy Archives: Soviet Counterinsurgency Operations and the Ukrainian Nationalist Movement: Selections from the Secret Police Archives,* eds., Volodymyr Viatrovych and Lubomyr Luciuk (Montreal: McGill-Queen's University Press, 2023).

22 The palace gardens had California Redwoods when I visited in 1960.

23 S. M. Plokhy, *Yalta: The Price of Peace* (New York: Viking, 2020), pp. 58-61.

2. Imperial Revivalism Is Older Than Putin

Prime Minister Georgi Malenkov and several other Soviet leaders. Khrushchev became First Secretary of the Communist Party in September 1953, but did not succeed in ousting Malenkov until January 1955.

Crimea had long served as a tool in Kremlin power struggles. For years Khrushchev thought that expanding Ukrainian territory could buttress Ukrainian elite support for himself and for the Soviet "Union." Khrushchev in 1954 orchestrated the transfer of Crimea from the Russian Soviet Republic to the Ukrainian Soviet Republic. Khrushchev also saw the transfer as a way of fortifying and perpetuating Soviet control over Ukraine. In 1954 the population of Crimea—some 1.1 million—was roughly 75 percent ethnically Russian. Some 860,000 ethnic Russians living in Crimea would be joining the large Russian minority in Ukraine (making a total of 18 percent in 2000).

Box: Khrushchev's Great Granddaughter Remembers

Nina Khrushcheva, now a professor in New York's New School, recalls that "my great-grandfather felt a strong kinship" with Ukraine. "He had worked there as a miner in Donbas during the 1910s and often wore the brightly embroidered Ukrainian folk shirts. His wife, my great-grandmother Nina, was an ethnic Western Ukrainian and proud of it.[24] [...] Yet curtailing Ukrainian national pride was always the Kremlin's objective. Even while he was rebuilding the economy, Khrushchev was supposed to make sure that nationalism and anti-Soviet sentiment were kept at bay. In 1939, he oversaw the uneasy, and brutal, acquisition of Western Ukraine from Poland.[25]

"One document from that time, which I found in my family home, quotes my great-grandfather saying, 'If we hung a few militant oppositionists in Lviv's main square, others will be less tempted to rebel.' And this is from a man who genuinely liked Ukraine and

---

24 On my request, in 1964 Nina sent my four-year old daughter a large Father Frost (*Ded Moroz*) doll.

25 Nina Khrushcheva, "Putin's Ukraine-Russia war exposes an arrogant historical revisionism," *NBC News*, March 4 2022, at https://www.nbcnews.com/think/opinion/ukraine-nuclear-power-plant-burns-putin-rewrites-history-ncna1290827?cid=sm_npd_nn_tw_ma

helped it rise from the ashes after the war."

Professor Khrushcheva continued: "Svetlana Alexievich, the Nobel laureate in literature [in 2020], who is half-Ukrainian, has often told me stories about the region's strong animosity toward Russians.[26] It was focused on, she recently explained, 'not just your great-grandfather, but those with Ukrainian ties who succeeded him. Leonid Brezhnev and Mikhail Gorbachev would always put the center first. We chafed at their domineering power attitude.'"

"While growing up," Khushcheva recalled, "I would often spend summers in Kyiv, visiting relatives there. I still remember being mocked for my perceived Moscow 'superiority'— though I don't think I displayed any. The fact that I was Russian was enough . . . Today, that sense of superiority toward Ukrainians seems ingrained in the Russians. Putin stiffly gives orders to conduct a Ukrainian 'special operation' (his euphemism for war) while seated alone at one end of a large white table. His entourage agrees from a distance, clustered around at the table's other end, in a giant hall in the Kremlin. It looks too much like the times of Stalin."

A Ukrainian essayist recalled that in the 1970s and early 1980s the specter of extinction was stalking Ukraine. It took the Chernobyl disaster in 1986 to end our social paralysis and take our security into our own hands. "In those police years, those who dared to speak Ukrainian in public could be at any moment humiliated with the Russian colonialist phrase '*Govorite po-chelovecheski!*' ('Speak human!')." Any discontent about the superiority of everything Russian was labeled Ukrainian nationalism. Oksana Zabushko complained the West ignored imperial domination and abuse by Boris Yeltsin and Putin of non-Russian peoples not only in Ukraine but also in in Tatarstan, Chechnya, and other Russian "republics." The dark side of Russia is due not only to its Communist but also to its imperialist heritage. Aware of this pattern, on October 18, 2022, Ukraine's Parliament declared the Chechen Republic of Ichkeria "temporarily occupied by the Russian Federation."[27]

---

26 Living in Belarus, Svetlana Alexievich, writes in Russian about life in Soviet times.

27 Oksana Zabuzhko, "The Problem with Russia, "*The New York Times,* February 20, 2023.

2. Imperial Revivalism Is Older Than Putin

When I visited Kyiv in 1960, Khrushchev—by then the leader of the entire USSR—drove down a major street without any fanfare. Thousands of residents lined the pavement to watch. Faces impassive, they did not cheer but—a prudent caution—did not show disdain. Visiting Crimea in the 1960s and 1970s, I saw nothing suggesting it was anything but Russian.

Ukraine, like most of the USSR, experienced stagnation under Khrushchev's successor, Leonid Brezhnev, 1964–1982, and his successors, 1982–1985. Their successor, the reformer Mikhail Gorbachev promoted "restructuring: and "openness" to cope with mounting economic and political malaise in the USSR.

In contrast to the rapid growth of mass movements in the Baltic and Transcaucasian republics in the Gorbachev era, in Ukraine the national revival stimulated by *glasnost* developed only gradually. A language law in autumn 1989 for the first time gave Ukrainian official status as the republic's state language. A campaign to fill in the "blank spots" in history aimed to restore public awareness of neglected or suppressed historical events and figures such as Hetman Ivan Mazepa.[28]

A religious revival emerged in 1988, greatly stimulated by celebrations of a millennium of Christianity in Kyivan Rus. As bishops and clergy emerged from the underground, demands grew for the re-legalization of the Uniate Byzantine rite Catholic Church and for restoration of the Ukrainian Autocephalous Orthodox Church.

The year 1989 witnessed a transition from social mobilization to mass politicization in Ukraine. A popular front known as *Rukh* took shape, nurtured by the Writer's Union of Ukraine. In 1989 the *Zeleny Svit* ("Green World") environmental movement evolved into a potent political force. But every step toward national revival and autonomous self-organization encountered bitter resistance from the Communist Party of Ukraine.

Ukrainians in 1990 saw the beginning of parliamentary democracy. The first competitive elections to the

---

28 For details, see Lubomyr A. Hajda and Andry Matuch at https://www.britannica.com/place/Ukraine/Independent-Ukraine

Ukrainian parliament (which replaced the former Supreme Soviet), held on March 4, broke the Communist Party's monopoly on political power in Ukraine. After the short-lived coup d'état by hardliners in Moscow, the Ukrainian parliament, in emergency session, declared the full independence of Ukraine on August 24, 1991—approved by a referendum on December 1.

On December 8, 1991, the presidents of Russia, Ukraine, and Belarus signed the Belovezha Accords. This agreement declared the dissolution of the USSR by its founder states and established the Commonwealth of Independent States (CIS). Some Russians hoped the CIS could be a way to reconstruct the erstwhile union, but Ukrainian leaders saw it as a means toward a "civilized divorce."

On December 25, 1991, Gorbachev announced his resignation as Soviet president. The hammer-and-sickle flag was lowered over the Kremlin and replaced by Russia's pre-revolutionary tricolor. Boris Yeltsin, already elected president of Russia in 1990, became the country's undisputed top leader. The Russian Federation assumed the USSR's permanent seat on the UN Security Council and all Soviet embassies became Russian embassies. On December 31, 1991, the Soviet Union was formally dissolved.

Ukraine After Independence

Many observers believed that an independent Ukraine could readily integrate with Western democracies, but this turned out to be a difficult process. Citizenship was extended to the people of Ukraine on an inclusive (rather than ethnic or linguistic) basis. Ukraine received widespread international recognition and developed its diplomatic service. A pro-Western foreign policy was instituted, and official pronouncements stressed that Ukraine was a "European" rather than a "Eurasian" country. The state symbols and national anthem of the short-lived, post-World War I Ukrainian National Republic were reinstituted.

Independent Ukraine avoided political violence in the 1990s, but its record was poor with regard to economic reform, law enforcement, crime prevention, health care, and education. The country was still ruled and managed by members of the erstwhile

Soviet nomenklatura who posed as born-again Ukrainians. Unlike Poland and Hungary, Ukraine had no elite able to replace the old cadres and establish its authority over a large but "cleft" country. Civil society was underdeveloped, political parties weak, objective news media rare, and poverty widespread. As in Russia, oligarchs became richer while most people remained poor

While independent Ukraine was acquiring the attributes of statehood, it faced a number of contentious issues that severely strained the fledgling country: the nature of its participation in the CIS, nuclear disarmament, the status of Crimea, along with control of the Black Sea Fleet and its port city of Sevastopol. While engaging passions on both sides of the border, these issues also helped to define Ukraine's new relationship with Russia.

What to do with the huge nuclear weapon arsenal left over from Soviet times? In 1994 Ukraine agreed to give up its 1,900 strategic nuclear warheads and let them go to Russia. In return, Kyiv sought and obtained three assurances. First, it wanted compensation for the highly enriched uranium in the nuclear warheads, which could be blended down for fuel in nuclear reactors. Russia agreed to provide compensation. Second, Kyiv wanted payment for the substantial costs entailed in eliminating ICBMs, ICBM silos, and bombers. The United States agreed to cover those expenses. Third, Ukraine wanted guarantees of its security once it got rid of the nuclear arms. In their 1994 "Budapest Memorandum" the United States, Russia, and Britain committed "to respect the independence and sovereignty and the existing borders of Ukraine" and "to refrain from the threat or use of force" against the country—explicit commitments Putin's Kremlin has rudely and viciously broken.

PUTIN'S AGGRESSIONS

Starting in 2004, a series of events raised worries in Moscow about the future of Ukraine. In November-December a so-called Orange Revolution overturned an election in which Western-oriented Viktor Yushchenko faced Viktor Yanukovych, supported by Moscow. The election reflected a tug-of-war between those seeking closer ties with the European Union and NATO and those favoring tighter alignment with Russia. Yushchenko mysteriously suffered dioxin poisoning in September, but survived, his face disfigured. After two rounds of voting awarded the election to Yanukovych, protesters dressed in orange, Yushchenko's campaign color, took to the streets and forced a revote in December, which Yushchenko won. This was the second so-called color revolution in a post-Soviet state—a year after Georgia's Rose Revolution. In 2010, however, Yanukovych mounted a comeback and won the presidency again, He outfitted his estate in ways that would have impressed Marie Antoinette.

In November 2013, Yanukovych scuttled a planned association agreement with the EU, triggering a wave of popular protest that came to be known as the Euromaidan movement. In February 2014, after scores of demonstrators were killed by government security forces in Kyiv and with parliament voting to impeach him, Yanukovych fled to Russia. His estate became a museum called "Yanukdisneyland," but in 2022 it provided a refuge for local villagers uprooted by war.

Yanukovych gone, Ukraine's parliament established an interim government. Within days it was confronted with a crisis in the autonomous republic of Crimea. Unidentified gunmen, "little green men," later confirmed to be Russian troops, occupied key sites throughout the peninsula. Over the next two weeks, pro-Russian paramilitary groups solidified their hold on the peninsula and organized a widely criticized independence referendum. On March 18, 2014, Russian President Putin formally annexed Crimea. Crimea became a "republic." *Respublika Krym joined* twenty-one other "republics" of the Russian Federation's now 85 federal "subjects," with Crimea and the city of Sevastopol added as separate entities.

In April 2014, unidentified troops carrying Russian weapons and equipment seized government buildings in Donetsk and Luhansk. In September, Russian units entered Ukraine to push back Ukrainian forces close to regaining control of Donbas.

Two accords signed in Minsk aimed to halt the fighting, Russian and Ukrainian negotiators on September 5, 2014, concluded the first Minsk Agreement. However, its terms were not implemented, and fighting continued along the line of contact. This war over the Donbass region took some 15,000 lives in the eight years before the February 2022 invasion.

2. Imperial Revivalism Is Older Than Putin

Snap parliamentary elections in October 2014 permitted pro-Western parties to claim victory at the polls. In December, Ukraine dropped its status as a nonaligned country, a posture it had adopted in 2010 under pressure from Russia. Leaders in Kyiv pledged to work toward membership in NATO.

Fighting intensified during a rebel offensive in January 2015. In February a second Minsk Agreement was signed by Putin and Petro Poroshenko, a Ukrainian businessman and politician who served as the fifth president of Ukraine from 2014 to 2019. Their accord was shepherded by French President Francois Hollande and German Chancellor Angela Merkel. It outlined thirteen steps to end the war, including an immediate cease-fire and the withdrawal of all heavy weaponry in order to create a "security zone."

Neither Minsk accord worked. Obscured behind the fine print were two contradictory visions. Kyiv wanted full sovereignty over Donbas while Moscow wanted to make permanent the puppet regimes established while Russian forces remained, as happened in Crimea. Russian control of Donbas, Putin hoped, could be a wedge to deepen divisions throughout Ukraine.[29] As we see in a later chapter, Putin used the most vulgar language to demand that Kyiv accept the second Minsk accord, like it or not.

After Russia recognized the Luhansk and Donetsk people's republics on February 21, 2022, Putin declared that the Minsk agreements "no longer existed" and that Ukraine, not Russia, was to blame for their collapse. Russia then invaded Ukraine on February 24.

Many residents of Crimea and other parts of Ukraine close to the border have felt an affinity to Russia. Many citizens of Ukraine and Belarus used Russian as their first language, but many—even before Putin's invasions—did not feel themselves Russian. Evidence of Russian brutality in the fighting so alienated many Russophiles that many native Russian speakers preferred to use Ukrainian.

Religious identity remains an important cultural factor in

---

29 Chatham House research paper dated May 22, 2020, by Duncan Allan at chathamhouse.org/2020/05/a-conundrum-western-policy-and-russias-war-eastern-ukraine-0/introduction-minsk

both Russia and Ukraine. In 2015, according to a Pew survey, 71% of Russians and 78% of Ukrainians identified themselves as Orthodox—up from 30% in 1991. Indeed, Orthodoxy came to be identified with what it meant to be Russian. Putin supported the restoration of Christian monasteries and returning Orthodox properties confiscated during the Soviet era, The Russian Orthodox Church has been critical of the West, declaring that demands for human rights are an insult to the national and religious values of Russia.

With roughly 35 million Orthodox Christians, Ukraine now has the third-largest Orthodox population in the world after Russia and Ethiopia. In 2019, the leading authority for Orthodox Christianity, the Ecumenical Patriarch of Constantinople Bartholomew recognized the independence of the Ukrainian Orthodox Church, severing it from the Russian Orthodox Church with its close ties to the Kremlin. Moscow accused the United States of encouraging the break and the Kremlin promised to defend "the interests of Russians and Russian speakers." Speaking in Istanbul, the Patriarch in 2022 claimed that he had become a Russian target.

In 2019, a former comedian who once played Ukraine's president on television, Volodymyr Zelenskyy, defeated Petro Poroshenko to become Ukraine's president. The landslide victory of a Jew should have silenced accusations that Ukraine is run by Nazis, but did not.

In February 2021, Zelenskyy ordered a series of measures against pro-Moscow oligarchs such as Viktor Medvedchuk, chairman of Ukraine's largest pro-Russia political party and close ally of Putin. The government froze his financial assets for three years and shut down three pro-Russia TV channels controlled by Medvedchuk alleging that they broadcast "misinformation." In May 2021 Kyiv authorities lodged treason charges against Medvedchuk, claiming that he transferred oil and gas production licenses in Crimea to Russian authorities.

Putin opted for war and launched his "special military operation" on February 24, 2022.

As noted earlier in this chapter, self-organized fitness sustained Ukrainian resistance to Russia's invasions. From all walks of life,

2. Imperial Revivalism Is Older Than Putin

Ukrainians left their former occupations to do whatever they can for the common cause. They became tougher and more fit under extreme duress, but moral and material support from the West helped sustain Ukrainian resilience.

Tatars on the Brink

Russia invaded Ukraine, Putin said, to stop genocide of Russian speakers in Donbas. Russians were not in danger, but Putin's policies aimed at wiping out the Ukrainian and Tatar peoples and their cultures.

The Crimean Tatars have a long history of opposition to Russia, under whose rule many died, and most were dispossessed. Many returned from exile to Crimea in the 1990s and threw in their lot with Ukraine. In 2014, roughly 13% of Crimea's people were Tatars. After annexation, they found themselves again living under Russian rule.

Having opposed annexation in 2014, more than a hundred Crimean Tatars were imprisoned on politicized charges of "extremism" or "terrorism." Following Russia's full-scale invasion of Ukraine in February 2022, all freedoms in Crimea were further restricted. According to the UN human rights monitoring mission in Ukraine, at least 89 individuals were prosecuted for "discrediting the armed forces of the Russian Federation."

Refat Chubarov, head of the Crimean Tatar governing body, the Mejlis, in 2022 fled to Kyiv. He pointed out that Russian mobilization in occupied territories such as Crimea is an international war crime. The Fourth Geneva Convention prohibits an occupying power from compelling occupied populations to serve in its armed forces.

Ethnic targeting cuts deep. "Mobilization into the armed forces is a way of getting rid of undesirable people, it's a kind of murder," said a worker at the ZMINA human rights center in Kyiv. Once conscripts arrive at the front, their chances of survival are poor. Russia in 2022 conducted more than a dozen campaigns and enlisted over 30,000 people in Crimea. According to the Ukrainian general staff, at least 139 Crimeans have been killed fighting for Russia in Ukraine since February, and at least twenty-two became prisoners of war.

On September 21, 2022, Nariman Dzhelyal, one of the last representatives of the Mejlis still in Crimea, was sentenced to seventeen years in prison.

Putin says that the values of the various peoples in the Russian Federation converged into a harmonious "Russian World." But this did not happen for Tatars or the many other ethnic groups in the former tsarist and Soviet empires.

CHAPTER 3
WAS NATO TO BLAME?

Russia's president since 1999–2000, Vladimir Putin, stated in 2005 that he was determined to correct the "greatest geopolitical catastrophe of the 20th century"—as he called the breakup of the Soviet Union. In 2012, during his inauguration speech for what was (de facto) his fourth term in as Russia's president, he declared: The "life of our future generations depends on Russians' ability to become a leader ... for the whole of Eurasia."

Putin sought to be known as the restorer of Russia and leader of Eurasia. He claimed to be like Peter the Great, who won hegemony over the Baltic region and much of Ukraine in 1709 by defeating Sweden at Poltava—celebrated in a poem by Pushkin and an opera by Tchaikovsky recalling the treachery of Ivan Mazepa, the Ukrainian military, political, and civic leader who served as Hetman of the Zaporozhian Host, 1687–1709. Feeling betrayed by Peter, Ivan Mazepa joined the Swedes and then shared in their defeat.

Why did Russian forces invade Ukraine on February 24, 2022? One reason, President Putin said, was to prevent Ukraine—allegedly ruled by Nazis—from joining the aggressive military bloc known as NATO. The Kremlin condemns the Atlantic alliance for incorporating former Soviet allies such as Poland and former Soviet republics such as Estonia.

As seen in Chapter 2, Moscow's determination to reoccupy its former vassal states pre-dates the Putin presidency. The reality is that—soon after the Soviet Union's collapse—Russian strategists plotted to recover what they called the "near abroad"—the former imperial possessions of Tsarist and Soviet Russia. This campaign commenced in the early 1990s *before* NATO started to expand eastward.

Some Kremlin officials and some Western commentators assert that when German reunification was being negotiated in 1990, U.S. and European diplomats promised that if Moscow permitted East Germany to join West, NATO forces would never be stationed in the former German Democratic Republic. But this is a myth. Western leaders did *not* make such a pledge. Nor did they promise to keep former Soviet allies and union-republics (such as Estonia) out of NATO.[1] Former Soviet president Mikhail Gorbachev, his interpreter, and his foreign minister—each in separate statements denied that NATO expansion had been an issue in 1990 or that the West offered any kind of quid pro quo to Moscow for going along with German reunification.[2] These issues involved many stakeholders in many countries and many unknowns in a rapidly evolving east-west context.[3] Andrei Kozyrev, Russia's foreign minister, 1990–1998, under then-president Boris Yeltsin, told me in 2001 that Russian hostility to the West arose mainly from Russian domestic politics and not from NATO expansion.[4] Why? Accustomed to top-down rule, Russian leaders feared the eastward spread of democracy and openness.[5]

Svetlana Savranskaya and Tom Blanton at the National Security Archive disagree. They claim the documents show that statements by a bevy of Western leaders led Gorbachev and Foreign Minister

---

1 Mark Kramer, "NATO Enlargement—Was There a Price?" *International Security* 42, 1 (Summer 2017): 186-192, and his earlier "The Myth of a No-NATO-Enlargement Pledge to Russia," *Washington Quarterly* 32, 1 (April 2009): 39-61. Kramer used declassified materials not available to most previous commentators.

2 "Russland: Gorbatschow sieht in Nato-Osterweiterung keinen Wortbruch," *Zeit Online*, 9 November 2014;_ "Mihhail Gorbatshov: Baltimaad polnud enam mingid oiged liiduvabariigid," *Postimees* (Tallinn), 18 August 2001, p. 3; Pavel Palazhchenko, "Rasshirenie NATO i pretenzii k Gorbachevu," posted on Facebook, March 9, 2018; interview with Eduard Shevardnadze: 'We Couldn't Believe that the Warsaw Pact Could Be Dissolved,'" in *Der Spiegel International*, 26 November 2009—all cited by Kramer, "NATO Enlargement."

3 Peter Baker and Susan Glaser, *The Man Who Ran Washington: The Life and Times of James A. Baker III* (New York: Doubleday, 2020), pp. 338, 346, 357, 361, 367, 389, 392.

4 Harvard seminar on the tenth anniversary of the tripartite decision in December 1991 at the Viskuli dacha in Belarus to replace the USSR with the Commonwealth of Independent States. Michael Weiss, "Russia's Ex-Foreign Minister on His 'Totalitarian' Country," *New Lines*, March 9, 2022, at https://newlinesmag.com/reportage/russias-ex-foreign-minister-on-his-totalitarian-country/

5 Michael Weiss, "Russia's Ex-Foreign Minister on His 'Totalitarian' Country," *New Lines*, March 9, 2022, at https://newlinesmag.com/reportage/russias-ex-foreign-minister-on-his-totalitarian-country/

Eduard Shevardnadze to believe that NATO would not move one inch closer to Soviet borders after German unification.[6] The statements cited could have led to this interpretation, reflecting some wishful thinking and bonhomie on all sides, but there was no formal promise not to broaden NATO. What we do see are Western commitments to respect Soviet security interests and conduct Western policies in a spirit of inclusiveness.[7]

The former State Department planner George F. Kennan and many other Soviet experts opposed NATO expansion into the former Soviet sphere. It was unnecessary and provocative, they argued.[8] Decades later, we cannot be sure. If NATO had been more welcoming to Russia and not expanded up to Russia's borders, would Moscow have held back from efforts to reconquer its lost satellites? Countries like Estonia, Poland, and the Czech Republic wanted Western protection from a resurgent Russia. The Baltic republics and other Soviet-occupied states had suffered numerous deaths and deportations due to Soviet rule and did not want to repeat this experience.[9] Given the imperial urges of many Russian leaders, governments in liberated East Central Europe preferred to err on the side of caution.

COULD RUSSIA JOIN THE WEST? POLICY DILEMMAS FOR WASHINGTON

The West did not try to beat Russia while it was down. The evidence shows that the Clinton administration did respect Russian security

---

6 "NATO Expansion: What Gorbachev Heard," at https://nsarchive.gwu.edu/briefing-book/russia-programs/2017-12-12/nato-expansion-what-gorbachev-heard-western-leaders-early

7 Mark Kramer, "What Gorbachev *Really* Heard," *Journal of Strategic Studies* (Summer 2023).

8 I proposed neutralization of Eastern Europe in "An Austrian Solution for Eastern Europe," *The New York Times*, July 10, 1989, A18, reprinted in Paris, Vienna, and Tallinn; updated in my "An Alternative to NATO Expansion," *International Journal* 52, 2 (1997): 353–357. For a review of the literature, see J.R.I. Shifrinson, "The NATO Enlargement Consensus and US Foreign Policy: Origins and Consequences," in J. Goldgeier and J.R.I. Shifrinson, eds., *Evaluating NATO Enlargement* (New York: Palgrave Macmillan, 2023).

9 Clemens, *Baltic Independence and Russian Empire* (New York: St. Martin's, 1991).

interests, but that this orientation entailed many potential pitfalls.

The United States and most Western countries tried to help Russia become a prosperous and peaceful member of the world community. They believed that a free market and political democracy would grow together. Some Western economic advisers overestimated Russia's ability to jump "cold turkey" into free enterprise, as Poland did, but their motives were benign. They did not foresee how former Communist officials and managers would become billionaires with no sense of social responsibility.

Boris Yeltsin, who became Russia's first elected president in 1990 (before the Soviet Union's collapse), talked like an aspiring democrat. But on October 3-4, 1993, he dissolved parliament and ordered tanks to shell the White House where it was located—the same building near which he had stood on a tank to defy the hardline coup in August 1991.

The complexities facing U.S. policymakers were manifest in a phone call that President Bill Clinton placed to Yeltsin one day after the shelling. Clinton called Yeltsin to express U.S. support and inquire about the Russian president's plans for the upcoming elections and political settlement after the constitutional crisis. Yeltsin put all the blame on his opponents. He told Clinton that these fascists "brought to Moscow a gang of people" from the Transdniester region and Latvia (actually, special forces of the Russian army), and gave them machine guns and grenade launchers to "fire on peaceful civilians." Yeltsin said he had no alternative but to use force. Yeltsin expressed regret that "some people were killed"—"thirty-nine on our side" (estimates of total casualties ranged into the hundreds). But he assured Clinton that now both the transition to democracy and to market reform would move faster. He might call for early presidential elections because "no real rivals to me are visible." He did not mention that his political rivals Vice President Aleksandr Rutskoy and Chairman of the Supreme Soviet Ruslan Khasbulatov were in prison, that the prosecutor general had been forced to resign, and the Constitutional Court was suspended after its chairman declared Yeltsin's decree abolishing the parliament unconstitutional.

3. Was NATO to Blame?

Moscow in 1993 traded its prospects of democracy for renewed, revanchist imperialism. When President Boris Yeltsin decided to move against his opposition in the Russian parliament, he used the military to crush it. With the help of the military generals who backed him in his assault on the parliament, Yeltsin dismantled Russian parliamentary democracy and rewrote the constitution to secure presidential authoritarianism. He paid back the generals by destroying Chechnya. Yeltsin's undemocratic move set the precedent for Russia to use violence at home and abroad to strengthen personalized rule.

Russia lost the first Chechen War of 1994-1996 due to the Russian army's weakness and the resilience of Chechen leader Dzhokhar Dudayev's command. Although Russian and international human rights organizations and European Union states condemned Russia's crimes against humanity, Yeltsin successfully sold the war to the Clinton White House as an internal conflict against "banditry." Instead of condemning Yeltsin, Clinton instead compared him to Abraham Lincoln fighting the Confederates. Since Clinton's priority was nuclear arms reduction instead of pushing Russia to comply with international law, as European states advocated, the United States provided financial assistance to Russia instead—partially for denuclearization.[10]

None of this seemed to lower Clinton's confidence in Yeltsin. Clinton never asked about the loss of life among civilians and the opposition. Instead, he told Yeltsin, "You did everything exactly as you had to…." Yeltsin thanked him for everything and said, "I embrace you with all my heart."[11]

Enter Secretary of State Warren Christopher, the first senior Western official to visit Moscow after Yeltsin's dissolution of the Parliament and the October 3-4 bloodshed. The U.S. Chargé

---

10 Boyakoz Kassymbekova, "The Road to Democracy in Russia Runs Through Chechnya," *Foreign Policy*, 3/11/23 at https://foreignpolicy.com/2023/03/11/russia-chechnya-democracy-ukraine-putin-kadyrov/

11 https://nsarchive.gwu.edu/briefing-book/russia-programs/2018-10-04/yeltsin-shelled-russian-parliament-25-years-ago-us-praised-superb-handling. Memorandum of Telephone Conversation: Telcon with President Boris Yeltsin of Russian Federation, Oct 5, 1993. William J. Clinton Presidential Library declassification 2015-0782-M-1

d'Affaires and future Ambassador to Russia James Collins sent Secretary Christopher a briefing cable in advance of his visit. Collins was far more cautious than Clinton about Russian democracy. Although 92 parties were registered for the election, that did not in itself guarantee free and fair elections.

What Chargé d'Affaires Collins called Yeltsin's new "half-baked" constitution concentrated the "preponderance of authority in the hands of the chief executive . . . Many reformers worry about establishing a new Russian democracy so heavily tilted toward presidential power." Collins also noted the continuing ban on nationalist and right-wing parties and their newspapers. Collins expressed concern that Boris Yeltsin's "face during his October 6 speech was proof the Russian President had cast his hardline opponents into a personal anathema." Collins also raised concern about the methods used by Moscow police and city government in implementing the state of emergency, such as "systematic police cleansing of non-Russian people from Central Asian and Caucasian states," and racist remarks about dark-skinned people by Moscow Mayor Yuri Luzhkov. In the end of the cable, Collins cautioned that although the actual voting is likely to be fair, "the question will be the democratic content of the entire electoral process."[12]

In a follow-up cable, Collins reviewed foreign policy issues that Christopher would face when he talked with Yeltsin and his Foreign Minister Kozyrev. New elections were scheduled for December 1993 and Yeltsin wanted all the support from the West he could get. Yeltsin and Kozyrev wanted Russia to be seen as a partner with whom the West consults and does not just take for granted. Russians knew that the U.S. internal debate about NATO expansion was reaching a crucial moment. They wanted assurance that the door was open to Russia—not just to East Europeans. "What the Russians hope to hear is that NATO is not moving precipitously, and that any policy NATO adopts will apply equally to them." Collins said that Russians' "neuralgic" attitude stemmed from the fear they will "end up on the wrong side of a new division of Europe."

---

12 Cable from American Embassy Moscow to Secretary of State: Secretary's Visit to Moscow: Domestic Political Dynamics. Oct 19, 1993. Source: Department of State Declassification, Date/Case ID; 6 MAR 2003 200001030

Christopher needed to make sure the Russians knew that the U.S. was actively promoting Russia's "complete reintegration into the family of Western states."[13]

Secretary Christopher and his special ambassador Strobe Talbott went to Moscow after meetings in Budapest. They met with Foreign Minister Kozyrev before visiting Yeltsin at his country residence. Christopher raised concerns about the fairness of the upcoming elections and mentioned that the United States had $12 million to contribute and could send election monitors. Kozyrev welcomed this as a way to guard against fraud by Communist-leaning local authorities in rural areas with "the old kolkhoz mentality."

Christopher worried about a free press since the order banning opposition newspapers had still not been lifted. Kozyrev said nothing about the press but volunteered that only six or seven political organizations would be banned from participating in the elections. Regarding NATO, Christopher told Kozyrev that the U.S. was sensitive to the Russian position and had developed a new proposal, the Partnership for Peace (PFP), open to all countries on an equal basis. He implied that the PFP was an alternative to expansion, at least for the time being. Christopher also asked for Russian cooperation in securing the withdrawal of nuclear weapons from Ukraine.[14]

The Clinton administration wanted to show that it accepted Russia into what Collins termed the family of Western states. But Washington had deep misgivings about the state of Russian democracy. If admitted to NATO, would that create one happy family across the Atlantic and Eurasia? Or would it undermine an alliance intended during the Cold War to keep Russia from attacking the West?

Poisoned and then imprisoned by the Putin regime, in 2022 the dissident Vladimir Kara-Mursa expressed regret about the Clinton administration's ambivalence. It was not until 1995, Kara-Mursa said,

---

[13] Cable from American Embassy Moscow to Secretary of State: Your October 21-23 Visit to Moscow-Key Foreign Policy Issues. Oct 20, 1993. Source: U.S. Department of State. Date/Case ID: 04 MAY 2000 200000982

[14] Secretary Christopher's Meeting with Foreign Minister Kozyrev, Oct 25, 1993. Source: U.S. Department of State. Date/Case ID: 11 MAR 2003 200001030

that Washington let Russia know it would consider its application to become an alliance member under certain conditions. The delay seemed an "eternity in view of the rapid changes that were taking place in Russia.... Opportunities were squandered during this time. One factor that contributed significantly to the failure of Russian democracy was that, unlike the other ex-Warsaw Pact countries, we never had the prospect of Euro-Atlantic integration. Had we had it, it would have been a tremendous driver for reform, just as it was in the Czech Republic, Slovakia, Poland or the Baltic states." When the Putin era ends, "this mistake must not be repeated."[15]

How Yeltsin Rose to Challenges

Yeltsin was not an easy man to deal with. He became impetuous as he engaged with whatever challenge confronted him. He was confident he could master whatever problem emerged, such as parliament's demand that he resign in 1993; Chechnya's assertion in 1994 of independence from the USSR; the broad opposition Yeltsin faced in 1996 to his reelection as president. Such challenges functioned like shock therapy.[16] In the late-1990s, however, prescription drugs for severe heart ailments and excessive drinking sometimes rendered him incoherent.

Having left office, Strobe Talbott wrote that Yeltsin—like former Soviet president Gorbachev— "was loath to use force or risk instability as the world's largest territorial state dismantled itself." By contrast, Vladimir Putin, starting in 1999, pursued a "scorched-earth strategy in subduing Chechen secessionists."

Cornell historian Matthew Evangelista sharply disagreed: "It was Yeltsin in late 1994 who first chose force to crush Chechnya's separatist movement, by launching a devastating war that entailed massive indiscriminate bombing of the capital city Grozny and smaller Chechen towns. Many thousands of civilians—Russian and Chechen alike—perished, and tens of thousands became refugees or internally displaced people."

---

15 Vladimir Kara-Mursa, "Putin's Regime Will Collapse," *Zeit Online*, September 7, 2022.

16 Timothy J. Colton, *Yeltsin: A Life* (New York: Basic Books, 2008), pp. 305, 394.

Yeltsin's "war of choice" to put down a mainly secular movement for autonomy sowed the seeds of the subsequent Islamist terrorism that wracked the region and reverberated in places so distant as Boston with its Marathon bombing by Chechens.[17] In April 1996, almost a year and a half into the Chechen war, at a summit meeting with Yeltsin in Moscow, Talbott's boss President Bill Clinton effectively endorsed Russia's resort to force. "I would remind you that we once had a Civil War in our country," said Clinton, fought "over the proposition that Abraham Lincoln gave his life for, that no State had a right to withdraw from our Union."

Evangelista believed it was "past time to recognize that the corruption and violence we condemn in Putin's Russia began with Yeltsin, rather than with his hand-picked successor."[18]

In reply, Talbott agreed that Yeltsin's military operation against Chechnya in 1994 was an act of mass cruelty, and the resulting alienation of his liberal supporters was a self-inflicted blow to his presidency that weakened him politically. Talbott said his "reference to Yeltsin's aversion to force concerned his resistance to revanchists bent on adjusting the borders of the USSR's constituent republics to bring as many ethnic Russians as possible into an expanded, predatory, post-Soviet Russian Federation. Yeltsin's opposition protected the Soviet Union from a decade-long bloodbath like the one that accompanied the breakup of Yugoslavia."

"When it came to Chechnya, Yeltsin was dealing not with a newly independent state [such as Estonia or Ukraine] but with militant secessionism within the Russian Federation. He first tried to quell the movement with punitive raids targeted against rebel strongholds, but that strategy ended in debacles and further advances by the guerrillas. With more patience, subtlety, and time, Yeltsin might have negotiated a settlement that would have kept Chechnya in Russia. Even if a peaceful compromise was impossible, Yeltsin

---

17 Russian authorities warned the FBI in 2011 about Tamerlan Tsarnaev, one of two Chechen brothers responsible for the bombing. Reuters, March 25, 2014.
18 The Evangelista-Talbott exchange is in *New York Review of Books*, January 18. 2018. It began with Talbott's "The Man Who Lost an Empire," *NYRB*, December 21, 2017, a review of William Taubman, *Gorbachev: His Life and Times* (New York: W. W. Norton, 2017),

should have found means other than an all-out invasion that caused many thousands of casualties among Chechen civilians. Two years later he tried to make amends by granting Chechnya a high degree of autonomy, renouncing the future use of force, and accepting the elected nationalist president, Aslan Maskhadov."

Talbott added that his memoir, *The Russia Hand* (2002), acknowledged that the Clinton administration "knew little about the Chechens' side of the story and was inclined to accept Moscow's—a shortcoming that skewed our analysis and policy. I also expressed regret over missing a chance to persuade President Clinton not to compare Yeltsin to Abraham Lincoln. That said, those of us who met with Yeltsin in the early and mid-1990s could see that he was frustrated and enervated by the lethal chaos in the Caucasus. We had quite a different impression of Vladimir Putin when, as prime minister in 1999, he launched the Second Chechen War. After several murderous and still not fully explained bombings in Russian cities, Putin ordered a relentless air campaign against Chechnya. That assault was much more brutal than Yeltsin's and ended with the installation of Chechen leaders so thuggish, violent, and deeply entrenched that they have operated with impunity even in Moscow itself. Yet Putin's popularity skyrocketed in Russia, clinching his succession to Yeltsin and anticipating what he is and does today."

Yeltsin, like Putin as he invaded Ukraine, had an unrealistic confidence in the power of Russia's armed forces and the ineptitude of their foes. Operating from a shared hubris, Yeltsin's advisers told him to expect a short war lasting ten days.[19] Putin in 2022 thought he could take Kyiv and its leaders in under two weeks. His forces, like those who invaded Russia in June 1812 and June 1941, were not equipped for winter weather and other challenges.

"Compatriots" in the "Near Abroad"

Many other Russian leaders, if not Yeltsin, were wedded to the former empire and strove to rebuild it. After a decade at the helm, Yeltsin became weaker and his family more corrupt. On New Year's Eve 1999, he transferred power to former KGB agent Vladimir Putin.[20]

---

19 Colton, *Yeltsin,* p. 290.

20 Putin earlier advertised his respect for Yuri Andropov—head of the KGB before

3. Was NATO to Blame?

Long before Putin took the helm, Russian strategists espoused a policy that was both revanchist and revisionist—oriented toward revenge and recovery of lost lands and glory. Two phrases sum up the revanchist approach: "near-abroad" and "compatriots [*sootechestveniki*]." Influential policy experts in Moscow declared that Russia had a right and a duty to protect its interests in the near-abroad—the former union-republics of the USSR such as Estonia, Ukraine, and Kazakhstan. The term implied that these borderlands were not independent in the way that a foreign country such as Italy is independent. In the mid-1990s the Russian Duma passed legislation to assist "compatriots"—former citizens of Russia or the USSR and their descendants--and to help them to form political action councils. Yeltsin refused to sign these bills. His advisers rightly argued there was no basis in international law for such intervention in the internal affairs of other states. But the Duma overruled Yeltsin and the compatriot legislation has been revised, updated, and tightened under the Putin regime.[21]

There were and still are many persons in most former Soviet republics (and even Old Believers in Alaska) whom the Kremlin could view as Russian compatriots. For example, half of Latvia's residents and two-fifths of Estonia's were native Russian speakers in 1991; also, one-third of Kazakhstan's people. Many in Kazakhstan moved back to Russia after the Soviet break-up. In the Baltic lands, many older Russian-speakers refused to learn the local language or even to apply for a residence permit. Younger Russian-speakers in the Baltic republics were more willing to adjust to the new ways and learn the local language.

Why did Yeltsin keep Russian military units in the Baltic states for several years after the Kremlin recognized their independence? There were no buildings in Russia to house them, Yeltsin explained, suggesting a need for foreign aid. A Russian admiral whom I met in Tallinn in 1990 told me he planned to move back to Rostov to live

---

becoming paramount leader of the USSR. On continuity between the former KGB and FSB, see Mark Kramer, "If It Looks Like the KGB, and Acts Like the KGB...." *The Washington Post*. March 19, 2020.

21 Clemens, *The Baltic Transformed: Complexity Theory and European Security*, Foreword by Jack F. Matlock, Jr. (Lanham, Md.: Rowman & Littlefield, 2001), pp. 182-185.

with his parents, even though the city was badly polluted.

To reduce friction with Moscow, Estonia and Latvia agreed in the early 1990s to forgo claims to border regions seized for Russia in Stalin's time. But their accommodations did not diminish revanchist attitudes in Russia.

Nazi Rule in Ukraine?

A third reason for the special military operation, Putin said, was to de-nazify Ukraine and its leadership and halt their genocide of Russian-speakers. Anticipating this campaign, on September 11, 2008, the Russian Ministry of Foreign Affairs alleged that Ukrainian attempts "to heroize the accomplices of fascism," violate "the rights of Ukraine's Russian-speaking population" and "oust the Russian language from the public life of the country, science, education, culture and the mass media."

The government newspaper *Zavtra* in October 2022 pictured the struggle against Nazi Ukraine:

Russian Troops ("Z") Defeating Ukrainian Nazis

Source: "No Let-up on the Ukraine Front," Aleksander Prokhanov, "Russkii Marten," Zavtra. October 24, 2022, at https://zavtra.ru/blogs/na_ukrainskom_fronte_bez_peremen (accessed 12/4/2022).

3. WAS NATO TO BLAME?

Brutality toward Jews has been a leitmotif of European politics, even before their 1492 expulsion from Spain. The reality is that antisemitism and far-right movements exist in many countries including the United States and Russia.[22]

Far-right parties won only 2% of the vote in Ukraine's 2019 parliamentary elections—less than in many European countries. Later, Ukraine voters chose a Jew as their president. Volodymyr Zelenskyy and his government have worked to protect minorities like Crimean Tatars and LGBTQ+ people, who are persecuted in Russia. There is no evidence of recent mass killings or ethnic purges in Ukraine.

Meanwhile, the Putin regime cultivated its own homegrown Nazis. Responding to Ukraine's Orange Revolution in 2004, the Kremlin mobilized a bevy of right-wing youth groups it called *Nashi* ("Ours") to counter democrats and leftists.

The origins of this relationship date to the late 1990s, when Russia was shaken by a wave of racist violence committed by neo-Nazi skinhead gangs. The Putin regime tried to "manage nationalism" by coopting radical nationalist militants, including neo-Nazis, as a counterweight to growing liberal forces. In 2005, Nashi took in football gang members and skinheads from the neo-Nazi underground.[23]

Threatened by Russian oppositionist Aleksei Navalny, the Kremlin in 2008–2009 began to work with *Russkii Obraz* ("Russian Image" or "RO" for short), a hardcore neo-Nazi group known for its

---

22 From the Smithsonian Castle in 1976, I watched uniformed Nazis, guarded by local police, march down the grassy mall toward the Washington Monument. More like them took part in the January 6 insurrection at the U.S. Capitol in 2021, According to Bloomberg News. January 11, 2023, "It's not just statements by rapper Ye and basketball star Kyrie Irving, or politicians cozying up to White supremacist groups: Antisemitism is seeping into the U.S. workplace. Jewish workers in industries as varied as PR and supply chain logistics expressed a sense of increasing discrimination, including overhearing antisemitic remarks from co-workers. That backs up data from bodies including the Anti-Defamation League."

23 Robert Horvath, "Putin's fascists: The Russian state's long history of cultivating homegrown neo-Nazis," *The Conversation*, 3/21/22 at https://theconversation.com/putins-fascists-the-russian-states-long-history-of-cultivating-homegrown-neo-nazis-178535

slick journal and its band "Hook from the Right." A co-founder of RO, Nikita Tikhonov, became leader of BORN ("Fighting Organization of Russian Nationalists"), a terrorist group that committed a string of murders of public figures and antifa militants. The victims included the renowned human rights lawyer Stanislav Markelov and journalist Anastasia Baburova. Tikhonov was convicted of their murders in 2011.

NASHI IN "OUR VICTORY" CLOAKS CELEBRATE A 2007 ELECTION WIN

In 2014, RO's Aleksandr Matyushin helped to terrorize supporters of the Ukrainian state in Donetsk. He went on to become a major field commander there. RO's Anna Trigga worked for the Internet Research Agency, the trolling factory that interfered in the 2016 U.S. presidential election and tried to foment anti-Muslim hatred in Australia. RO's Dmitrii Steshin, war correspondent for a mass circulation tabloid, disseminated lies blaming Ukrainian false-flag operations for atrocities committed by Russian forces.

The Kremlin also cultivated neo-Nazis in the West, for example, "experts" who expound conspiracy theories on RT, the Kremlin's cable TV. Some Westerners serve the Kremlin as "monitors" who applaud fraudulent elections. From an apartment in St. Petersburg, the American Roman Wolf, aka Rinaldo Nazzaro, ran "The Base," a white-supremacist organization that described itself as an "international survivalist and self-defense network" that trains members for race war. Since its founding, the Base has been active in North America, Europe, South Africa, and Australia.[24] Nazzaro resigned in 2022, regretting his work had not achieved stronger results.

For a dictator who is dismantling democracy and constructing an authoritarian regime, neo-Nazis are useful accomplices.

The main basis for Putin's false claim that Ukraine's government is run by neo-Nazis has been the Azov Battalion, a far-right nationalist Ukrainian paramilitary and political movement, This paramilitary organization took shape in 2014 before integrating into the Ukrainian National Guard as a Special Purposes Regiment. Following integration, Azov Regiment veterans broadened the movement to include a political wing, the National Corps, and a paramilitary wing, the National Militia. It keeps extensive transnational ties with other far-right organizations. The Battalion recruits far-right foreign fighters via white-supremacist sites in the U.S., Russia, and Europe. Though Azov remains a fringe movement in Ukraine, it is a larger-than-life brand among many extremists.[25]

The Mapping Militants project at Stanford University reported that the Azov Battalion's first violent attack was in April 2014 when it clashed with Russian-backed separatists in Donetsk. In 2022 the movement fought Russian forces in Kyiv, Kharkiv, and Mariupol. In August 2022, Azov special forces in Kharkiv attacked Russian forces outside the village of Ternova. A commander claimed the attack destroyed several vehicles, an outpost, an ammunition depot, and killed seven Russian combatants.[26]

RT reported that on October 1, 2022, Stanford University hosted several Azov representatives, including two former POWs recently released by Russia. The former U.S. ambassador to Russia,

---

24 https://www.counterextremism.com/supremacy/base (accessed 1/10/23).
25 Rita Katz, "Neo-Nazis are exploiting Russia's war in Ukraine for their own purposes," *The Washington Post*, March 14. 2022.
26 Stanford University, https://cisac.fsi.stanford.edu/mappingmilitants/profiles/azov-battalion#text_block_33831

professor Michael McFaul, was there. Two weeks later, Anatoly Antonov Russia's ambassador to the U.S., rebuked Stanford for hosting an event featuring fighters from the Azov Battalion. "It would appear that in its maniacal drive to tarnish and cancel Russia, the U.S. is prepared to glorify Nazism."

The idea that one should hear all sides to a conflict may seem strange to the ambassador. He did not comment on the Kremlin's manipulation of far-right organizations, discussed above, and recruitment of criminals from prisons to fight in Ukraine.

So Why is Putin in Ukraine?

In 2019, Ukraine's constitution was amended to commit the country to membership in NATO and the EU. In June 2020 Ukraine was named a NATO Enhanced Opportunities Partner—joining Australia, Georgia, Finland, Jordan, and Sweden for possible cooperation in NATO-led missions and exercises. NATO made clear, however, that the new status did "not pre-judge any decisions on NATO membership." In September 2020, Zelenskyy approved a new National Security Strategy to develop a partnership leading to NATO membership. Even as war enveloped the region in 2022–2023, however, the prospects of NATO membership for Ukraine and Georgia looked very remote.

The United States and other NATO powers were reluctant to arm Ukraine. The Obama administration authorized only non-lethal military assistance. In 2017, the United States approved lethal weapons for Ukraine, but Donald Trump tried to condition military assistance on Kyiv's finding dirt on Hunter Biden.[27]

Long concerned about Russian militarism, President Biden sought to deliver substantial aid to Ukraine, stopping short of crossing a threshold that could provoke World War III. Biden tapped U.S. intelligence to warn that Russia planned to invade. He

---

27 A couple months into the job, Zelenskyy got a phone call from U.S. President Donald Trump asking for information on the son of Joe Biden, whom he expected to face in the 2020 presidential election. Democrats saw this as an effort to make aid to Ukraine conditional on Zelenskyy's help in a partisan contest. House Democrats impeached Trump, but Senate Republicans acquitted him.

authorized U.S. troops to train Ukrainians, He authorized delivery of anti-tank and anti-aircraft defenses. As the war dragged on, rockets that could hit Russian forces in Ukraine—delivered with assurances they would not be used against targets in Russia. Not until 2023 would the United States provide Ukraine with Patriot anti-missile systems or modern tanks.[28]

Why is Putin in Ukraine? The facts summarized in this chapter dovetail with the conclusions of Professor Alexander Motyl at Rutgers University: "Ukraine is an important security interest of Russia only because Russians have made it into an important security interest." Russians could just as easily "unmake" it and, instead, treat Ukraine as nothing more than a neighbor. Ukraine is as much of an objective threat to Russia as Canada is to the United States. Even NATO poses no objective threat to Russia's security. Most of its members have completely neglected their militaries since the collapse of the Soviet Union in 1991. Ukraine's resistance and independent Ukraine's very existence is thus a threat to Putin's imperialist project—not because it actually threatens Russia's existence, but because they are perceived by Putin as threatening his and his imperial project's existence.[29]

This analysis does not say that Putin's decision to invade Ukraine was due only to his quest for empire and that Western policies played no role. Life is complex. We must avoid psychology's attribution error--ascribing the behavior of others to their essential nature and ignoring the situations they face. Still, Putin seemed not to care much about NATO. He said little when Sweden and Finland applied to join. What really bothered him was the fact of a democratic country next to Russia.[30]

---

28 Germany and other NATO members did not offer their best tanks until the United States led the way. Europeans then discovered that their dreams of eternal peace led them not to keep all their tanks functional. Many decided they could not afford to transfer many of their limited supply of working tanks to Ukraine.

29 Alexander J. Motyl, "How Putin's Russia invented a Ukrainian threat, and why," *EUObserver*, 12/14/22 at https://euobserver.com/opinion/156539 (accessed 1/12/23).

30 Remarks by Anna Grzymala-Busse, Director of Stanford's European Center, to visitors from the NATO Parliamentary Assembly, September 26, 2022.

CHAPTER 4
RUSSIAN VALUES IN A "RUSSIAN WORLD"

Putin and his acolytes strove to negate everything associated with Ukraine. Against this negativity, they cast Russia in the most positive terms. Its values, they said, emerged from more than a millennium of struggle in which the ways of neighboring cultures coalesced to form a unique "Russian World"—*Russkii Mir.*

When Putin first came to power, he began to modify the official ideology with his 2000 National Security Strategy calling for the protection of Russian cultural, moral, and spiritual traditions. The Kremlin presented Russia's identity as no less important to defend than its physical integrity.

Putin portrayed Western values and politics as a Trojan horse and instead promoted a Russian culture rooted in tradition but strengthened by modern technologies. Putin revived Count Sergei Uvarov's 19th century doctrine of "Orthodoxy, Autocracy, and Nationality." The result was the creation of a national identity in which Putin and Russia became interchangeable.[1] This outlook paralleled Patriarch Kirill's efforts to make his Orthodox Church the fulcrum of Russian society.

Putin's chauvinism hurt Russia as well as Ukraine and undermined every principle of world order and global humanism. In some ways it paralleled the cult of Adolph Hitler and his German Volk.

AGAINST THE WEST: RUSSIA'S SPIRITUAL AND MORAL VALUES

In the late 1980s, Soviet President Mikhail Gorbachev (1931–2022) called for policies based on "universal values" rather than those of class or Communism.[2] Now, the wheel turned again as the Putin

---

1 Carlo J. V. Caro, "Vladimir Putin's 'Orthodoxy, Autocracy, and Nationality,'" *The Rule of Law Post,* August 31, 2022 at https://www.penncerl.org/the-rule-of-law-post/vladimir-putins-orthodoxy-autocracy-and-nationality/

2 He was buried September 3, 2022, in a farewell ceremony at Novodevichy

regime endorsed a moral code wordily referred to as "Fundamentals of State Policy for the Preservation and Strengthening of Traditional Russian Spiritual and Moral Values." It aimed to counter Western liberal influences that plant ideas and values deemed alien to the Russian people and destructive of Russian society. These negative values include the cult of selfishness, permissiveness, and immorality, along with efforts to denigrate patriotism, service to the Fatherland, procreation, and creative work. Putin also accused the West of demeaning Russia's positive contribution to world history and culture. The West's corrosive ideology was said to harm the national interests of the Russian Federation. Against it, the Kremlin would clamp down on Western missionary activity and other alien influences on Russian soil.[3]

This picture of Western and Russian values agrees with that depicted by Aleksandr Dugin, a somewhat mystical writer, born in 1962, who laid out his vision of Russia as an "eternal Rome" in the far-right newspaper *Den'* in the early 1990s.[4] His 29-year-old daughter Darya Dugina died when her SUV detonated near Moscow in August 2022—an event that sparked a mix of possible explanations. Kyiv, however, denied any role.

In 2014, when Putin invaded Ukraine for the first time, Dugin had already developed an entire arsenal of language for the occasion. He had called for the creation of a "Russian World" —a geographically non-specific concept that imagined Russia on a

---

cemetery attended by thousands of mourners but snubbed by Putin. The Kremlin's refusal to formally declare a state funeral reflected its uneasiness with the legacy of Gorbachev, venerated worldwide for bringing down the Iron Curtain but reviled by many at home for bringing on the Soviet collapse.

3   My book *Can Russia Change?* first appeared in 1990, at a time when Mikhail Gorbachev as well as many observers believed then that the entire Soviet system needed profound changes. But many experts forecast—correctly—the old ways would persist. The structures of Communist rule fell away in 1991–1992, but the deepest currents of political culture remained. A new lust for personal wealth as well as for power posed huge dangers to Russia, its former vassal states, and the West.

4   In the early 1990s, Dugin co-founded the National Bol'shevik Party with Eduard Limonov. See Tata Isabella Burton in https://www.washingtonpost.com/outlook/2022/05/12/dugin-russia-ukraine-putin/ Donald Trump consultant Steve Bannon was also attracted to the same "Traditionalist" school that influenced Dugin.

civilizational mission rooted in traditional values and the Russian Orthodox religion. Annexing eastern Ukraine was seen as a big step in building or rebuilding the Russian World.[5]

In January 2022, the deputy editor of Russia's last major independent newspaper, *Novaya Gazeta* (subsequently relocated in Riga) noted that Putin's call for 'Moral Values" claims that "collectivism" is inherent in the Russian people. However, Putin says nothing about the universal values praised by Gorbachev and common to some religions today.[6] It avers that Russian values emerge from more than a thousand years in which the religious and other values of the many peoples now living in the Russian Federation have converged into an amalgamated "Russian World." Putin's "spiritual" values text never speaks of serving God. Rather, it sacralizes the Fatherland. In reality, it demeans both culture and religion by treating them as a "strategic resource" —another asset in Russia's armorarium.[7]

The draft presidential decree prepared by the Ministry of Culture in accordance with the National Security Strategy, was expected to be signed by the president in May 2022, but first there was to be some public discussion. In March, some three hundred leading figures from all walks of life from across the country gathered all day in an elegant Moscow hotel. Nearly all gave the project their enthusiastic approval. The only dissidents were representatives of theatrical and museum workers, who feared another layer of thought control by greedy bureaucrats. Cultural workers said the "protective" decree was extremely vague. It simplistically supported good values and opposed bad ones. Except for collectivism, it mentioned no values specifically Russian. Artistic sensitivity would suffer. The

---

5   Masha Gessen, "The Mysterious Murder of Darya Dugina," *The New Yorker,* August 26, 2022.

6   Some religions have denied universal values. Some Christians have claimed that the Bible justifies slavery and that whites are God's Chosen people. Hindus find a rationale for the caste system in their most revered texts. Religious as well as ethnic wars continue, e.g., Sunni Muslims versus Shiia. Chinese atheists try to extirpate religion and culture. Jews have been persecuted for millennia–in part because of their religion. Israeli Jews and Arab fight over land as well as religion.

7   "Dukno-nravstvennye tsennosti kak strategicheskii resurs Rossii," *РУССКИЙ ДОЗОР* (03/07/22). *DOZOR [PATROL]* provides military news online.

"protective" decree would, sacrifice artistic creativity to enhance the power of apparatchiks in the Institute of Heritage under the Ministry of Culture.[8]

Novaya Gazeta surmised that since the draft decree provides for an "interdepartmental coordination body," Big Brother might soon demand establishment of a Ministry of Values as well as a Ministry of Truth.

The draft document endorsed patriotism but said little about faith or hope and nothing at all about charity or loving one's neighbor. While the draft document did not mention any particular Russian values except collectivism, it appeared in Ukraine that some Russians placed a high value on rape, shooting handcuffed civilians in the back of the head, bombing schools and hospitals, and looting—everything from nuclear power plant machinery to Disney-branded sheets from private apartments.[9]

On November 8, 2022, Putin made it official—a return to Russia's traditional spiritual and moral values would be an official priority. The Kremlin's reputed "brain center," the Institute of Social Research, conducted a roundtable on these issues by highly placed political and social scientists. Most of them, according to the newspaper *Kommersant'*, agreed that a return to traditional spiritual values would consolidate society—both older and younger generations—more effectively than any attempt to formulate a "national ideology" to replace what was lost with the Soviet demise. Any effort to impose such an ideology risked civil war, while imported foreign ideas threatened national sovereignty and would weaken Russia in international competition. One demographer reminded the roundtable that Russian values included families with many children, devotion to children, and respect for elders. For now, however, many young people preferred to celebrate western holidays such as Saint Valentine's Day and Halloween (unheard of when I studied in Moscow in 1958–1959), while older people still liked to remember "October" [1917] and "The Day of the

---

8 Ol'ga Fedianina on cultural politics and the art of censorship in *Kommersant'*, February 9, 2022, p. 11.

9 Austrians I met in 1952–1953 had similar stories about the behavior of the Red Army occupiers in 1945–1946.

Cosmonauts."[10] Not afraid to give contradictory messages, the same day that *Kommersant'* regurgitated the roundtable, it also featured colorful pictures and stories about the Thanksgiving Day parade in New York City,

Having labored to amplify the ostensible values of their boss, most roundtable participants probably retired to enjoy other Russian traditions, especially when the sponsor covered the costs of food and drink.

The Orthodox Patriarchate and Military Values

The Moscow Patriarchate of Russian Orthodoxy also backed Putin's version of patriotism. That symbol of modern Russian militarism, the Cathedral of the Armed Forces, was erected in 2018 in Odintsovsky district, about an hour's drive west of Moscow. There, angels hover above images of artillery, religious icons are adorned with Kalashnikovs; the Virgin Mary strikes a pose reminiscent of a "Great Patriotic War" poster. The entire edifice is clad in khaki-colored metal. In the spirit of *Gott mit uns*, the cathedral mosaics suggest that God has blessed not just the Red Army in the Great Patriotic War but also Russian military actions in 1956 Hungary, 1968 Czechoslovakia, and 1979 Afghanistan, as well as President Putin's adventures in Chechnya, Georgia, Crimea and the "fight against international terrorism in Syria." A 28-year-old server at the cathedral observed that "only Russians are capable of sacrificing themselves to save humanity, just like Jesus did." Combined with militarized youth groups such as the Youth Army (*Yunarmiia*), the cathedral and its surrounding Patriotic Park prepare Russians for heroic wars in the future.[11]

---

10 Anastasiia Kornia, "Rossii predlozhili smenit' orientatsiiu," *Kommersant'*, No. 219, November 25, 2022, p. 3.

11 The temple's mosaics are dedicated to wars against Russia's enemies, beginning with Dmitrii Donskoi's battles in the 14th century. A blank row is reserved for wars yet to come. Protests arose when one of the mosaics depicted Vladimir Putin and Defense Minister Sergei Shoigu. The images were removed after the president said that someday grateful descendants might appreciate his contributions, but it was still too early for that. On another mosaic, the inscription "Crimea is ours" was replaced with "We are together."

At the initiative of Minister of Culture Vladimir Medinskii, the Russian Military-

In March 2022, Russian Orthodox Patriarch Kirill (known in the Baltic as a long-time KGB agent and in Moscow as boss of an illegal cigarette smuggling ring) rapturously blessed Putin's invasion of Ukraine as a crusade against Western heathenism and gay pride, triggering rebukes by some Russian clerics and Orthodox leaders in Ukraine and beyond.

The *russkii mir* outlook, orchestrated by Patriarch Kirill as well as Dudin, reinforced Putin in his campaign to destroy the Ukrainian state and people. The Russian church, as Rutgers professor Alexander Motyl has suggested, seems to have lost its own soul.

Putin may be hoping that the same fate awaits the Russian people as it did the spaceship builder protagonist in Yevgeny Zamyatin's sci-fi dystopia *We,* banned by Soviet censors in 1921, but published in the West in various translations.[12] Not until surgeons removed both his soul and imagination, could the rocket engineer in the blissful community of *We* live in harmony with the mandates of the Great Benefactor.

Russia's *Prezident*: Risen Savior or War Criminal?

The International Criminal Court is flooded with detailed reports of Russian war crimes in Ukraine, along with abundant evidence that the entire "special military operation" has been instigated and directed by Russian Federation's president. Vladimir Putin may be a war criminal to many in the West, but for ardent Russian ultranationalists, he is a risen Christ.

What claims to be a newspaper of the Russian state, *Zavtra* [*Tomorrow*] on Easter 2022 portrayed the war on Ukraine as a crusade in which President Putin carries the cross of the "Russian Cathedral" to the top of Golgotha where it fights the American "fortress." Editor Aleksandr Prokhanov covered the first page with the headline, "He is truly risen!" with a picture of Christ accompanied by heavy artillery, a tank, and smoking buildings.

Historical Society *(Rossiiskoe voenno-istoricheskoe obshchestvo* or *RVIO*) was formed December 29, 2012 by Order 1710 of President Putin with the declared intent of facilitating the study of Russia's military history and thwarting efforts to distort it. See https://rvio.histrf.ru/.

12 Summarized below in Chapter 11.

4. Russian Values in a "Russian World"

Here is the picture https://zavtra.ru/blogs/voistinu

Prokhanov denounced Gorbachev's late 1980s *perestroika* (restructuring) campaign for nailing Russia to the cross and compared Boris Yeltsin's 1990s Russia with putting Christ into his grave. By implication, Putin's emergence is a resurrection.

Prokhanov is seen by some Russians as an articulate clown, like the ardent nationalist Vladimir Zhirinovsky, who was honored in death by President Putin on April 6, 2022. Putin laid a bouquet of red roses near the coffin and bowed his head for a moment of silence for the leader of the ultranationalist opposition that Putin exploited to advance his own goals, while keeping up appearances of democratic pluralism.

Prokhanov who was once a foe of Putin but later functioned as part of the systemic, government-approved PR network. Prokhanov had earlier criticized Putin as being too liberal but became his strong supporter after annexation of Crimea. Some observers characterized *Zavtra* as "brown-red"—Hitlerite-Stalinist. The paper descended from the ultra-conservative newspaper *Den'* [*Day*], founded by Prokhanov in 1990, but soon shut down by Boris Yeltsin's administration. *Zavtra* is not *the* official voice of the Kremlin but on newsstands it is displayed next to *Izvestiya, Pravda,* and *Komsomol'skaya Pravda*, while the liberal *Novaya Gazeta* is no more except online from outside Russia. Most of the surviving print and electronic media trumpet whatever message the government wants. *Zavtra* maintained that Putin, if not actually the crucified Christ, is a man of God whose actions are blessed by the Orthodox Church.

Prokhanov stated that Russia is not a helpless victim of foreign doctors. He boasted that no one can kill the homeland of Stalin, the venerable church reformer Sergei [14th century miracle worker of Radonezh], academician ["biosphere"] Vladimir Vernadskii [first president, Ukrainian Academy of Sciences], Lake Baikal and Mother Volga, and the Baikal-Amur Railway, deemed unviable in the 1990s but a subject of renewed interest in recent years.

Owned by a Gazprom magnate, the business daily *Kommersant'* continued to publish many articles that deviated from Kremlin orthodoxy. On November 25, 2022, for example, it published a detailed chronology of Russian censorship of foreign publications, from 1700 through 1985, noting that the renowned physicist Petr Kapitsa complained to Stalin he was being cut off from the foreign journals essential to his work. Another article, citing an IMF study, said that "sanctions are working." Another detailed what was known about a new U.S. bomber—a veritable flying wing. There were many articles about aspects of the Ukraine special operation. They included Boris Johnson collecting medical supplies for Ukraine; agreements by Poland and Latvia to do more for Ukraine; a Russian oil refinery in Sicily in danger of bankruptcy. From these and other tidbits, a Russian reader could connect the dots to get closer to the big picture.

Contrary to Prokhanov and other devout supporters of the president, banker Oleg Tinkov announced that, with Putin ascendant, Russia "as a country no longer exists." On April 19, 2022, oligarch Tinkov published an antiwar post on Instagram, calling the invasion of Ukraine "crazy" and deriding Russia's military: "Why would we have a good army," he asked, if everything else in the country is dysfunctional "and mired in nepotism, servility and subservience?"[13]

---

13 Immediately punished for disloyalty, Tinkov was forced to sell his shares in a

4. Russian Values in a "Russian World"

The False God of Tsar Vladimir

The notion *Bog s nami*, "God is with us," has been part of Vladimir Putin's Russian nationalist revival, a boast that is sacrilegious and untrue. The Putin administration has waged a zealous and accelerating campaign to throttle alien influences. It has shut down human rights organizations such as Memorial (founded with strong support by Sakharov) as alleged foreign agents.

Beginning in 2021, the Russian Academy of Sciences and State Duma discussed ways to restrict influences emanating from abroad. Some officials proposed that any contact between an Academy scientist and a foreigner must be authorized by the head of his/her institute; that a third Russian scientist must be present at any meeting with a foreigner; and that a meeting report must be submitted to the directorate. All correspondence with foreign scientists should be monitored by the institute's directorate. The possibilities of "digitalization" were marching toward Orwell's predictions about an all-powerful Ministry of Truth.

Some Putin supporters seemed to lose contact with reality. The newspaper *Zavtra* (*Tomorrow*), May 5, 2022, still claiming to be the "newspaper of the Russian state," ran a front-page story by its editor, Aleksandr Prokhanov, entitled "Glory to the Lord! Allah Is Great!" [*Slava tebe, Gospodi! Allakh Akbar*!] illustrated with the image of two fighters—a square jawed Russian youth and an older, white bearded militant likely to shout "Allakh Akbar!" after every explosion. Is he a Chechen or Syrian mercenary? Prokhanov explains nothing about this man's presence except to add "Allakh Akbar" to the final words of his disquisition on Russia's greatness. Perhaps all this is to show solidarity between Russian Orthodox Russians and some Muslims. Yes. Islam is on the rise in Russia's south, but it is not obvious that many Russians would feel solidarity with a Muslim white beard.[14]

---

major bank at far below their market value. *The New York Times*, May 1, 2022.

14 Alisa Shishkina, "Russia Seeks Pathways for Disaffected Young Muslims," *Europe's Edge* (*May 23, 2022*) at https://cepa.org/russia-seeks-pathways-for-disaffected-young-muslims

https://zavtra.ru/upl/20000/alarge/pic_17128265d19.jpg

Whatever else, Putin's special operation shakes the world. To quote Prokhanov: "Russian regiments from the Crimea, Bryansk, Rostov entered Ukraine, and the blows of heavy columns shook the world . . . . The old world shakes off its plaster, and under it appear unprecedented, unprecedented constructions of a new, unknown humanity"—a hill crowned with a Russian cathedral, terrifying with its mystery, numbing with its unexpected appearance. "The 21-st century becomes the Russian century . . . Again, from the black abyss of Russian timelessness, the true, primordial Russia rises, conceived by the Lord as an empire between three oceans. It resides among Russia's forests, ridges and great rivers, among temples, palaces, and huts, the innermost Russian essence. The dream of a mighty, flourishing, divine and just kingdom, where there is no darkness, but only the radiant Tabor light. This Russian Dream, obscured by unprecedented suffering, terrible defeats and falling into the abyss, every time brought Russia out of timelessness, created a great state out of it."

Prokhanov continued: "Today, Russia, thrown back from its historical borders, wounded, bloodied, goes on a counterattack. It attacks the West and regains its heritage. There is also a fierce battle going on within Russia. The billionaires who fled from Russia, losing their untold wealth, now sponsor a Kremlin 'peace party'. They demand a cessation of hostilities and wish Russia's defeat so they can return to Russia and drink into its oil and gas, diamonds, and prolong its suffering."

This negative appraisal of oligarch peaceniks may have been reflected in the mysterious deaths of at least ten Lukoil, Gazprom, and government officials between August 25, 2022, and spring 2023 after they expressed misgivings about the special military operation.

Prokhanov boasted that this peace party of billionaires was countered by Russia's military industrial complex—"its heavyweight Russian industrialists, the heads of corporations, supplying tanks and planes to the front, patching sanctions holes, mobilizing Russian engineers, managers, entrepreneurs to create a new sovereign economy, tearing it out of humiliating perfidious globalism." Overnight, however, "a lightweight, evil-tongued population of laughers and singers, caustic accusers, vicious haters, and refined Russophobes ... fled to Israel."

Now that the "liberal dictatorship of the Yeltsin years has cracked, Russian culture, strangled in the 1990s, begins to rise from under the iron plate, looks at the world with hard, penetrating eyes, sends its artists, writer, singers to Russian battalions fighting near Kharkov [Kharkhiv] and Odessa [Odesa]. This fight is cruel, just as the fight of Russian people for their dream has been cruel in all ages...."

Who is Russia's foe? According to Prokhanov, "the West is not only the flow of heavy howitzers and Javelins sent to Ukraine. Not only parliaments and prime ministers, introducing endless anti-Russian sanctions one by one. Not only TV magnates who have taken over the airwaves, turning the European peoples into crowds of brutalized senseless Russophobes. The West is a huge, mysterious, thousand-dimensional entity, consisting of intelligence agencies, military factories, intellectual headquarters, magic centers, religious and philosophical circles, hidden structures that contain the ancient demonic idea of world domination ... with which the demon tempted Christ on top of the temple."

"Russia and the West cannot live side by side," Prokhanov continued. "The American dream, as defined by neocons, is a fortress built on top of a mountain, from where the whole conquered world is visible, on which, in case of disobedience, cruise missiles rain down."

"The Russian Dream is a temple on a hill"—Prokhanov wrote—"on the heavenly hill of Russian history consisting of our victories, defeats, great misfortunes and transformations. And on the top of this hill there is not a fortress, not a pillbox, not a fortified area, but a delightful temple, like the Savior Church on Nereditsa Hill near Novgorod or the Intercession Church on the Nerl near the ancient capital of Vladimir. The domes of this temple touch the crystal blue. And this azure, the divine light of Tabor (Matthew 17) in all ages pours into our families, garrisons, universities, overcoming the deep darkness, not allowing us to perish."

This interpretation of Tabor light by Orthodox theologians was rejected by the Western Church in the 1340s, regarding its interpretation as an attack on the papacy. A related article in *Zavtra* denounced Pope Francis, because his proposal for an Easter ceasefire in 2022 would have permitted the West to send more arms to Ukraine.

Prokhanov concluded: "Today the Russian Temple and the American fortress are fighting in the world. The Russian Temple in the hour of trouble and violence turns into a fortress. The West and Russia have come together in a merciless battle. We will win this battle, because the temple is stronger than the fortress, because the world is conceived as harmony, not violence, as justice, not outrage . . . Today, Russian battalions, breaking through the defenses of the Ukrainian troops, break through the wall of the American fortress. And a Russian whirlwind, Russian light, will burst into this hole. The Russian Dream will win. Glory to you, Lord! Allakh Akbar!"

Continuing to scavenge the past for contemporary wisdom, Prokhanov wrote that each founder of a Russian empire—Saint Vladimir, Ivan Grozny, Peter the Great, and Stalin—all shared one virtue: each was like Stalin [*Stalinym*]. The founder of the fifth Russian empire, Vladimir Putin, is becoming another Stalin [*Stalinym stanet Vladimir Putin*]. But the West has bribed and compromised Russia's elites with Coca Cola and Broadway music. The West's inventions such as Ekho, Memorial, and Boris Yeltsin must be consumed in fire.[15] Like his predecessors, Putin must create a new elite and purge our *rodina* of decay.[16]

There are fanatics with fantasies is in many countries, but few endorse unprovoked aggressive war. If the fantasies of Russian nationalists like Prokhanov, do not materialize, they may need therapy for cognitive dissonance or worse.

After Ukraine, according to a professor at the Diplomatic Academy of the Russian Foreign Ministry, Russia had to "de-Nazify" six additional countries—Estonia, Latvia, Lithuania, Poland, Moldova, and Kazakhstan.[17] This same list of targets was repeated by a KPRF (Communist) deputy in the Moscow city duma.

METAPHYSICS AND REALPOLITIK

Who believes what? Do Putin, Kirill, and Dugin take seriously the belief that the Russian Orthodox Church and Russian state are a virtual Third Rome representing the only correct interpretation of Christianity and the rightful guardian of Slavdom—indeed, the protector of humanity from the wiles of Western materialism and gay culture? Or is this worldview merely a pretense for mobilizing Russian citizens (including millions of non-Russians) under a totalitarian dictatorship and reconstituting the former tsarist/Soviet empire—while reconstituting Russia as a major global power? On balance, probably a pretense.

Putin's outlook is surely influenced by personal experiences—a tough childhood on the streets of Leningrad; an impetuous fight that delayed his entry into the KGB; his real-time experience of the East German collapse; looking for a job after the Soviet demise. Of course, Russia's history and character also shape Kremlin

---

15 Ekho radio, not a government station, was shut down in March 2022 but, by October, was broadcasting from Berlin.

16 Prokhanov, "Russkii Marten," *Zavtra*, October 24, 2022.

17 *Voennoe Nezavisimoe Obozrenie [Independent Military Review]*, April 21, 2022.

ambitions.[18] Putin seems to approve the romantic ideas of Russia's 19th century mystics such as Konstantin Leontiev, who taught that Russia is "to head some new Eastern realm giving the world a new culture, so that the Slav-Oriental civilization may replace the passing civilization of Latin-Germanic Europe."[19] Leontiev, however, also questioned the relevance of Slavophilism and urged Russia to become a socialist autocracy. Though he lived for a time as a monk on Mount Athos, toward the end of his life, influenced by Vladimir Solovyev, he was attracted to Roman Catholicism. Adding to his career of brilliant complexity, he also worked in the censor's office and wrote deep analyses of Lev Tolstoy's works.

Russian confidence in its role as the Third Rome helps explain its continued insistence on trying to punch above its weight in GDP or demography. As Prokhanov made clear in *Zavtra*, Russia's claim to a unique destiny is not based on its achievements in freedom or prosperity, but on its spiritual culture and ability to endure suffering.[20]

The wild assertions of Prokhanov echo those of 19th century Slavophiles such as Fyodor Tyutchev (1803–1873), a diplomat who is also regarded as Russia's leading poet after Pushkin and Lermontov.[21] From age nineteen, Tyutchev worked in Russia's legation in Munich, where he reveled in the salon culture of Bavaria's capital, then aspiring to become the Athens of the North.[22]

---

18 Vatro Murvar, "Messianism in Russia: Religious and Revolutionary," *Journal for the Scientific Study of Religion* 10, 4 (Winter 1971): 277-338.

19 Konstantin Leontiev, *Vizantium i slavianstvo* (Moscow: Univ. tip. [Katkov], 1876). There are more than a dozen references in the Harvard Library to works by Leontiev and about him by Russian and Western scholars, A recent book is Glenn Cronin, *Disenchanted Wanderer: The Apocalyptic Vision of Konstantin Leontiev* (Ithaca: Cornell University Press, 2021).

20 Kirill Kovalenko, 'Why No One Gets Russia,' *The Diplomat*, December 8, 2014.

21 Tyutchev was the topic of Strobe Talbott's senior thesis at Yale. Putin once asked Talbott what he thought of Tyutchev—the Russian president had absorbed his briefing on Clinton's Russia adviser!

22 Tyutchev (or Tiutchev), like other Russian metaphysical poets, was inspired by the pantheistic writings of Friedrich Schelling, Goethe, and Friedrich Schiller. Many Russian poets as well as scientists studied and lived in Germany. One of Russia's first metaphysical poets, the polymath, Mikhail Lomonosov (1711–1765), for whom Moscow State University is named, studied at two German

4. Russian Values in a "Russian World"

Tyutchev stayed abroad for 22 years, writing and speaking French better than Russian. Still, he became an ardent Slavophile. He urged Czechs, Poles, and all Slavs to merge with Mother Russia. Living comfortably most of time on his government salary, he wanted to bribe Western periodicals to publish favorable comments about Russia and rebut the critical reports of some visitors such as the Marquis de Custine. His efforts were applauded by Slavophiles but not by Foreign Minister Karl Nesselrode and Tsar Nicholas I, who were trying to improve ties with Austria (which ruled Czechs and other Slavs).

Having concluded that bribed propaganda had little effect, Tyutchev sought a positive and all-embracing political vision proclaimed to the world. He dreamed of a grand campaign to win hearts and minds involving active encouragement and support for Western opinion-makers sympathetic to the Russian cause. As for the widespread suspicion that Russia was bent on world domination, nothing was further from the truth, he maintained: "We want only to exist."

Not beyond contradictions, Tyutchev preferred living in Europe to Russia. Campaigning for Orthodox Christian values, he lived and traveled as a veritable Don Juan while admiring the industrialization and modernization of Switzerland and other European lands. Another contradiction was the contrast between Tyutchev's romantic poetry (such as *Videnie—Vision*) and his support for dirty tricks to promote an imperial Realpolitik. Toward the end of his life, he obtained a job in St. Petersburg as a censor, where—another incongruity—he opposed censorship of most Russian as well as foreign publications.

Tyutchev, like many other Slavophiles (including Fyodor Dostoevsky) justified his worldview as a defense of the Third

---

universities for five years, 1735–1741. The young poet whom Eugene Onegin slays in Pushkin's novel-in-verse had recently returned from Göttingen bursting with ideas and feelings. See D. C. Schindler, *The Perfection of Freedom: Schiller, Schelling, and Hegel between the Ancients and the Moderns* (Eugene OR; Cascade Press, 2012); Sarah Pratt, *Russian Metaphysical Romanticism: The Poetry of Tiutchev and Boratynskii* (Stanford: Stanford University Press, 1984); Roger Conant, *The Political Poetry and Ideology of F. I. Tiutchev* (Ann Arbor: Ardis Essay Series, No, 6. 1985); John Dewey, *Mirror of the Soul: A Life of the Poet Fyodor Tyutchev* (Mount Buckhorn Weston Gillingham, UK: Brimstone Press 2017).

Rome—Russian Orthodoxy as the correct form of Christianity, anchored to mysticism and hostile to the rationalistic impulses of Thomas Aquinas and Martin Luther (who, as a young man and translator, wanted everyone to read the Bible and think about its meaning without a priest). While Dostoyevsky (1821–1881) originally felt that the purpose of the Russian man was to reconcile European contradictions, he later came to believe that Russia was not European and that its mission consisted in uniting Slavs, looking towards Asia, and civilizing/conquering that continent.[23] Nihilism—introduced to Russian society through the work of Ivan Turgenev to awaken a sense of rebellion and reconfigured by Dostoyevsky as threats to Imperial Russia from theories originating in Western Europe—foreshadowed how Putin and the Orthodox Church would perceive Western values as threatening contemporary Russia as well as the measures they have taken to confront those Western ideas.

---

23 See above, note 1: Caro, "Vladimir Putin's 'Orthodoxy, Autocracy, and Nationality.'"

CHAPTER 5
PUTIN LAYS WASTE TO RUSSIA AS WELL AS UKRAINE

As a New Year 2023 began, the clock in the Kremlin's Spassky Tower struck midnight. The Russian national anthem played. Channel One TV kicked off 2023 with a pop song: "I'm Russian and I will go all the way . . . I'm Russian, to spite the world." Next on the patriotic pops list came, "I was born in the Soviet Union, I was made in the USSR!" On another channel, a Moscow-installed official from Russian-occupied Donbas declared, "I wish us all peace. But peace will only come after our victory."[1]

Instead of celebrating the success of Russian civilization in war, however, Russians should be attending a solemn requiem for its demise. When President Putin launched his special military operation, he expected to take Ukrainian territory in weeks, nullify its sovereignty, wipe out the very idea of its national identity, and turn what remained into a failed state ready for absorption by the Russian Federation. More than a year after Putin's invasion, Ukraine's statehood and its identity were stronger than ever, and all the things that Putin intended to inflict on Ukraine were afflicting his own country. Putin's war was turning Russia into a failed state, with uncontrolled borders, private military formations, a fleeing population, moral decay and the possibility of civil conflict and his own demotion.

Great civilizations can whither—even when built on the material and human foundations of a potential superpower. Today the civilizations of India, China, the West, and Islam are all in jeopardy. But what has happened to Russia, the world's largest state and fulcrum of Eurasia? Tsarist Russia, for all its negative traits, had redeeming features. It gave rise to some of the greatest music, dance, and literature in human history—a flowering that gasped for air in Soviet times but has nearly stopped breathing in Vladimir

---

1 Steve Rosenberg, "Ukraine war: New year in Putin's Russia—nothing is normal," BBC, January 1, 2023, at https://www.bbc.com/news/world-europe-64138731

Putin's petrostate. Xi Jinping's China, still one of the world's great powers, has lost nearly all the intangible qualities that energized China's civilization, at least for its upper classes.

BRAIN DRAIN

More than 16 million Ukrainians were displaced by fighting in 2022–2023—half of them internally and half abroad. Some 3 million went to Russia—one million of whom were forcibly deported or kidnapped; about 1.5 million went to Poland and one million to Germany; lower numbers went to other European countries and North America.

Hundreds of thousands of young Russian men, some with their families, fled Russia to avoid conscription. Many drove their own cars; a few bicycled; some paid exorbitant prices to fly out—many to Turkey.

Thousands of scientists and other intellectuals along with hundreds of ballet dancers and other artists left or tried to leave Russia, ashamed of Putin's wars and unhappy with his repression. Some Russian scientists worried that "there is no future for science in Russia." Adding a fillip to the exodus, the rectors of 250 Russian academic institutions approved a statement endorsing Putin's "difficult but correct" decision to "de-nazify" Ukraine.[2] It appeared that such officials would stop at nothing to keep their jobs, salaries, and perks.

More than 10 percent of Russia's tech workforce left the country in 2022. Many found office space in Armenia, with good access to the Internet and to international banking. The mass flight of tech workers turned Russian IT into another casualty of war. Meanwhile, Russia struggled under an unprecedented wave of hacking, puncturing the myth of its cyber superiority.[3] It is possible, of course, that Putin was glad to be rid of malcontents and to pursue

---

2 Peter Dickinson, "Not just Putin: Most Russians support the war in Ukraine," *Atlantic Council*, March 10, 2022, at https://www.atlanticcouncil.org/blogs/ukrainealert/not-just-putin-most-russians-support-the-war-in-ukraine/ Dickinsom's interpretation of the data is challenged here in Chapter 6.

3 Joseph Merin, "Hacking Russia was off-limits. The Ukraine war made it a free-for-all," *The Washington Post*, May 1, 2022.

autarky, supported by a majority of Russians who, in 2022, seemed to approve his every word and deed.

Vadim Smyslov, a former editor at *GQ Rossiia*, described what led him to move to Tbilisi. "As a journalist, I wanted transparency. But while soldiers on the southern front seized Ukrainian villages, people on the home front were being muzzled. Russian media were prohibited from calling the war anything other than a 'special military operation'. On March 3 [2022], Putin signed into law a bill banning 'fake news', with fines of up to €13,000 and 15 years in prison. The police began to stop people on the street to search their phone chat histories for the words 'war', 'Ukraine', and 'Zelensky'. In Moscow a man was detained for holding a bank card that had the word *mir* (peace) printed on it—the name of Russia's equivalent of Visa and Mastercard. Another man found himself in a police cell for wearing sneakers that were blue and yellow, the colors of the Ukrainian flag."[4]

Having flown to Tbilisi with his hiking backpack, Smyslov began to spot the faces of people he had once written about—Kantemir Balagov, a filmmaker twice nominated at the Academy Awards ... noted biologist Ilya Kolmanovsky ... the contemporary artist Dagnini ... the sculptor Nikita Seleznev ... the literary bloggers Zhenya Kalinkin and Daria Kasyan. Smyslov learned that the cult Russian rock singer Zemfira flew to Paris immediately after giving a performance in Moscow that she ended with the song "Don't Shoot." From Paris, Zemfira continued to speak out, writing a track called "Meat," about a war that turns "people's bodies into rotting flesh." Her friend Renata Litvinova shot the short anti-war film *When Will You Ever Learn?* in which she recites the lyrics, in Russian, from Pete Seeger's *Where Have All the Flowers Gone?"*

Smyslov recalled that in "2015, the newspaper *RBC* published an investigative piece on Putin's daughter, Katerina Tikhonova, and less than a year later the editor-in-chief Maxim Solius was fired.... In 2021, journalist Andrey Zakharov discovered that Putin had fathered an illegitimate daughter. Six months later Zakharov was declared a foreign agent. He left the country after noticing that he

---

4 Vadim Smyslov, https://www.gq.com › story › russia-cultural-brain-drain, June 13, 2022.

was being followed in Moscow . . . . In 2017, the regime turned on another director, Kirill Serebrennikov, whose films had been selected to compete at the Berlin, Venice, and Cannes Film Festivals. Ever since, Serebrennikov has been under investigation in Russia for fabricated charges of large-scale fraud . . . . Letters of support for the director were written by such cultural figures as Cate Blanchett, Ian McKellen, and Mikhail Baryshnikov." But he left for Berlin. The Bolshoi Theater removed Serebrennikov's production *Nureyev* from their program—the story of Rudolf Nureyev, another artist who fled the Soviet Union in 1961 for the security of Europe, leading Soviet newspapers to call him a "traitor to the Motherland."

Ilya Kolmanovsky, the scientist, also in Tbilisi, articulated the magnitude of Putin's crimes. "It's one thing for Putin to be a mafioso dictator who has his opponents killed from time to time," he explained. But now we if we're talking about "the embodiment of evil that has the capacity to destroy the world. [W]ith time, people will come to understand that Putin's invasion was also an attack on Russia."[5]

Germany is now a major destination for Russians and Ukrainians fleeing the war—a contrast to the eighteenth century when Peter the Great and Catherine imported Europe's best and brightest. For decades the Russian Academy of Sciences consisted mainly of Germans. Blind to the big picture, Putin says that he, like Peter, is merely taking back Russia's historic possessions. Now Putin pushes back to the West the very persons on whom Russia's future depends. Some 200 Russian and Ukrainian dancers are training with the State Ballet in Berlin, which provides them even with shoes.

Perhaps these potential émigrés in Berlin will follow the path of Sergei Diaghilev whose *Ballets Russes* transformed dance theatre from Paris to New York to San Francisco and Australia by its synergy of world-class choreography by Michel Fokine and George Balanchine, the costumes and sets of Henri Matisse, Pablo Picasso, Georges Rouault, Léon Bakst, and Natalya Goncharova, the dancing of Vaslav Nijinsky and Anna Pavlova—all done to the music of Rimsky-Korsakov, Claude Debussy, and Igor Stravinsky.[6]

---

5   Ibid.

6   All these complex interactions are beautifully described and illustrated in a film by

5. Putin Lays Waste to Russia as Well as Ukraine

Here is Osipova—imagined at the Temple of Poseidon:

Diaghilev never returned to Russia; his Ballets Russes never performed there—land of his birth. This would resemble the case if Louis Armstrong and his orchestra toured Russia but chose never to come home. A later generation of Parisians and New Yorkers enjoyed and learned from the dance marvels of Soviet-era defectors Rudolf Nureyev, Mikhail Baryshnikov, and—today—Natalya Osipova. At Nureyev's funeral in Paris in 1993, Oleg Vinogradov, Artistic Director of St. Petersburg's Marinski Ballet observed that "What Nureyev did in the West, he could never have done here." When Osipova joined Britain's Royal Ballet, she cited the broader and more diverse repertoire as her primary motivation.

---

the National Gallery of Art at https://www.youtube.com/watch?v=lmsR8eR2-MI.

Where is the cultural milieu that gave humanity the symphonies and operas of Glinka, Mussorgsky, Tchaikovsky, and Rimsky-Korsakov? Their works are still played—often by Russian masters with superb technical skills—but where is the deep creativity that spawned *Swan Lake* and *Boris Godunov*? When I look at the Metropolitan Opera's productions of *Prince Igor* or *Eugene Onegin*, I weep for the civilization that gave rise to their birth but is no more. Thanks to Putin's war, two Putin-sympathizers, conductor Valery Gergiev and pianist Denis Matsuev were dropped from performances by the Vienna Philharmonic Orchestra at Carnegie Hall and Naples-Arts. For *Turandot* in 2022, the Met replaced a pro-Putin Russian diva with a Ukrainian.

Stalin and his successors suppressed, killed, or drove into exile many of the Soviet Union's best and brightest. Stalin smothered two world-class composers, Sergei Prokofiev, and Dmitri Shostakovich. Risking censure for "degenerate modernism," Prokofiev wrote *Romeo and Juliet* in 1935 but did not get it produced until 1940. Defying official and popular anti-Semitism, Shostakovich managed in 1962 to have his *Symphony No. 13* performed—its five segments meant to illustrate the meanings of five poems by Evgeny Yevtushenko including *Babi Yar*, described later in this chapter.

It goes without saying, of course, that a country's artistic achievements do not somehow compensate for its criminal brutalities—past or present. Indeed, many of Russians' artistic achievements since 1917 saw daylight in spite of the regime's pervasive brutality.

THE KREMLIN VS JEWISH AND OTHER "NONCONFORMISTS"

What happened to the literary milieu that gave the world some of its greatest ever poets and novelists—Pushkin and Lermontov (both killed in duels), Tolstoy, and Dostoevsky (whose first novel, before he was sent to Siberia and wrote about crazies, focused on the dreams of an eleven-year old orphan girl, *Netochka Nezvanova*)? Several major Russian poets continued working in Soviet times. Vladimir Mayakovsky begged, "Make me a part of the Five-Year Plan!" When Stalinist controls tightened, however, he committed suicide in 1930, as did his more romantic comrade, Sergei Esenin (spouse for a time to Isadora Duncan), in 1925.

The Kyiv-born writer Anatoly Kuznetsov explained the problem for writers and artists: "'Socialist realism' requires an author to describe, not so much what really happened, as what ought to have happened, or at any rate, what might have happened. This method, false and hypocritical in intention, has in fact destroyed Russian literature...." Soviet censors removed more than a quarter of his book about massacres of Jews before allowing its truncated and desiccated version to appear in 1966.[7]

The many Jewish giants on the Soviet cultural scene were shaped both by their family's origins in the Pale of Settlement and by their struggles to function in the evolving political environment—or flee from it.[8]

After Stalin's death in 1953, Nikita Khrushchev permitted a cultural "thaw," but he continued to impose his conservative provincialism on the arts from the top down. In response to American jazz, Khrushchev stated: "I don't like jazz. When I hear jazz, it's as if I had gas on the stomach. I used to think it was static when I heard it on the radio." As for commissioning artists during the mid-1950s cultural thaw, Khrushchev declared: "As long as I am president of the Council of Ministers, we are going to support genuine art. We aren't going to give a kopeck for pictures painted by jackasses."

When I visited Moscow's Tretyakov Art Gallery in 1958, the works of Chagall, Kandinsky, and other avant-garde painters were kept in a dark storage room. I needed a lantern to see them. Now, of course, they are displayed—in part to draw tourists.

In 1960 I met a leading "nonconforming, unofficial artist" Oskar Rabin (1928–2018), who then lived and worked in a barracks near Moscow. He told me: "I face three problems here. I am part-Latvian; I do modern art—not socialist realism; and my passport says I am Jewish, Hebrew—*evrei*." Oskar's father was from Ukraine and his mother from Latvia, but both had Jewish surnames.

---

7   *Babi Yar: A Document in the Form of a Novel; New, Complete, Uncensored Version* (New York: Farrar, Straus and Giroux, 1970), p. 14.
8   Gary Shteyngart, "Beyond the Pale," *The New York Review of Books*, February 9, 2023, pp. 10-12 as he reviews Sasha Senderovich, *How the Soviet Jew Was Made* (Cambridge: Harvard University Press, 2022).

In 1974 Rabin and other nonconforming artists exhibited their work in a field near Moscow. The Kremlin (then led by Leonid Brezhnev) bulldozed the art and exiled Rabin. Having moved to Paris, he painted an imaginary Soviet passport. It included the heading: ***place of death.*** He filled it in, "*Beyond our borders…in Israel???*" Liberated in Europe, Rabin's paintings sold well in Paris and London. He died in Florence in 2018.

During a 1962 show in Moscow of contemporary art, Nikita Khrushchev looked around and began to hurl insults at the artists, labeling them "degenerates" and calling their work "shit." When Khrushchev accused sculptor Ernst Neizvestny of wasting metal that was valuable for industry, the artist defended the integrity of his work, saying, "I'm not afraid of your threats." The two men later took a liking to each other. The artist moved to New York in 1976 and died there in 2016. A black and white marble statue by Neizvestny graces the tomb of Khrushchev in Moscow. Putin called the émigré artist's death "a grievous loss for Russia's culture and for world culture as a whole." Like Rabin, Neizvestny was born into a Jewish family and had studied in Riga.

The novelist-poet Boris Pasternak won a Nobel Prize in literature in 1958, but the Khrushchev regime did not permit him to accept it. When I translated a few pages of *Dr. Pasternak* from a smuggled American edition for some Moscow University students, they asked me, "Is it anti-Soviet?" When I replied "yes," they said the authorities were right to ban the book and isolate the author. Fearing he might win the prize, Pasternak wrote to a friend: "One step out of place—and the people closest to you will be condemned to suffer from all the jealousy, resentment, wounded pride and disappointment of others, and old scars on the heart will be reopened."

One of Stalin's favorite writers, Mikhail Sholokhov, brought up in the "land of the Don Cossacks," won the Nobel in 1965 (despite repeated accusations of plagiarism) for his novels about the Russian Civil War. Aleksandr Solzhenitsyn also won a Nobel in 1970 for his novels exposing life in the gulag. Expelled from the USSR by the Brezhnev regime in 1974, Solzhenitsyn moved to Vermont, but returned to (post-Soviet) Russia toward the end of his life.

5. Putin Lays Waste to Russia as Well as Ukraine

Leningrad poet Josef Brodsky (1940–1996) ran afoul of Soviet authorities and was expelled from the USSR in 1972. In 1987 he won the Nobel Prize in Literature and was appointed U.S. Poet Laureate in 1991. When asked who he is, Brodsky replied "I'm Jewish, a Russian poet, an English essayist, and, of course, an American citizen." But he was deeply critical of an independent Ukraine breaking away from "Great Russia" and revitalizing its own language.

The bravest man I ever met, Eduard Kuznetsov, tried in 1971 to hijack a Soviet passenger plane to ferry some Soviet Jews, denied exit visas, to Israel. His plan was foiled. He knew that his plot might have been penetrated by the KGB and that, if thwarted, he could receive the death penalty for high treason, which is what happened. Kuznetsov's *Prison Diaries* (1975) describes his hopes and worries. Exchanged for Soviet spies in the United States, he avoided execution. He met me in Santa Monica, and we talked for two days. He later settled in Israel.

Andrei Sakharov, a father of the Soviet H-bomb but later the country's leading campaigner for human rights, is probably the greatest Russian of all time. His wife, Yelena Bonner, and her daughter organized an archive of Sakharov's papers at Brandeis University and later at Harvard. The documents include KGB reports on the movements and the ideas of Bonner's husband.[9]

One of the world's greatest cellists, Mstislav Rostropovich (1927–2007), provided refuge to Solzhenitsyn in his dacha near Moscow in 1974, but was then banned from performing except in provincial towns. Like Solzhenitsyn, the cellist and his singer wife escaped to the West in 1974. From 1977 until 1994, Rostropovich was music director and conductor of the National Symphony in Washington, D.C.

As in the 1920s, the cultural treasures lost to repression in the last decades of Soviet rule proved a boon to the West.

---

9 There is more on Sakharov in Chapters 10 and 12.

Russians and Babi Yar: Was Yevtushenko Wrong?

One of the leading dissident poets in the Khrushchev era, Yevgeny Yevtushenko, was born in Siberia in 1932. He departed post-Communist Russia in 2007 for the University of Tulsa and other U.S. colleges. He was the most vital—most alive—person I have ever met. He told me that Russian audiences in the 1990s no longer appreciated poetry and could no longer afford books. One of his last public performances was in a Boston Synagogue in 2017.

When Yevtushenko visited Kyiv in 1961, he saw the 40-foot deep *yar* (ravine), several blocks long, where Germans (helped by Ukrainian collaborators), in September 1941 shot and buried 33,771 Jews in 36 hours—and, in the next several years killed another 100,000 to 150,000 Jews, Roma, Communists, and Soviet POWs. Yevtushenko then wrote a poem named for the massacre's location, *Babi Yar.*

Evgeny wanted to alert his fellow Soviet citizens to these horrors that the Kremlin had covered up. He was not the first to write about Babyn Yar (as it is called in Ukrainian). It had already been memorialized in verse by several other poets and a suppressed symphony—the composer fired from his post and the poems denounced as bourgeois-cosmopolitan and anti-Soviet. One of the poets, Mykota Bazhan, won the Nobel prize in literature in 1970, but the Kremlin kept him from accepting it.

In 1944 a teenager in Kyiv named Anatoly Kuznetsov lived near the ravine and began to write down his impressions and memories. He ultimately assembled notes, interviews, and documents into a book, *Babi Yar: A Document in the Form of a Novel.* It was serialized, in censored form, in the Soviet journal *Yunost'* (*Youth*) in 1966. In 1969 Kuznetsov defected to the U.K. and published the unexpurgated version, including the final lines of his original manuscript, which had been cut by the censor: "I wonder if we shall ever understand that the most precious thing in this world is a man's life and his freedom. Or is there still more barbarism ahead? With these questions I think I shall bring this book to an end. I wish you peace."

5. Putin Lays Waste to Russia as Well as Ukraine

Born and raised in Siberia, Yevtushenko was definitively "Russian." Having visited and thought about Babi Yar, however, the empathetic poet wrote that he felt like the Israelites in Egypt, like the crucified Jesus, like Dreyfus, like Anne Frank, "like each old man" and "every child" shot dead at Babi Yar.

For these feelings, Yevtushenko said, "In their callous rage, all antisemites must hate me now as a Jew. For that reason, I am a true Russian."[10] Evtushenko wrote:

No monument stands over Babi Yar.

A steep cliff only, like the rudest headstone.

I am afraid.

Today, I am as old

As the entire Jewish race itself.

I know the kindness of my native land.

How vile, that without the slightest quiver

The antisemites have proclaimed themselves

The "Union of the Russian People!"

I wander o'er the roads of ancient Egypt

And here, upon the cross, I perish, tortured.

And even now I bear the marks of nails.

O, Russia of my heart, I know that you

Are international, by inner nature.

But often those whose hands are steeped in filth

Abused your purest name, in name of hatred.

I'm thrown back by a boot, I have no strength left,

In vain I beg the rabble of pogrom,

To jeers of "Kill the Jews, and save our Russia!"

---

10 www.pbs.org/suschwitz. Copyright © 2004-2005 Community Television of Southern California (KCET).

My mother's being beaten by a clerk.
In vain I plead with these pogrom bullies
While they jeer and shout,
Beat the kikes and Ukrainians. Save Russia!

"And I myself," Evgeny continued, "am one massive, soundless scream above the thousand buried here. I am each old man shot dead. I am every child shot dead. Nothing in me shall ever forget! The 'Internationale,' let it thunder when the last antisemite on earth is buried forever. In my blood there is no Jewish blood. In their callous rage, all antisemites must hate me now as a Jew. For that reason, I am a true Russian!"

Sorry to say, Evgeny was wrong about Russia and Jews. Yes, many Russians are outgoing and "international," but many are deeply antisemitic and xenophobic. Part of old Russia remains, as we see in Putin's war, where a would-be imperial master labors to impose a "final solution" on a people seeking only to go their own way. Indeed, antisemitism has been endemic in what Yale historian Timothy Snyder called the "bloodlands," with its chapter on "Stalinist antisemitism."[11] Ukrainian civilians and soldiers massacred more than 100,000 Jews in 1918–1921. Stalin distrusted his Jewish foreign minister Maksim Litvinov and his assistant, Boris Shtein, who—returned from exile—in 1958 became my academic adviser at Moscow University, quite nervous lest I do something to embarrass him and the history department. In 1953, Stalin prepared a purge of Jews he believed part of a Doctors' Plot against his life and the lives of other Soviet leaders.

One of my two closest friends at Moscow University in 1958–1959 was Jewish. When I returned to Moscow a decade later, those two had parted. The non-Jew denounced the Jew as untrustworthy. "On a spy mission he might stick a knife in your back."

Nearly all the Russian-speakers I have met in Boston and at Walden Pond in recent years are Jewish. Most are highly educated but left the USSR because of multiple forms of discrimination.

---

11 *Bloodlands: Europe Between Hitler and Stalin* (New York: Basic Books, 2010).

5. Putin Lays Waste to Russia as Well as Ukraine

One explained why he never got his Ph.D. in history. To deny him a degree, the examiners asked him, "What is the name of the cemetery where Karl Marx is buried?"

Ukrainians, led by a Jew, have become Putin's Nazis—those who must be purged for their alleged genocide of Russian-speakers. Thus, genocide for genocide. As Gessen writes: Putin and his followers now brand "real or imagined challengers to their power as Nazis. Like all Russian propaganda, this line intentionally sows chaos. The effect is to produce a preferred historical narrative and a sense of nihilism—a consensus that good and evil are indistinguishable, that nothing is true and everything is possible." Fighting a war of annihilation, Russians have adopted as a symbol the letter Z which, in Cyrillic, looks and functions like a crippled swastika. When Evtushenko in the 1960s talked of antisemites, he could have been describing aspects of Putin's Russia. Gessen quotes the filmmaker Ilya Khrzhanovsky: "Babyn Yar is not in the past—it is now." But, she added, even he didn't realize then that "now" meant *now*.[12]

Of course, Russians still speak in many voices. Against every form of militant chauvinism, the Russian rapper Oxxxymiron sings against war and to raise funds to assist needy Ukrainians. Banned in Russia, he and his team perform abroad, for example, in Istanbul and Berlin.[13]

Maskirovka

Masking—hiding both strengths and weaknesses—has long been a Russian forte. The Soviet regime masked its losses in the "Great Patriotic War" for decades. The Putin regime masks its losses in the "Special Military Action" against Ukraine. Hiding the magnitude of these losses also masks the shortcomings of Kremlin decision-making and planning. It also obscures the ugly indifference of Russian leaders to human life.

In Ukraine, as in World War II, Russia masked its bad planning and battlefield defeats by pushing more soldiers—many poorly

---

12 Masha Gessen "Memorial," *The New Yorker*, April 18, 2022.
13 https://www.youtube.com/watch?v=CFKhLYqUA0Q).

trained and equipped—into extreme danger, if not nearly certain death. Far more chaotic than Stalin's command structure, Putin's permitted three private armies to fight alongside his regular forces. He allowed the erstwhile "Kremlin chef" Yevgeny Prigozhin to recruit convicts as cannon fodder. Neither Moscow nor Kyiv has released reliable numbers, but Western agencies in 2023 reported that Russia's casualties, dead and wounded, probably exceeded 250,000--a smaller per capita toll than Ukraine's losses, closer to 150,000 (civilian and military), from a much smaller population struggling to survive.

Victory against Nazi Germany was achieved at enormous human cost—at least 26 million Soviet lives, military and civilian, compared to 419,400 total U.S. losses and 450,000 British. Stalin and his successors masked the war's death toll for more than sixty years with what Russian historian Igor Ivlev in the *War Historical Archive* in 2012 termed a "General (or Generalized) Lie."[14] Thus, in 1946 the Stalin regime said that the USSR lost 7 million in the war. Twenty years after the war, the Supreme Soviet admitted 20 million dead, of whom 8.7 million were soldiers. In the early 2000s, other Russian estimates put the number of civilians killed at 18 million.

Many of these numbers, Ivlev wrote, undercounted Soviet losses by 50% or more. He found that total Soviet losses from 1941 to 1945 were 38.5 million, of whom 20.5 million were military—not the 8.7 million reported by the Ministry of Defense for twenty years. However Ivlev accepted earlier reports that civilian dead amounted to about 18 million.

Ivlev reached this grim reckoning by adding bits and pieces of official information not totaled by the authorities. He checked these totals against census data from before and after the war, including the number of children born after the pre-war census, but who perished in the war—some 1.3 million. From Young Communist League and Communist Party records, Ivlev learned how many party members donned uniforms and how many survived—7 million of 16 million. Of 18 million civilian deaths, 10.6 million were not party members.

---

14 "General'skaia Lozh'," *Voenno-Istoricheskii Arkhiv 9* (153)(September 2012): 41-58.

Other contributions to the total: The 900-day siege of Leningrad cost 642,000 Soviet lives.[15] Some 2.7 million Soviets died laboring in German detention. Ivlev does not mention that many of those in German detention were later arrested and incarcerated (like Solzhenitsyn) or executed by Soviet forces. Neither Ivlev nor the other sources cited here mention the nearly 3 million Soviet citizens, including Tatars from Crimea, who died in wartime and post-war deportations, massacres, and other kinds of repression carried out by Stalin's agents—not Hitler's.

Far more females survived the war than males. In 1939 there were about 7 million more females than males in the USSR. Forty-five years after the war—in 1959--the imbalance was 21 million more females. Thus, the male deficit continued for nearly half a century. but was smaller than in February 1946 when 26 million more women voted than men.

In the pages following the Ivlev article, the journal published a rebuttal by Viktor N. Zemskov: "On the Dimensions of Human Losses in the USSR in the Great Patriotic War (In Search of the Truth),"[16] Zemskov concluded that total Soviet losses were about 16 million of whom 11.5 were civilians and 4.5 million military. He noted that normal mortality would have ended the lives of many citizens regardless of the war.

Zemskov granted that 16 million dead was a huge loss, but he accused those posting higher war losses of ulterior motives—degrading the Soviet [Stalin's] leadership, the military authorities, and the entire Soviet system. He even claimed that they wanted to magnify the successes of Nazis and their (unnamed) accomplices [*posobniki*].

Viktor N. Zemskov, born in 1946, was known also for deflating estimates of the total numbers of those repressed by Stalin. He reported that from 1921 to 1953, only 4 million suffered. Of that number, nearly 800,000 were executed; 2.6 million sent to the camps

---

[15] Nina Khrushcheva put the Leningrad toll at 1.5 million on 3/4/22 at https://www.nbcnews.com/think/opinion/ukraine-nuclear-power-plant-burns-putin-rewrites-history-ncna1290827?cid=sm_npd_nn_tw_ma

[16] *Voenno-Istoricheskii Arkhiv 9* (153)(September 2012): 59-71.

[*lageria*]; 414,000 exiled; while 216,000 experienced other measures. What happened to those in the gulag camps, he did not say.[17]

The competing articles by Ivlev and Zemskov were published in 2012—after Russia's attacks on Chechnya and Georgia, but before Putin's military operations in Crimea, Donbas, and the rest of Ukraine. Viktor Zemskov died in 2015, but Ivlev was not silenced. His website in 2023 had him organizing an 8-volume collection entitled *Army of the Fatherland, 1939-1960,* of which one thick volume was for sale.

A colleague of Ivlev, the parliamentarian *Nikolai* Zemskov informed the State Duma in 2017 that Soviet losses in World War II numbered nearly 42 million.[18] Citing Gosplan documents, Zemskov said that during the war the Soviet population declined by 52,812,657 from which he subtracted 10,830,000 in natural decline. Actual losses were 19,410,000 service personnel and 22,570,000 civilians.

Vladimir Medinskii, Putin's Minister of Culture, 2012-2020, also entered the disputation.[19] According to Medinsky, every fifth person in the USSR died as a result of World War II. The total Soviet population was reduced by 37.2 million people during the four years of the war. The aggressor was fully responsible for all these losses, regardless of whether these people were victims of extermination, fell on the frontline, or died behind the lines because their living standards dropped dramatically. "Natural cause" deaths were 11.9 million during the war to which we must add 1.3 million children who died shortly after they were born because of the spike

---

17 V. N. Zemskov, "Politicheskie repressii v SSSR (1917-1990)," *Rossiia* 21, 1-2 (1994): 107-124.

18 Nikolai Zemskov, "Patrioticheskoe vospitanie grazhdan Rossii," 2/15/2017, no longer accessible. Nikolai Zemskov, then an MP from the dominant United Russia Party, was reporting on the national project "Establishing the fate of the missing defenders of the Fatherland." He was also co-chairman of the movement "Immortal Regiment of Russia" and Putin appeared with him at its founding ceremony.

19 Vladimir Medinskii, *Rossiia nikogda ne sdavalas': mify voiny i mira* (Moscow; Knizhnyi Mir, 2016); see also his article, "Every fifth person: The USSR's loss of civilian, military life during World War II," *The Jakarta Post*. 4/28/21, at https://www.thejakartapost.com/academia/2021/04/28/every-fifth-person-the-ussrs-loss-of-civilian-military-life-during-world-war-ii-.html.

in child mortality. After all these calculations, Medinskii claimed that experts arrived at the final figure of 26.6 million lives lost (37.2 million − 11.9 million + 1.3 million).

Why was it important for the world to know these numbers? Medinskii denounced the incessant attempts, within and outside Russia, to erase or reverse the Soviet Union's role in defeating Nazi Germany. No one should forget, he wrote. who was to blame for every single one of the many lives lost. Medinskii reported that the rehabilitation of Nazism had slinked back into our world. The European Union went so far as to accuse the USSR of unleashing World War II. Eastern Europe and the Baltic states officially declared that the USSR did not liberate them from Nazism but rather occupied them and enslaved their people. So Russia needed to announce the Soviet Union's loss of life and material in the war and have these numbers memorized by all.[20]

Having studied Soviet documents and Russian writings, the British economist Mark Harrison also accepted estimates of 26-27 million total losses.[21]

---

20 Dr. Medinskii was said by a faculty committee at St, Petersburg University to have plagiarized all three of his theses for advanced degrees, but the committee was overruled by higher powers. Paradoxically, much of Medinskii's prolific output aimed at correcting myths and distortions of Russian history. At his initiative, the Russian Military-Historical Society *(Rossiiskoe voenno-istoricheskoe obshchestvo* or *RVIO)* was formed on 29 December 2012 by Order 1710 of President Putin with the declared intent of facilitating the study of Russia's military history and thwarting efforts to distort it. For updates, see https://rvio.histrf.ru/. In 2021 Medinskii was named Chairman of the Interdepartmental Commission on Historical Education of Russia. Starting in 2021, he served as a personal assistant to the president, contributing to talk about *russkii mir* and "civilization." For a critique of how the party of power steers history, see Sergei Kremlev, Anti-Medinskiĭ : oproverzhenie : kak partiia vlasti "pravit" istoriiu (Moscow: IAuza-press, 2012).

21 Mark Harrison, "Counting the Soviet Union's War Dead: Still 26–27 Million," *Europe-Asia Studies 71*, 6, July 2019, 1036–1047. Harrison endorsed E.M. Andreev et al, (1990) "Otsenka lyudskikh poter' v period Velikoi Otechestvennoi voiny," *Vestnik statistiki* (1990*)* 10. Andreev's disagreements with Ivlev arose in part from divergent estimates of the Soviet population in 1939 and estimates of wartime deaths from natural causes. Taking account of two factors not included in most other estimates--emigration and the birth deficit due to absent males—A, J. Rieber estimated a total loss of 35 million in his *Stalin as Warlord* (Yale University Press, 2022), p. 219. Harrison's earlier book, *Soviet Planning*

Whether Soviet losses in World War II were 16 or 26 or 38.5 or 42 million, their magnitude underscored the heavy price paid for survival and victory.[22] Their scale confirmed that Stalin was not only cruel but also a fool. Having weakened the Soviet body politic, the economy, and military leadership, Stalin appeased Hitler and then ignored warnings of an imminent German blitzkrieg. The only way he could stop and drive back the Germans was by pushing millions of human beings into the maw of the Nazi war machine. Thanks to a large and relatively compliant population—plus substantial aid delivered on U.S. merchant ships, many of them torpedoed en route--this approach ultimately worked. One of every two Germans killed by the Red Army died from a U.S. bullet, according to another Russian historian.

While Stalin eventually got the free world to ally with him against Hitler, Putin has alienated NATO and the EU so they help Ukraine to resist and repulse. The battlefields saw the *quality* of Western weaponry and economic might combined with Ukrainian skill and spirit pitted against the *quantity* of human life and bombs Putin mustered. Guided by the arrogance of personal power and hubris, Putin--like Stalin--proved himself not just brutal but foolish.

Is Russia Eurasian, European, or One-of-a-Kind?

Is Russia-closer to China or to Germany? Or is unique, defying any simplistic categorization?

In 1802 a Russian diplomat and educator, Vasyli Malinovsky, published in St. Petersburg his *Essays [Traktaty] on War and Peace*. Written in Russian while he served in England, the *Essays* took it for

---

for Peace and War (Cambridge University Press, 1985) allowed for 27 to 29 million civilian deaths but kept to the low-ball 7.8 million estimate of military losses. Taking account of two factors not included in other analyses, emigration and the birth deficit due to absent males—A. J. Rieber estimated a total loss of 35 million in his *Stalin as Warlord* (Yale University Press, 2022), p. 219. For a detailed comparison of dozens of Russian and non-Russian sources, see "World War II Casualties of the Soviet Union" in *Wikipedia*.

22 Germany lost about 7 million; Japan, 3 million, China, 15 to 20 million; Poland, 6 million—17% of its 1939 population. Lithuania and Greece also lost more than 10% of their populations; the United States, 0.32%. My family lost one Marine on Saipan, 80 years later, he is still remembered.

granted that Russia is part of Europe. Malinovsky proposed a union or alliance *[soyuz]* of Russia with Europe's other great powers—a sort of world government to maintain the peace.[23]

An admirer of English liberalism, Malinovsky knew that Russia did not have a representative government, but he pushed for change from inside the system. He proposed to the reform-minded foreign minister, Viktor Kochubey, scion of a Crimean Tatar family, a project for freeing the serfs–one of the first emancipation proposals in Russia.[24]

Malinovsky helped to establish, fund, and administer a classically oriented prep school, the Lyceum, for sons of the nobility adjoining the imperial palace at Tsarskoe Selo near St. Petersburg. Malinovsky died in 1814, but Russia's greatest poet, Aleksandr Pushkin, studied at the lycée where, he recalled (in *Evgeny Onegin*, VIII), his muse appeared to him as he strolled in the palace gardens and its mysterious valleys, in springtime listening to swans and enjoying fountains spraying into quiet places. He grew up at the lycée, not rebellious but curious. Some of his classmates, however, became mutinous army officers (Decembrists) who, having seen Paris, in December 1825 demanded a constitution as a new emperor, Nicholas I, took the throne after the death of Aleksandr I. Many were arrested and sent to Siberia. Though Pushkin himself was trained to look outward, he once warned, "In foreign ways, Russian grain does not grow." For his unconventional views, nonetheless, he was exiled for a time to Odesa and Moldova.[25]

---

23 V. F. Malinovsky graduated from the philosophy faculty of Moscow State University, where his father once worked. He was reported to have excellent knowledge of Greek, ancient Greek, Latin, Turkish, French, and English. From an early age he was attracted to the fight against despotism. Having strong command of English, he was appointed to the staff of the Russian diplomatic mission to England. Next, he was appointed to the peace congress at Yassi to conduct diplomacy at the end of the Russo-Turkish War. In 1800, Malinovsky was appointed as consul to the Moldavian principality, Upon return to Moscow in 1802, Malinovsky published the journal *Autumn Evenings* (*«Осенние вечера»*), where he printed his essays "On War," "Love of Russia," "History of Russia," "Personal Side."

24 For more on Kant's vision, turn to chapter 10 below.

25 Aleksandr II, successor to Nicholas I did not free Russia's serfs until 1861— two years *before* Lincoln liberated America's slaves. Tsarist Russia had no

Is Russia part of Europe? According to what George Robinson, former secretary general of NATO told *The Guardian* in 2001, Vladimir Putin wanted Russia to join NATO but did not want his country to have to go through the usual application process. The former Labour defence secretary who led the Atlantic alliance between 1999 and 2003 said that Putin made it clear at their first meeting that he wanted Russia to be part of western Europe—"that secure, stable prosperous west that Russia was out of at the time." The Labour peer recalled an early meeting with Putin, who became Russian president in 2000. Putin asked, "When are you going to invite us to join NATO?" Robertson replied, "Well, we don't invite people to join NATO, they apply to join NATO." To which Putin replied, 'Well, we're not standing in line with a lot of countries that don't matter.'" [26]

While Malinovsky foresaw an alliance between Russia and Europe's other great powers, most of Europe turned against Russia after it made war on Ukraine. On March 16, 2022, in a somber ceremony in Strasbourg, France, the Russian flag was lowered from its staff in front of the *Palais de l'Europe*, formally ending Russia's membership in the continent's oldest intergovernmental organization and marking the rupture between Vladimir Putin's regime and the democratic world. The decision to expel Russia from the Council of Europe—a body established after World War II to safeguard peace, the rule of law, and human rights–was taken by European lawmakers and diplomats in response to Putin's invasion of Ukraine, which the Council classified as a "crime against peace" under the Nuremberg statues and as "aggression" in the United Nations definition of the term.

Putin, like Napoleon, tried to expand his personal power and his realm too far. He laid waste to Russia as well as Ukraine, causing

---

constitution until 1906, when Tsar Nicholas II reluctantly agreed to share power with a bicameral parliament, but he soon prorogued the first and second Dumas, There were four constitutions in Soviet times—1918, 1924, 1936 (the "Stalin Constitution"), and October 1977 ("Brezhnev Constitution"). While Boris Yeltsin had the army shell the parliament into submission in 1993, a new constitution emerged with strong presidential powers. A package of constitutional changes approved in 2020 included an amendment allowing Putin to run again for the presidency in 2024—and stay in power until 2036.

26 *The Guardian*, November 4, 2001.

havoc worldwide in countries that try now to accommodate millions of Ukrainian refugees; that depend on Russian gas and oil; or need grain and fertilizer shipped from Black Sea ports. Besides their collapsed economy and living standards, Russians suffer spiritually. Many of its citizens are chagrined to say, "I am Russian."

For The BBC correspondent Steve Rosenberg told the BBC his impressions of Moscow in April 2022 compared with the city where he taught English 30 years before. A female medical doctor whom he met in a supermarket confided, "The hardest thing of all is living in a society that doesn't want to know the truth about events in Ukraine. People are too busy worrying about their mortgage payments, paying off their debts. They're not interested in what's going on around them. But I think that what's happening in Ukraine is terrible. I'm ashamed to be Russian."[27]

Rosenberg visited the giant war museum that celebrates the Soviet Union's victory over Nazi Germany in "The Great Patriotic War." What Rosenberg found "disturbing is how the 'Special Military Operation' has found a place in this museum, how it's being honored here." On the museum's website, the spelling of the word "museum" has been altered to feature the letter Z. In the museum shop you can buy Z mugs and badges declaring "Putin is My *PreZident*." The purchasers may not care who was Diaghilev or that few Russians ever saw his creations or that he never returned to Russia.

Russia in the World

What happened to Russia? Since roughly 1917 its cultural achievements have been disappearing—the dark legacy of a series of thuggish autocrats, from Lenin to Putin, claiming that they knew best about everything.

The war in Ukraine isolated Russians from the world and insulated them from information.[28] Putin's courts in 2022 named

---

27 "Ukraine war: The Russia I knew no longer exists," April 22, 2022, at https://www.bbc.com/news/world-europe-61188783

28 Land borders to the European Union became nearly closed to Russians with tourist visas, while getting a visa became more expensive and time-consuming. Flights to Europe became two or three times more expensive.

Meta, the owner of Instagram, an "extremist organization." In February 2022, some 32 million people a day were using Instagram, the second most popular social media site in Russia. By early April, that number halved, and by early December the number dropped to just 7 million. Average user- time fell from 41 minutes a day to 15. A law "on sovereign Russian internet" forced providers to install special devices to control traffic and to allow the state to block VPN services. Users wondered in 2023 if and when YouTube might become a target.[29]

In the modern world economic development is shaped not only by resources but by human capital. Ignoring this fossilizes economic development. So Russia's economy will stagnate. Western markets are closed and in Asia there is intense competition. Instead of proactive investment in innovation and technology, the Putin regime has spent ever more on its military.

Russia sank into is a passive position on the battlefield and lost in many domains. Modern wars are necessarily hybrid wars, covering military, economic, political, diplomatic, public opinion, propaganda, intelligence, and information. Zelenskyy and his diplomats are masters of PR. Russia's president and his foreign minister look and talk like thugs. Russia can no longer decide when and how the war will end. Putin might like to end the war and hold on to what it has gained. But Kyiv works to regain all territories seized by Russia, including Crimea. The street artist Banksy captured the dynamics in 2022:

---

29 "Cost of War," The Bell, January 10, 2023, at https://thebell.io/en/cost-of-war/

5. Putin Lays Waste to Russia as Well as Ukraine

https://twitter.com/ngumenyuk/status/1591360212887547904/photo/1

One asset for Putin was the passivity of most Russians. While 40 percent of Americans are content to be followers of authoritarian leaders,[30] as many as 80 percent of Russians may fit this category. Passivity on the home front permitted Putin to continue the war, but poor morale and passivity on the front lines was a downer.

Russia's image suffers when those whom the world honors are harassed or worse at home. In 2022, three opponents of the Ukraine war shared in the Nobel peace prize: Yan Rachinsky, head of the Memorial Human Rights Center (shut down by the Russian Supreme Court and Prosecutor in 2021), the Ukrainian Center for Civil Liberties, and Ales Bialiatski, founder of the Viasna-96 Human Rights Center but imprisoned in Belarus. Russian authorities told Rachinsky to reject the award, but he accepted it anyway and gave the Nobel lecture. He told Stephen Sackur at the BBC, "In today's Russia, no-one's personal safety is guaranteed."

The Nobel committee explained its award: "The Peace Prize laureates represent civil society in their home countries. They have for many years promoted the right to criticize power and protect the fundamental rights of citizens. They have made an outstanding effort to document war crimes, human right abuses, and the abuse of

---

30 John E. Dean and Bob Altemeyer, *Authoritarian Nightmare: The Ongoing Threat of Trump's Followers* (Brooklyn: Melville House, 2020).

power. Together they demonstrate the significance of civil society for peace and democracy."

Bialiatski's Nobel lecture, read by a colleague, stated: "It just so happens that people who value freedom the most are often deprived of it. I remember my friends—human rights activists from Cuba, Azerbaijan, Uzbekistan, I remember my spiritual sister Nasrin Sotoudeh from Iran. I admire Cardinal Joseph Zen from Hong Kong. Thousands of people are currently behind bars in Belarus for political reasons, and they are all my brothers and sisters. Nothing can stop people's thirst for freedom.

"In my homeland, the entirety of Belarus is a prison. Journalists, political scientists, trade union leaders are in jail, there are many of my acquaintances and friends among them. The courts work like a conveyor belt, convicts are transported to penal colonies, and new waves of political prisoners take their place...."

"Now the permanent struggle of good and evil has unfolded almost in its purest form throughout the region. The cold wind from the East collided with the warmth of the European renaissance. It is not enough to be educated and democratic; it is not enough to be humane and merciful; we should be able to protect our achievements and our Fatherland. It is not for nothing that in the Middle Ages the concept of the Fatherland was linked to the concept of freedom.

"I know exactly what kind of Ukraine would suit Russia and Putin—a dependent dictatorship. The same as today's Belarus, where the voice of the oppressed people is ignored and disregarded. Russian military bases, huge economic dependence, cultural and linguistic russification—that's the answer, on whose side is Lukashenka. The Belarusian authorities are independent only to the extent that Putin allows them to be. Consequently, it is necessary to fight against 'the international of dictatorships.'"

Putin's special military operation harmed Belarus as well as Ukraine and Russia.

CHAPTER 6
ARE RUSSIANS AGAIN "DIZZY WITH SUCCESS"? ARE CHINESE?

The West is challenged by one country with the world's largest arsenal of nuclear warheads and another that could soon have the world's largest GDP. Adding to their material power, their presidents have claimed to be best friends. But what lies behind their military and economic assets? How do their subject live? What is the quality of life for Russians and Chinese? Some answers may be found in measures of their *intangible* achievements and shortfalls.

Judging by Kremlin-backed studies of public opinion, life in Russia in 2023 has become as it was in 1935 when Iosif V. Stalin proclaimed, "Life has become better. Living has become better, comrades. Living has become happier." A few years earlier, in 1930, he praised collectivization, but cautioned Communists not to become "dizzy with success." He claimed "Even our enemies are forced to admit that the successes are substantial. And they really are very great. It is a fact that by February 20 of this year, 50 per cent of the peasant farms throughout the USSR have been collectivized . . . We *overfulfilled* the five-year plan for collectivization by more than 100 per cent." Not only did Stain pronounce a "very great" success, but he asserted that collectivization was totally voluntary: "The successes of our collective-farm policy are due, among other things, to the fact that it rests on the *voluntary character* of the collective-farm movement and on *taking into account the diversity of conditions* in the various regions of the USSR."[1] Some Western apologists for Stalin praised collectivization. But when Stalin wrote of success, the murder/exile/starvation of four to five million Ukrainians was already underway.

If we take Putin's media at face value, the Kremlin's special military operation (SMO) in Ukraine has also been a great success. Not only is this what the media say, but it is what most Russian

---

1 Stalin, "Golovokruzhenie ot uspekov. K voprosam kolkhoznogo dvezheniia," *Pravda,* March 2, 1930.

citizens believe—if we accept reports by some of Russia's top sociologists and experts on public opinion.

Putin's official polling organization reported in 2023 that citizens' attitudes to all things political became more positive in the year after the SMO began. From February 2022 to January 2023, support for the SMO increased from 65% to 68%. Indeed, 75% of respondents approved incorporating annexed territories into Russia's borders. Trust in Russia's leader increased from 65% to 78%. Approval of the president's actions rose from 60% to 75%. Acceptance of his legitimacy rose from 53% to 73%. Acceptance of the Russian Federation government's legitimacy, however, was lower. It increased from 35% to only 49%.[2]

In 2023, some 79% of respondents expressed their willingness to assist citizens in the new territories and Russian soldiers (two rather distinct categories lumped into one), and 73% of respondents approved their school age children writing letters of support to soldiers. Another 73% welcomed sending soldiers "Christmas" gifts (by whom and to whom not specified).

How did respondents feel about protests alleging a decline of living standards or unjust government actions? Critical attitudes declined from 21% in 2021 to 12% in 2022, even after the partial mobilization of youngish males. On the positive side, the share of respondents satisfied with their own circumstances rose from 48% in 2021 to 57% in 2002. Only 8% of respondents wanted to move abroad. A good 90% said *nyet* to emigration. Satisfaction with things in one's own region increased from 49% in 2021 to 60% in 2022.

Note that these surveys do not break down responses by region. Non-Russian republics such as Bashkortostan, Dagestan, and Komi are known to resent the mobilization and high death rates of their young men conscripted into the SMO. It is doubtful their views count for much in the official statistics.

Can Russia cope with the exodus of foreign companies? 70% of respondents said yes. Respondents believed that Russia can cope

---

[2] https://wciom.ru/analytical-reviews/analiticheskii-obzor/reitingi-doverija-politikam-ocenki-raboty-prezidenta-i-pravitelstva-podderzhka-politicheskikh-partii-20221125, November 25, 2022; updated to January 2023 by V. Maimonov, *God SVO: Sotsial'no-politicheskie posledstviia.pdf.*

better in the airline industry and with industrial equipment (68% and 67%) than with everyday electronics or automobiles (59% and 52%). They ignored the rationale for an international division of labor expressed by Sergei Chemezov, boss of Russia's largest military-industrial complex, *Rostekha*, in the business publication *PBK*, on June 15, 2022.[3]

Does Russia now have a large influence in international affairs? Positive opinions rose from 62% in 2021 to 78% in 2023. What will be Russia's place in 15 years? Answers were muddled.

Does the RF government have a long-term strategy for development? In 2021 only 40% said yes; but in 2002 the *da* vote rose to 54%. What share of your friends and family believe the government has a clear long-term development plan? Only 29% answered in the affirmative in 2021, but nearly half gave a positive assessment in 2022—46%.

The All-Russian Center for Public Opinion Research showed that Russia today, as in Stalin's 1930s, is practically giddy with success. But the pollsters reveal nothing about the age, gender, or location of respondents. *Most important, they do not disclose how many people refused to answer the questions. How many were simply afraid to say anything negative about their own situation or Russia's?*

Critics of Russian opinion polls, such as Cornell University's Bryn Rosenfeld point out that since only five percent of respondents contacted are willing to participate in interviews, the polls are a worthless barometer of what people actually think.[4] The risks of answering polls honestly are too high because no one can guarantee anonymity. Far safer to refuse to participate at all. The five percent willing to respond to pollsters presumably have nothing to fear because they genuinely support the regime.

Sociologists Anna Biriukova of Aleksei Navalny's Anti-Corruption Foundation and Elena Koneva of ExtremeScan, Cyprus,

---

3 https://www.rbc.ru/opinions/economics/15/06/2022/62a87e589a7947cbf332c253 (accessed 2/25/23).

4 For his views and those of other specialists, see *Russian Analytical Digest* No. 292, 2/22/23 at https://css.ethz.ch/content/dam/ethz/special-interest/gess/cis/center-for-securities-studies/pdfs/RAD292.pdf

conducted research that showed that, while *most* Russians do support the actions of the Russian authorities, they are considerably fewer than 70-80 percent. Their research showed that, while 35 percent of Russians did not support Putin's military operation in Ukraine in the summer of 2022, the number increased to 47 percent by February 2023.[5]

The official survey results showed that most respondents felt no reason to protest about anything. But in January 2021, there were protests in 198 towns and cities across Russia in support of opposition leader Aleksei Navalny—the largest anti-government demonstrations since the legislative elections in 2011 and Putin's re-election in 2012. Then, on March 6, 2022, ten days after the SMO began, police arrested more than 4,600 protestors. According to the Russian human rights group OVD-Info, the year 2022 saw more than 21,000 Russians arrested (many beaten and tortured) for anti-war actions, with more than 370 facing criminal charges under the new "false information" law.

The official surveys made no effort to square their findings with the Corruption Perceptions Index of Transparency International showing that, year after year, Russia has been one of the most corrupt places in the world.[6] The Russian Interior Ministry reported that the average bribe amounted to 9,000 rubles in 2008 but jumped to 236,000 rubles in 2011. Could anyone but criminals be content with this situation? Russia's index rank deteriorated from 90th place in the world in 2004 to126th place to 137th in 2023--worse than Belarus at 91st and Ukraine at 116th. Russia's placement tied with that of Mali (where Russian mercenaries protected the regime) and with Paraguay, the most corrupt country in Latin America except for Putin's amigos in Venezuela, 177th—just above worse-ranked Somalia at 180th. North Korea, purveyor of munitions to Putin's forces, placed 171st.

Not just the system but its top leader was profoundly corrupt. Putin had at least two gold-plated palaces—one on the Black Sea

---

5 Jaroslaw Martyniuk and Alexander Motyl, 3/22/23 at https://euobserver.com/opinion/156857

6 https://www.transparency.org/en/press/2022-corruption-perceptions-index-reveals-scant-progress-against-corruption-as-world-becomes-more-violent

and one near Moscow at Valdai, which he shared with his younger mistress and their children, often reached by a heavily armored train. Bank officials in Switzerland were charged with facilitating Putin's money laundering.[7]

Ukraine at 116th tied with Algeria and Zambia in on the Corruption Perceptions Index in 2022, but—even in wartime—climbed twenty places since 2009. Ukraine's parliament enacted a National Anti-Corruption Strategy in June 2022, but investigators uncovered profiteering by officials in the defense and other ministries in January 2023. In 2023 Denmark and Finland ranked 1st and 2nd—the most honest of 180 countries; the United States placed 24th—just ahead of Taiwan and Bhutan, but up two places since the Trump era, China, tied with Cuba at 65th.

These somewhat contradictory surveys give mixed answers to big questions: To what extent do the citizens of Russia *actually* approve Putin's leadership and his war? If he were challenged by someone claiming to do a better job, would the crowd stand by Putin or go for a fresh face? Might the Russian public be just as polarized as the American?

BENEATH THE EXTERNALS OF MATERIAL POWER

How do people really live? One major indicator is the United Nations Human Development Index. It assesses three factors that enhance human choice—health, education, and income. Switzerland and Norway scored highest on the HDI in 2022; Russia ranked 52nd and China 79th. Down from earlier highs, the USA fell to 21st.

China's Communist Party brags about how many people it lifted out of poverty in the past four decades, while refusing to mention how it had thrown the entire nation into abject poverty under Mao Zedong. Xi Jinping says he has defeated poverty, but discussion of economic hardship is taboo, scrubbed from the internet and banished from the news. Li Yuan reported that in March 2023 "the Cyberspace Administration of China, the country's internet regulator, announced that it would crack down on anyone who

---

7 "Bankers in Swiss trial for helping 'Putin's wallet'" at https://www.bbc.com/news/world-europe-64885959, 3/8/23.

publishes videos or posts that 'deliberately manipulate sadness, incite polarization, create harmful information that damages the image of the Party and the government, and disrupts economic and social development.'" It bans sad videos of old people, disabled people and children. Behind the ban is a government eager to keep all talk about China positive."[8]

The HDI says nothing about politics. With regard to political rights and civil liberties, the nonpartisan Freedom House reports year after year that Russia and China, are "not free"—like other Communist or post-Communist states, from Belarus to North Korea to Cuba.[9] A leading Soviet-era dissident and former *New York Times* bureau chief in Moscow agreed in 2023 that Putin's repression was more oppressive than Brezhnev's in the 1970s-1980s.[10]

The Global Innovation Index (World Intellectual Property Organization) placed Russia 47th in the world in 2022—far behind many countries with lower GDP per capita; China, however, ranked 11th—the only middle-income country in the top 30.[11] All the numbers cited here reflect conditions as countries confronted Covid-19 and just before Russia's invasion of Ukraine, They are probably in the correct ballparks but need to be adjusted to changes in the real world and improvements in scientific methodology.

These factors are both cause and effect of other variables. Finland is the least fragile state in the world; Yemen, the most fragile. Of 177 states, Russia is far more fragile than most of Europe—78 places from the bottom, even Belarus and Ukraine were less fragile in 2022—91st and 92nd from the bottom; China was just above the halfway mark—96 places; the USA, more fragile than most Western countries at 138; least fragile—the most stable—was Finland at 177.[12]

---

8 "Why China's Censors Are Deleting Videos About Poverty," *The New York Times*, May 8, 2023,

9 https://freedomhouse.org/report/freedom-world (accessed 3/7/23).

10 Natan Sharansky, "Why Putin's repression is worse than what I endured under the Soviets," *The Washington Post*," May 8. 2023 and Serge Schemann, "Things in Russia Aren't as Bad as the Bad Old Soviet Days. 'They're Worse'," *The New York Times*, May 8, 2023.

11 https://www.wipo.int/global_innovation_index/en/2022/ (accessed 3/7/23).

12 https://fragilestatesindex.org/global-data/

6. Are Russians Again "Dizzy with Success"? Are Chinese?

The claim that most Russians are content with the quality of their life is not credible. 'The World Happiness Index (based on Gallup World Poll data) asks respondents to rate their satisfaction with the quality of their life. It shows that Russians' satisfaction ranks at 78th in the world—one place lower than Turkmenistan and 14 places behind Belarus. Putin's subjects were malcontent. Much of their putative GDP per capita went to oligarchs.Not surprisingly, the report shows Lebanon and Afghanistan to be the least happy while Finland and Denmark—the most honest—are also the happiest. The United States and UK rank 16th and 17th on satisfaction with their quality of life.[13]

Finland and Denmark, least corrupt, also topped the Happiness Index, which asks people to evaluate their quality of life on a scale from 1 to 10. Here the USA ranks 16th; China, 71st; and Russia, 76th. Least happy, no surprise, is Afghanistan, which may have become even more unhappy since the last survey in 2021.

How do these measures of intangibles match up with material wealth? Very roughly. Russia and China had similar per capita incomes in 2022—$14,700 and $13,630—much higher than Belarus at nearly $10,000 and Ukraine at nearly $5,000. Finland and Denmark rated the most happy, with incomes ($51,000 and $66,000) much lower than Norway ($89,000) or the United States ($78,400). The highest per capita incomes were in Ireland ($107,000) and Switzerland ($95.000).[14]

The Nordic countries performed best overall, while the West's two major challengers, Russia and China, did poorly in cultivation of human and humane values. Except for China, the numbers for most Communist or ex-Communist comrades were weak in GDP as well as human development—Russia, Belarus, North Korea, Cuba, Vietnam, Laos, and Venezuela.

Assuming that public discontent in Russia and China is unable

---

13 https://worldhappiness.report/ed/2022/happiness-benevolence-and-trust-during-covid-19-and-beyond/#ranking-of happiness-2019-2021

14 https://www.imf.org/external/datamapper/NGDPDPC@WEO/OEMDC/ADVEC/WEOWORLD. All these numbers changed by year and by source, See also https://www.theglobaleconomy.com/rankings/GDP_per_capita_current_dollars/

to change the ruling elites and their policies, this dismal picture will persist—bad for its victims and not good for the West.

Reinforcing this negative picture for Russia and China is the distribution of Nobel prizes. Russian writers (including one Belarusian) have won six in literature—all but one condemned by the Kremlin; Soviets or Russians won four in peace, one banned from accepting it in 1958 and another, Mikhail Gorbachev in 1990—later persona non grata in the Kremlin; the other two, in 2021 and 2022, also ostracized by Moscow. Russians, some working abroad, won eleven prizes in physics or chemistry, and two, one working abroad, in economics. One Chinese scientist, a woman, received a Nobel in medicine; another Chinese, in jail, won the Nobel Peace Prize; two won in literature—one living abroad and another, often banned, whose pen name is "Don't Speak." Some other Chinese-born scientists won Nobels in physics and chemistry while working abroad. The future of science, according to Russian and Chinese fiction of recent decades (discussed in Chapter 11 below), will amplify totalitarian controls deeper and broader than those in *Brave New World*.

Four of Europe's smallest countries—Sweden, Switzerland, Austria, and the Netherlands have each won more than twice as many Nobel prizes as China and nearly as many as Russia. Indeed, Sweden won 33 compared to Russia's total of 32—even counting all the Russian-born laureates denounced by the Kremlin. The United States, with 406 prizes, won more than a dozen times the Russian total; the UK, Germany, and France each won from four times to twice as many as Russia.

Public Opinion in Ukraine

Some 70% of all Ukrainians interviewed by Gallup in September 2022 said their country should continue fighting until it wins the war with Russia. Majorities of Ukrainians from all major demographic subgroups favored continued fighting to win the war. But 76% of Ukrainian men did so compared to 64% of women. On the other hand, one in four Ukrainians favored negotiating to end the war as soon as possible.[15]

---

15 Mohamed Younis, "9 Charts on the Russia-Ukraine War," 2/24/23 at https://

6. Are Russians Again "Dizzy with Success"? Are Chinese?

Support for continuing to fight was stronger in regions farthest from the ground war and weaker in parts of Ukraine where people were closest to the action. Backing for the war effort was highest in the capital, Kyiv (83%), and in the West (82%), Central (78%) and North (75%) regions of the country. Much smaller majorities in the country's East (56%) and South (58%) supported continuing the war. About 91% said that victory would entail Ukrainian forces' retaking all territory that Russia seized since 2014, including Crimea.

Nearly all Ukrainians disapproved of Russia's leadership. Before 2014 and 2022, Ukrainians largely approved of Russia's leadership—approval ratings soared as high as 61% in 2010. But in the aftermath of Crimea in 2014, just 5% of Ukrainians approved of Russia's leadership. Since then, approval never topped 13%. In 2022, less than half of 1% approved.

For Ukrainians, the leadership of the U.S. and China were on similar footing in 2021, with approval ratings of 37% and 36%, In 2022, however, China's rating tumbled to a new low of 14%. Although China considered Ukraine a strategic partner, China's failure to condemn Russia's invasion hurt its image in Ukraine. China abstained from joining the United Nations General Assembly on October 12, 2022, as it condemned the annexation of parts of Eastern Ukraine. In September 2022, a record-high 66% of Ukrainians said they approved of U.S. leadership—nearly double the rate in 2021.

Over eight in ten Ukrainians (84%) surveyed in September 2022 approved of the job that President Zelenskyy was doing, the highest on record for him—or any leader in Ukraine in the previous decade. Only the country's military elicited more support than the president. Nearly 94% of Ukrainians expressed confidence in their armed forces. Confidence in the country's judicial system, honesty of elections, and freedom of the media reached all-time highs in 2022.

In September 2022, 71% of Ukrainians said their standard of living was getting worse. Although the war with Russia dealt a serious blow to their economy, with the IMF estimating that the

---

news.gallup.com/opinion/gallup/471155/charts-russia-ukraine-war.aspx

country's GDP would shrink by 35% in 2022, these troubles did not dampen Ukrainians' confidence in their leaders. Before Russia invaded Ukraine in 2022, a record-high 35% of Ukrainians said they would like to leave Ukraine permanently. In early 2023, that percentage dropped to 9%.

In 2022, most Ukrainians expected their country to join NATO (64%) and the European Union (73%) in the coming decade. More than half (54%) approved of the job being done by the NATO leadership.

Public Opinion in the United States

Nearly one year into the war, Gallup found that in early January 2023 Americans' support for Ukraine had held steady.[16] A stable 65% of U.S. adults preferred that the United States support Ukraine in reclaiming its territory, even if that prolonged the conflict. Meanwhile, 31% said they would rather see the U.S. work to end the war quickly, even if this allowed Russia to keep its territory. Democrats were far more supportive than Republicans and independents—though majorities of all three parties favored Ukraine's continuing to fight to reclaim its former territory.

A plurality of Americans (39%) said the support being offered to Ukraine in the war was the right amount, but 30% thought the U.S. was not doing enough, while 28% said the U.S. was doing too much. Nearly half of Republicans, 47%, said the U.S. was doing too much, while 48% of Democrats said American involvement was about right. Most of the rest of Democrats, 41%, said the U.S. was not doing enough. Independents were evenly divided between the two camps. Democrats were more likely than independents and Republicans to think the U.S. was not doing enough.

A Russian social scientist noted that Biden's election prospects in 2024 would gain if the United States could exit the war by then.[17]

---

[16] https://news.gallup.com/poll/469328/one-year-later-americans-stand-ukraine.aspx

[17] Nikolai Popov in *Nezavisimaya gazeta*, March 1, 2023.

CHAPTER 7
WHAT DO PUTIN AND XI OWE THEIR VICTIMS?

Evil-doers should pay for their evil. By this logic, Russia owes Ukraine huge sums to compensate for death and destruction—not just for damage done in the recent years but over the past century. China's Communist Party also owes huge debts to its subjects—Han Chinese as well as Tibetans, Uyghurs, and other minorities. Both Putin and Xi owe unfathomable debts to all humans for pulling us away from genuine human development toward rule by power-mad tyrants.

All heads of state at the UN World Summit in 2005 affirmed the *responsibility to protect* all populations from genocide, war crimes, ethnic cleansing, and crimes against humanity. The responsibility is three-fold: first, each state must protect its own populations; second, the international community must assist other states to protect their populations; and third, the international community must act when a state is manifestly failing to protect its populations.[1] As the United Nations saw in 2022–2023, Russia—like China and the other permanent member of the Security Council—can veto any enforcement it dislikes.

Still, all nations are sworn to honor the responsibility to protect. Instead of protecting their own and other peoples, Moscow and Beijing have seriously abused their own peoples and others. Outsiders have tried to help protect the victims of Putin and Xi—trying to do so without triggering even greater tragedies.

PRECEDENTS

Reparations is not some new invention. After the Punic wars, Rome extracted indemnities from Carthage. In 1807 Napoleon imposed indemnities on Prussia. In 1815 France had to pay indemnities for damage done by Napoleon and in 1871 for a war provoked by Bismarck. In each case, France paid in full and ahead of schedule—to get rid of Prussian occupiers. In 1919, France and the United

---

[1] https://www.un.org/en/chronicle/article/responsibility-protect

Kingdom demanded that Germany pay for the deaths and destruction caused by Kaiser Wilhelm's forces in World War I. The Soviet Union demanded reparations from Hitler's Germany and took what it could get from East Germany—worth perhaps $20 million in late 1940s dollars, far more than U.S. investments in the Marshall Plan.

Furthermore, the past is not past. European exploitation of African, Middle Eastern, and Asian peoples wreaked damage whose effects persist. Chinese have not forgotten the Opium Wars and imperial spheres of influence followed by years of Japanese occupation. Central Asians and other peoples on Russia's periphery cannot forget centuries of Russian domination.

Indigenous peoples and descendants of slaves in the Americas rightly demand compensation for the evils perpetrated by whites in Europe and in North America. Major universities—Glasgow, Georgetown, Brown, Harvard, and others—now recognize that their founding and survival were funded by slavery.

How can whites make up for past cruelty and injustice from which they benefited? When Britain banned slavery in the 19th century, it compensated slave owners for loss of property. But what about those who suffered and died as slaves—and their descendants? French warships anchored near Port-au-Prince made sure that Haitians compensated French banks and slave masters for their losses after Haitian troops won their country's independence. Burdensome French loans, sometimes forcibly imposed, set off a cycle of underdevelopment that has made today's Haiti poorer by tens of billions of dollars. Former Haitian president Jean-Bertrand Aristide in 2010 launched a campaign demanding that France repay the money it extracted.

Hilary Beckles, a Barbadian historian and chairman of the reparations commission for CARICO, estimated the European debt to the region just for "200 years of free labor" at seven trillion British pounds. Jamaica is seeking $10.6 billion—equivalent to the fees that Britain paid slave owners to populate the island. One lawmaker argued in 2021 that Britain owes those slaves' descendants, at a minimum, their ancestors' purchase price.[2]

---

2 Max Fisher, "The Long Road Ahead for Colonial Reparations," *The New York*

7. What Do Putin and Xi Owe Their Victims?

British historian Jason Hickel observed in 2018: "Chalk up the billions of hours that enslaved Africans worked on British plantations, pay it at a living wage. Tally up compensation for the 60 million souls sacrificed to famine, And you realize that if Britain paid reparations—real, honest, courageous reparations—there would be nothing left."

The Catholic Church in the United States, Canada, and Ireland is blamed for sexual and other abuses by its clergy and the deaths of Native American children in Catholic institutions.[3]

More generally, taking away a people's way of life and the environment where they lived amounts to cultural genocide and, even if not intended, leads to physical genocide. Native Americans have the worst public health statistics in the United States. Where traditional values and family structures are eroded, "rain check" handouts at age 18 risk being dissipated in beer and gambling.[4]

Some American blacks ask compensation not only for slavery but for the effects of continuing discrimination[5]—ideas that most Americans reject. Some say taxpayers who were never slave owners should not have to pay money to people who, since the 1860s, were not enslaved. In this spirit some Russians may say, "Ukraine was not my war. Let Putin pay."

Times, August 27, 2022.

3   In 2023, Canada agreed to pay C$2.8bn ($2.9bn) to settle a class-action lawsuit seeking compensation for the loss of language and culture caused by its residential schools. Government-funded compulsory boarding schools were part of a policy meant to assimilate children and destroy indigenous cultures and languages. The money will be paid to a non-profit trust independent of the government. https://www.bbc.com/news/world-us-canada-64362246.

4   See the story by Sterling HolyWhiteMountain, "False Start," *The New Yorker.* March 20, 2023, pp. 48-56.

5   How much is enough? In March 2023 Evanston, Illinois became the first city in the United States to pass a reparations resolution for black residents who qualified—$25,000 in cash benefits. Black residents that lived in Evanston during the period of harm, 1919-1969, or their direct descendants were eligible. In San Francisco, however, a committee said the city should pay every black resident $5 million. In March 2023, the city's Board of Supervisors weighed this proposal along with others such as grants to buy and maintain homes and exempting black businesses from paying taxes.

Whom, precisely, should be compensated—and how? Negotiations between Germany and its former colony, now the independent state of Namibia, illustrate the potential complexities. Between 1904 and 1908 German colonial officials and soldiers killed tens of thousands of Herero and thousands of Nama people in a campaign of extermination widely acknowledged as the first genocide of the twentieth century. The Herero and Nama peoples were just two among several other ethnic groups in the area—then and now. Since independence in 1990, the Namibian government has been dominated by Ovambo so that the Herero and Nama feel politically marginalized. In 2021, Germany reached a "reconciliation" settlement with the Namibian government, but the Herero and Nama object to it on several grounds. Germany offered $1.2 billion for development projects over 30 years. Herero and Nama representatives say this sum is much too small. They do not trust their own government to share it equitably. They want the money to be termed "reparations"—a condition rejected by Berlin lest it face similar demands by Greece and other German-occupied lands in World War II.[6]

The most relevant precedent for Ukraine and Russia is Iraq's payment of $52.4 billion to compensate individuals, companies, and governments who proved damages due to Iraq's 1990 invasion and occupation of Kuwait. The UN Compensation Commission, set up by the UN. Security Council after Iraq's seven-month occupation of the emirate and U.S.-led defeat of Saddam Hussein's troops in the Gulf War, received a portion of the proceeds from Iraqi oil sales.

---

6   In 2008, Herero representatives filed a class-action suit in the United States against three German companies that the Hereros said were party to "enslavement and genocidal destruction of the Herero tribe." The suit, filed in District of Columbia Superior Court, sought $2 billion in reparations. Germany claimed immunity because the 1948 Genocide Convention could not be applied retroactively. The suit was dismissed but opened the door to negotiations.

Herero and Nama now call for reopening negotiations with their direct participation, to address the poverty and marginalization that resulted from the genocide. Descendants of victims of mass murders in Namibia have called on Germany to "stop hiding" and discuss reparations with them directly, as they take their own government to court for making a deal without their approval. Thomas Rogers, "The Long Shadow of German Colonialism," *The New York Review of Books* LXX, 4 (March 9, 2023): 40-42.

The payment rate varied over 30 years and was most recently 3%. In all, about 2.7 million claims, with an asserted value of $352.5 billion were lodged, but the UNCC approved payment of only $52.4 billion covering 1.5 million successful claims. The largest claim approved by the UNCC was for $14.7 billion in damages incurred by the Kuwait Petroleum Corporation (KPC) after departing Iraqi troops set fire to oil wells. Payments were suspended between October 2014 and April 2018 because of the Iraqi government's security and budgetary problems in its fight against Islamic State insurgents. "With the final payment of compensation made on 13 January 2022, all compensation awarded by the Commission has now been paid in full," the Geneva-based body said in a statement following a closed-door meeting of its Governing Council.[7]

CALCULATING DEBTS: LIVES DAMAGED AND LOST

Russia should compensate Ukraine for lives damaged and lost as well as for material destruction. But what is one life worth? Estimates depend on time and place, sources, and methodology. The U.S. government values every life at nearly $10,000,000. Russia's national insurance agency in 2015 valued a single life at $72,000. Some Russian scholars observed that the value of a human life in Russia is significantly understated. Sociologists at Russia's National Research University Higher School of Economics reported in 2014 that the average value of a statistical life in Russia was about 50 million rubles or $1.6 million—a value comparable to that of some developing Asian countries.

Another way to see how the Kremlin values life is to see what it paid the families of soldiers killed in Ukraine in 2022. The official sum was the ruble equivalent of $126,000. In practice, however, compensation was much less. A family in Moscow receives three times more than in Buryat or other remote areas that contribute less to GDP and where living costs are lower. For each dead soldier, some regions (federal subjects) get the equivalent of $51,000 per

---

7 Mazhar Muhammad Salih, a financial adviser to Iraqi Prime Minister Mustafa al-Kadhimi, said that ending this obligation with the final payment boosted Iraq's credit rating and would facilitate future economic development. https://www.al-monitor.com/originals/2022/01/iraqs-credit-rating-lifts-final-reparations-payment-kuwait#ixzz7qrYfTTL6

dead soldier; others, just $17,000. So long as a soldier is reported missing in action—not dead—the family gets nothing.[8]

To get a sense of the big picture, assume that each life in Ukraine is worth just $1 million. Begin with the 22,000 killed between 2014 and February 2022. Add the low estimate of 100,000 civilians and soldiers killed in 2022-2023. Add reimbursement for those wounded and those displaced internally and abroad.

122,000 killed @ $1 million $122,000,000,000

122,000 wounded/incapacitated @ $1 million $122,000,000,000

16 million displaced @ $100,000 .... $1,600,000,000,000

Total damages to human life, 2014–2023 .... $1,844,000,000,000

This bill includes nothing for grief and PTSD or for losses of education, earnings, and fun. How put a price tag on the trauma in children who no longer speak and miss school and social development? How price the discomfort of elderly Ukrainians who feel helpless when they look at the mounds of vodka bottles and other trash left by departing Russians? The feelings of the elderly physically unable to go with their children and grandchildren to a safer location?[9]

The bill also omits any charges for the 9 million Ukrainians killed under Lenin and Stalin from 1917 to 1953. It omits any reimbursement to Western countries for the $100 billion or more in aid they gave to Ukraine to cope with Russian attacks. It asks nothing for Arabs and Africans who hungered and even died because Russia obstructed shipments of Ukrainian grain. It says nothing about the debt the Kremlin should also pay to its own subjects for the 200,000 or more soldiers killed or wounded in this unprovoked war and the sufferings of their families.

---

8   https://tvpworld.com/61415715/the-price-of-a-russian-soldiers-life-depends-on-where-he-is-from, 7/21/22

9   For a database of 305 videos showing the horrors of war in Ukraine, see https://www.washingtonpost.com/world/interactive/2022/ukraine-russia-war-videos-verified/?itid=hp-more-top-stories_p003_f004; also https://www.businessinsider.com/ukraine-war-in-numbers-year-russia-invasion-deaths-aid-tanks-2023-2 (2/26/23)

7. What Do Putin and Xi Owe Their Victims?

Who will compensate the foreigners caught up in a war after they came to study or work in Ukraine? Seven Sri Lankans were captured by Russian forces in May 2022 as they tried to walk from their homes in Kupiansk in north-eastern Ukraine to the relative safety of Kharkiv, 75 miles away. At the first checkpoint, they were captured by Russian soldiers. The Sri Lankans were blindfolded, their hands tied, and taken to a machine tool factory in the town of Vovchansk near the Russian border. It was the start of a four-month nightmare which would see them kept prisoner, used as forced labor, and tortured by drunken soldiers, beaten with rifles, toenails pulled out, and pressured for bribes. The group had come to Ukraine to find work or study. Now, they were prisoners, surviving on very little food, allowed to use the toilet just once a day for two minutes. On the occasions they were allowed to wash, showering was restricted to just two minutes. The men--mainly in their 20s—were all kept in one room. The only woman in the group, 50-years old, was kept separately—in isolation. Freedom for the seven finally came when the Ukrainian military began retaking areas in eastern Ukraine including Vovchansk.[10]

This bill also omits compensation for Chechens, Georgians, Tatars, and other minorities killed since the end of Soviet power in 1991. It omits any reckoning for the Chechens, Tatars, and others forcefully moved to Central Asia in the 1940s, many—perhaps half—of whom died during the moves.

Damage to Property and the Environment

It is difficult to gauge the value of what Russia has destroyed and what it will cost to rebuild. By mid-2022—just in the Kyiv area—damaged assets included 167 schools, 122 hospitals, nearly 900 miles of roads, and residential areas covering 7.451 million square meters.[11] The first two of these drawings by Alexander Motyl give a feel for the destruction in 2022. The third image shows Kyiv burning in September 1941 as the Red Army fled encirlement by German invaders.

---

10 https://www.bbc.com/news/world-europe-62948148 (accessed 9/20/22).
11 *Plan for the Recovery of Ukraine* at https://recovery.gov.ua/

https://mail.google.com/mail/u/0?ui=2&ik=dd9ce41e66&attid=0.3
&permmsgid=msg-f:1766510678861138064&th=1883e81a6173c
890&view=att&disp=safe&realattid=f_lhxgjcru2

7. What Do Putin and Xi Owe Their Victims?

https://mail.google.com/mail/u/0?ui=2&ik=dd9ce41e66&attid
=0.2&permmsgid=msg-f:1766510678861138064&th=1883e81a61
73c890&view=att&disp=safe&realattid=f_lhxgj40q1

https://mail.google.com/mail/u/0?ui=2&ik=dd9ce41e66&attid=
0.1&permmsgid=msg-f:1766510678861138064&th=1883e81a61
73c890&view=att&disp=safe&realattid=f_lhxgilo30

President Zelenskyy was probably correct to say on September 6, 2022, that more than $1 trillion will be needed to rebuild Ukraine. Declaring that it "will be the largest economic project in Europe of our time," he added that his estimate preceded the damage to Ukraine's infrastructure in late 2022–2023. Addressing potential investors, he listed what would need to be rebuilt:

> Infrastructure funds will find a large number of projects in the airports and in the construction of new roads and bridges. Real estate funds will receive a market with hundreds of millions of square meters of new housing, offices, logistics, and industrial real estate. Banks and financial institutions can enter the huge lending market for all these projects in Ukraine. Insurance companies will be able to offer new insurance products, taking into account the specifics of our region and our risks. Hotel operators will be able to reveal our great tourist and business potential.[12]

Street artist Banksy expresses hope in Ukrainian resilience:

---

12 https://www.ukrinform.net/rubric-economy/3565966-zelensky-more-than-1-trillion-needed-to-rebuild-ukraine.html (accessed 10/2/22).

https://twitter.com/Gerashchenko_en/status/1591186163397627905/photo/3

The value of environmental destruction is hard to calculate but surely runs into billions of dollars.[13] There is degradation from munitions and fires that poison water, air, urban and farmland; fish, animals, birds, and insects poisoned, starved, bombed, or shot. Agricultural and forest resources have been wasted.[14]

The longer the destruction continues, the higher the bill, Besides the destruction, there is product lost. In 2020, Ukraine's GDP grew by about $2 billion. If war costs it $2 billion in growth for each of five years, that adds up to $10 billion. In 2022, Ukraine lost at least one-third of its prewar GDP—more than the United States during its Great Depression.

Studies of Germany's reconstruction after World War II illustrate the complexities.[15] Rubble must be cleared—including crippled tanks and other machines.[16] Some rubble can be recycled but is it worth the trouble? How to keep rubble from leaking poisons? How much will workers be paid—unskilled and highly qualified? Where will they live? Can disabled persons be engaged? Price of building materials? Are they available nearby or do they come from far away? Variables by location, location, location.[17] Can some materials and designs be standardized? Speedy reconstruction versus making everything "green?" Should architects seek modern

---

13 The United States in 2021-2022 suffered more than $300 billion in damage caused by drought, fires, floods, cyclones other storms in 2021-2022. Source: National Centers for Environmental Information at https://www.ncei.noaa.gov/access/monitoring/dyk/billions-calculations (accessed 1/22/23).

14 Claims disputes continue about American use of Agent Orange that poisoned the environment of Vietnam as well as its people and U.S. troops. President Biden claimed his son Major Beau Biden may have contracted a fatal brain cancer from inhaling fumes from burn pits in Iraq.

15 Jeffry M. Diefendorf, *In the Wake of War: The Reconstruction of German Cities After World War II* (New York: Oxford University Press, 1993); also Werner Dűrth and Niels Gutschow, *Traűme in Trűmmern. Planungen zum Wiederaufbau zerstörter Städte im Westen Deutschland 1940-1950*. 2 vols. (Braunschweig: Fried, Vieweg & Sohn, 1988).

16 Some Russians may remember how they cleaned up rubble on unpaid holidays (*subotniki*), as I did with other Moscow students in 1958.

17 American insurance companies have algorithms for estimating the cost of rebuilding. They begin with the approximate price per square foot of land and structures in a given locality.

functionality or historic restoration?[18]

A Provisional Reckoning

Some $2 trillion will be needed to compensate Ukrainians for damage to human lives and material goods (buildings and infrastructure), and the environment—omitting any reckoning for emotional pain and intellectual/creative losses.

This issue is not fanciful. The UN General Assembly on November 14, 2022, adopted a resolution that calls for Russia to pay war reparations to Ukraine. The resolution stated that Russia "must bear the legal consequences of all its internationally wrongful acts, including making reparation for injury, including any damage, caused by such acts." It called for establishing an international mechanism for compensation for damage, loss and injury, as well as a register to document evidence and claims. Ninety-four countries voted for the resolution, 14 (including China and Cuba) voted against, while 73 (including India) abstained.

Presenting the resolution, Ukrainian Ambassador Sergiy Kyslytsya outlined the impact of the Russian war on his country, including bombing of residential buildings and infrastructure, the demolition of nearly half of the power grid and utilities, massive displacement, and atrocities such as murder, rape, torture, and forced deportations, the ambassador pointed out that Russia had supported the creation of the UN Compensation Commission in 1991 following Iraq's invasion and occupation of Kuwait. That commission, Kyslytsya noted, completed its mandate in February 2022, having paid out over $52 billion in reparations to victims.

---

18 One historian wrote that to rebuild the fire-bombed city of Dresden cost $218 million. But another wrote that just to rebuild a single church, the Frauenkirche, cost $250 million and the palace known as the "Versailles of Dresden," $350 million. Human variables as well as the price of materials must somehow be calculated for each region's geography and culture. Not far from Dresden, the Polish port town of Gdansk (German Danzig) on the Baltic Sea, also fire-bombed, was rebuilt in its Hanseatic glory after being wasted by war. Poles were known as skilled, industrious workers, later hired in neighboring countries such as Estonia to restore historic sites. With limited outside subsidies, they had to be efficient.

Russia's response to the UN resolution? Kremlin spokesman Dmitry Peskov accused the West of attempting to "formalize robbery" and violate the rules of private property and international law.

U.S. Treasury Assistant Secretary Elizabeth Rosenberg, said on November 22, 2022 that Kyiv would create "an international register of losses" to serve as an official record of all damages suffered by Ukraine, both individuals and institutions. Ukraine has also teamed up with Columbia Law School to establish an International Claims and Reparations Project whose team of scholars and experts will examine and propose legal frameworks for the payment of reparations.

Assets in Foreign Banks and in Pleasure-Dome Yachts

In early 2022, the Bank of Russia kept $127 billion of gold in its vaults. But Russia's central bank also had large amounts of money stored in assets of other countries—$80 billion in China, $71 billion in France, $58 billion in Japan, $55 billion in Germany, $38 billion in the U.S., plus $29 billion at international institutions. The hundreds of billions in foreign assets, which include government securities and foreign deposits, could have been used to prop up the ruble and stave off inflation, but was out of reach—frozen. The only major country to not freeze Russia's reserve funds was China, where Russia stored 13 percent of its funds.[19]

The European Commission sought an EU-wide way of using the 300 billion euros ($324 billion) in frozen Russian central-bank reserves and billions more belonging to sanctioned individuals. Western governments sanctioned more than 1,200 Russian individuals, more than 120 entities, and 19 banks since Russia invaded Ukraine. To make use of Russian assets, however, Western authorities had to demonstrate that particular assets were linked to crime.

NATO members might like to confiscate Russian assets but expropriating them without evidence of a crime would endanger

---

19 Analysis by Monica Hersh and Joe Murphy for *NBC News*, 3/17/22 at https://www.nbcnews.com/data-graphics/russian-bank-foreign-reserve-billions-frozen-sanctions-n1292153

Western companies. Seizing an asset is different from freezing it. Seizing requires an investigation linking the asset's owner to a crime, as Italy has done with some Russian assets.[20] Italy's Guardia di Finanza froze large amounts of money, villas, and yachts belonging to wealthy Russians. In August 2022, the Guardia seized assets worth $152 million belonging to the architect of Russian President Vladimir Putin's Black Sea palace. Lanfranco Cirillo, an Italian with Russian citizenship, will be tried in absentia in Italy on charges of fraud and money laundering—criminal offenses.

A New Marshall Plan?

If evildoers should pay for their evil, Russia should pay most of the bills for rebuilding Ukraine. But many in the West want to help Ukraine to recover and prosper. Some call for a new Marshall Plan—as if these words offered a magical formula for success. But conditions today are different from the late 1940s. Stalin then was a sullen onlooker, having opted not to join the European Recovery Program. Today, in contrast, Putin's Russia is virtually at war with the West. Europeans after World War II could rebuild on the foundations of economic and social systems that functioned fairly well before the war. They had the benefit of strong leaders such as Robert Schuman, Jean Monnet, and Paul-Henri Spaak—energized by Americans such as George C. Marshall and a U.S. Congress able to unite on foreign policy, for whom there are no counterparts today. Also, the grants and loans from the United States to Europe 1947–1952 were far larger than what Western governments are now providing to Ukraine. Much of the foreign aid now goes just to plug a monthly shortfall of $4 to 5 billion in the current Ukrainian government budgets.

The Marshall Pan or European Recovery Plan ranks as one of the most successful U.S. foreign policy initiatives ever. It helped Europeans to help themselves and, over time, also bolster U.S. interests. But money is no panacea. The United States spent more in Iraq and Afghanistan over twenty years than the Marshall Plan did

---

20 Elisabeth Braw, "Freeze—Don't Seize—Russian Assets," *Foreign Policy,* at https://foreignpolicy.com/2023/01/13/putin-sanctions-oligarchs-freeze-seize-assets/

in Europe over three or four years but achieved very little.[21]

The European Recovery Plan saw one country provide aid to many. A 21st-century ERP would involve many countries assisting just one—Ukraine—though it might also help neighboring countries affected by the war, such as Poland and Moldova.

Another approach to finance the reconstruction effort would be to tap the unallocated Special Drawing Rights at the International monetary Fund to use as hard-currency collateral for Ukrainian bonds. Such an intervention by Western governments and financial institutions would greatly increase Ukrainian creditworthiness and lower the cost of private-sector financing, while costing Western taxpayers little or nothing.[22]

Modernizing Ukraine's infrastructure could make it competitive inside the EU. Reconstruction should aim to "build back better" with an eye to meeting EU standards, but stringent controls must be introduced to thwart the endemic corruption plaguing Ukraine.[23]

Russia Must Pay, But How?

The war has damaged Russia as well as Ukraine. Russia's GDP may have reached $2 trillion in 2014 but it fell to $1.8 trillion in 2021 and to $1.6 trillion in 2023—declining more than 3 percent a year.[24] How can Russia meet its obligations with an economy not 3% of global GDP—not 1/16th that of the United States or of China? In 2022, Russia's revenues grew just 10% while expenditure increased by more than 20%.

Russia—despite its relatively small GDP, declining growth, and brain drain—could, over time, use its sales of oil and other

---

21 In Iraq, nearly $300 billion; in Afghanistan, close to $200 billion, according to Bloomberg.

22 Timothy Ash and Polina Kurdyavko, "Rebuilding Ukraine: A Historic Plan for Congress," Center for European Policy Analysis, 1/25/23 at https://cepa.org/article/rebuilding-ukraine-a-historic-plan-for-us-congress/

23 A number of high-ranking officials were fired for embezzlement and bribe-taking in early 2023.

24 https://tradingeconomics.com/russia/gdp

commodities to indemnify Ukraine. Despite the bite of sanctions, Russia in 2022 earned huge sums from foreign trade. Russia continued to be one of the world's leading exporters of crude oil petroleum, with an estimated value of $74.4 billion—with China, India, and Turkey the leading buyers. Russia's state-run energy giant Gazprom posted a record profit in the first half of 2022, even though shipments to Europe slumped. International car makers still depended on Russia for palladium and rhodium to make catalytic converters. French and other European nuclear plants relied on Russian uranium, while Belgium still played a key role in Russia's diamond trade. Russia earned at least $55 billion in 2022 from its export of coal briquettes, platinum, pig iron, asbestos, and nickel mattes. The only high-tech product at which Russia was a world leader, with 26% of the global market, was nuclear reactors—valued at $870 million in 2022.

Back in 2020, Russia imported $220 billion of products from the rest of the world, including cars, car parts, medicine, and computers—buying heavily from China, Germany, and Korea. The volume of Russia's imports plunged as sanctions and trade limits went into effect, but a few countries, including China and Turkey, deepened their relationships with Russia after the war began. China's total trade with Russia in 2022 was $15 billion—up 64%, due largely to imports. China and other countries—Turkey, India, Iran, North Korea—masked details of their exchanges with Russia.[25] During the last 20 years, Russia's economy became relatively less complex, moving from the 21st to the 43rd position in the ECI rank.[26]

---

25 Ana Swanson and Lazaro Gamio, "How Russia Pays for War," *The New York Times*, November 11, 2022.

26 Observatory of Economic Complexity at https://oec.world/en/profile/country/rus; data for 2020–before the war–are at https://atlas.cid.harvard.edu/countries/186.

7. What Do Putin and Xi Owe Their Victims?

Table 8.1 Trade of Leading Countries with Russia. January–October 2022

COUNTRY	Total Value in 2022	Change in 2022	Imports	Exports
CHINA	$15 billion	+64%	+98%	+24%
TURKEY	$6.2 billion	+198%	+213%	+113%
GERMANY	$4.8 billion	-3%	+38%	-51%
INDIA	$3.3 billion	+310%	+430%	-19%
USA	$1.5 billion	-35%	-20%	-84%

Russia' role in world trade is miniscule compared to that of China, the European Union, and the United States. Indeed, the value of Russia's trade in 2021 was less than India's—about the same as Singapore's. Still, the value of Russia's exports grew *after* it invaded Ukraine, even with some countries that opposed the war.

A surge in trade by Russia's neighbors and allies suggested one reason its economy remained so resilient after sweeping sanctions. Countries like Turkey, China, Belarus, Kazakhstan, and Kyrgyzstan provided Russia with many of the products that Western countries tried to cut off.[27] Unreported smuggling also helped.

Future trade prospects were complicated. Russia's oil revenues declined toward the end of 2022 as price caps took effect and EU demand collapsed. The Russian oil benchmark averaged $66.5 per barrel in November and $50.5 per barrel in early December. From December 15 to January 14, 2023, however, it fell to $46.8. The West's oil price cap was introduced in December 2022 at $60 a barrel—substantially lower than the early 2023 market price for benchmark Brent crude of about $85. On December 5, 2022, the EU started enforcing an embargo on Russian crude oil exports. The sanctions were supposed to curtail revenues and at the same time dissuade European shippers from moving fossil fuels to the rest of the world. But Moscow still profited from exports and European firms still facilitated much of the trade. In the month ended January 5, 2023, some 250 European tankers, most of them

---

27 Ana Swanson, "Russia Sidesteps Western Punishments, With Help From Friends," *The New York Times,* January 31, 2023.

Greek, left Russian ports carrying fossil fuels. In 2022, Greek-owned ships carried more carbons from Russia than did ships from nine other countries, including China and Russia, *combined*![28]

Demand for Russian energy dropped. Russia needed to find buyers for its gas. By mid-2022, Germany cut by half the amount of natural gas it imported from Russia, relying more on Norway and the United States. Russia lost more than half the physical volume of its former gas sales to Europe. By year's end prices of gas in Europe returned to pre-February 2022 levels. Europe acquired liquefied natural gas from North Africa, the United States, and the Middle East.

Unlike oil, carried by tankers at sea, much of Russia's gas leaves through pipelines that take years to construct and are costly to maintain. Gas exports to China increased, but Russia had just one existing pipeline to China, and it moved only a fraction of the volume of Russia's pipelines to Europe. To move gas by ship, Russia would need to build new facilities to liquefy the gas, another expensive and time-consuming process.

The war lowered global demand and prices for Russian oil and gas. This threatened Russian macro stability and deepened Russia's longer-term economic malaise.

Scholars at the Yale School of Management concluded that, as of July 2022, Western sanctions and the departure of over 1,000 global businesses were crippling the Russian economy. Russia lost companies representing ~40% of its GDP, reversing nearly all of three decades' worth of foreign investment and buttressing unprecedented simultaneous capital and population flight in a mass exodus of Russia's economic base. With the loss of its erstwhile main markets, Russia's position as a commodities exporter irrevocably deteriorated. Russia faced stark challenges securing crucial inputs, parts, and technology from hesitant trade partners. Despite Putin's delusions of self-sufficiency and import substitution, Russian domestic production came to a complete standstill with no capacity

---

28 *Investigate-Europe*, 1/27/23 at https://www.investigate-europe.eu/en/2023/europe-continues-to-finance-russias-war-in-ukraine-with-lucrative-fossil-fuel-trades/

to replace lost businesses, products, and talent; the hollowing out of Russia's domestic innovation and production base led to soaring prices and consumer angst. Russian domestic financial markets became the worst performing in the entire world. Cut off from international financial markets, Russia could not tap pools of capital needed for the revitalization of its crippled economy.[29]

The big picture for Russia's economy was unclear. Without profound changes, Russia's capacity to meet challenges creatively could not improve. Russia in 2021 ranked 47th in the world on the Global Innovation Index (where Switzerland, Sweden. and the USA ranked 1, 2, and 3). Ukraine, before the war, ranked only 57th, but it showed tremendous resilience in 2022.

The impact of sanctions on Russia would probably become more severe, but when and to what degree are uncertain. Still, Russia's ability to produce oil and other commodities would not suffer unless war or civil strife hit the homeland directly. Before the Ukrainian conflict, Russia enjoyed a favorable trade balance—$427 billion in exports versus $247 billion in imports in 2018. This kind of surplus increased during the first months after the invasion but shrank toward the end of 2022.

Russia's National Wealth Fund (NWF) fell to $148.4 billion as of January 1, 2023—down $38.1 billion in a month, as the government took out cash to plug its budget deficit. Along with heavy state borrowing at domestic debt auctions, the NWF was becoming the main source of financing for the budget deficit. It was originally intended to support pensions.

Putin claimed Russia had everything needed to withstand the cost of the war and sanctions. Military expenditure in 2023–2025 were planned to be 9.5 trillion rubles for military and national security while social spending was set to be 7.3 trillion rubles. Putin might command sufficient money to pursue his war for several years, drawing on Russia's reserves of gold, Chinese yuan, and euros. Overall, however, Russia's future looked bleak. It faces decades of economic stagnation and regression. Industrial production is

---

29 Jeffrey Sonnenfeld et al., "Business Retreats and Sanctions Are Crippling the Russian Economy," 7/20/22 at https://papers.ssrn.com/sol3/papers.cfm?abstract_id=4167193

likely to continue falling. High-tech items from the West—needed for some weapons and an IT economy—are no longer available. Many Western companies have pulled out; trade with the West has dwindled; and financing the war is draining Russia's budget. Numerous foreign airlines have ceased service to Russia. Thousands of Russia's best and brightest have fled.

One expert concluded: "The Russian economy's prewar potential was not overly large, with growth at 2–3 percent per year. The war against Ukraine and external restrictions have lowered it to about 1 percent. For now, the economy's development will be put into reverse, and it will take three to five years for that decline to come to a halt.[30]

Can Justice Be Done?

Much of Russia's present and future trade surpluses will be needed for domestic needs, but a large fraction can and should go to Ukraine. The major obstacle is not economic but political. Whoever bosses the Kremlin must agree.

The main problem is not Russia's ability bit its willingness to pay. Russia will not be occupied by victor nations like France in 1871 or Germany in 1945. The Soviet occupiers of East Germany just took what they wanted. The Putin regime admits to no war crimes, so it must be replaced before any agreement can be reached on reparations or other war-related issues.

The total due and the methods for repayment could be established by a UN agency like the Compensation Commission set up after Iraq's invasion of Kuwait. To avoid a Russian or Chinese veto, this procedure could be authorized by the UN General Assembly under the October 1950 Uniting for Peace Resolution 377 (V). Somehow a large segment of the Russian public must come to see the justice in these arrangements—unlike Germans after Versailles.[31]

---

30 Alexandra Prokopenko, "The Cost of War: Russian Economy Faces a Decade of Regress," 12/19/22 at https://carnegieendowment.org/politika/88664

31 Reparations can be mandated as part of international or national judicial processes, whether an interstate case at the ICJ, a claims commission established by the parties in question, a criminal case at the ICC or domestic criminal court,

Reports that Russian forces have systematically looted Ukrainian museums drive home the reality that many of Vladimir Putin's policies resemble those of Adolf Hitler.[32] Starting in spring 2022, individual Russian soldiers and units of Russian forces were stealing not just food and drink but also sheets, electronics and vehicles from Ukrainians. Like rape, torture, and murder, some of those actions could be blamed on lack of direction from military leaders, but repeated missile attacks on civilian dwellings and infrastructure required decisions at the top. Looting museums in multiple locations must be blamed on No. 1 in the Kremlin.

On March 17, 2023, the International Criminal Court accused the Russian president, Vladimir V. Putin, of war crimes and issued a warrant for his arrest. The court cited Putin's responsibility for the abduction and deportation of Ukrainian children, thousands of whom were sent to Russia since the invasion. It also issued a warrant for Russia's commissioner for children's rights, Maria Lvova-Belova, the public face of the Kremlin-sponsored program for transferring children out of Ukraine.

There is no way Putin can escape responsibility for every facet of the Ukraine disaster

It is unthinkable that Russia's leaders not be tried by an international tribunal for a wide range war crimes. It is also unthinkable that Russia—the country—not be compelled to pay for the damage it has inflicted on Ukraine. Neither process can happen until the Putin regime is replaced. This could happen, through a popular uprising or a coup d'état by insiders, but for now, neither outcome seems likely.

For Putin and his aides to be tried, and for Russia to start paying reparations, the country must be defeated—like Germany and Japan in 1945. The Russian public must be made to understand that their leaders were evil and conducted evil policies in Russia's name.

---

or an individual suit for damages in a national court. Laurie Blank, "War Reparations for Ukraine: Key Issues," *Just Security,* 5/2/22 at https://www.justsecurity.org/81341/war-reparations-for-ukraine-key-issues/

32 Anna Nemtova, "The Bitter Truth Behind Russia's Looting of Ukrainian Art," at https://www.theatlantic.com/international/archive/2023/01/russia-looting-ukraine-art-treasures-kherson/672790/

Many Russians have neither the time nor the means to be informed, but many are guilty of willful ignorance. What of the 250 rectors of Russian academic institutions who approved a statement endorsing Putin's "difficult but correct" decision to "de-Nazify" Ukraine? What of countless media personages who knowingly parrot Kremlin lies? What of the industry and business managers who see the debilitating consequences of war but do nothing to stop it? Many professionals could have done more to thwart or protest the "special military operation."

The final days of the Putin regime will differ from those of Hitler, Benito Mussolini, or Hideki Tojo. Unlike Germany, Italy, or Japan in 1945, Russia has not been directly attacked. Neither Kyiv nor its Western backers have invaded Russia. Putin will not be found by invaders, like Hitler, dead in an underground bunker. Nor will he be killed by antifascist partisans, like Mussolini, while trying to escape to a neutral Switzerland or Spain.

The necessary endgame is that a medium-sized country defeats a former superpower so decisively that its president loses all credibility and legitimacy. He is then replaced by another leader, or leaders, who try—like German statesmen Konrad Adenauer and Willy Brandt—to lead the country gradually back into the family of law-abiding nations. Defeated in war, Russia would still have the resources of a great nation.

Justice for Putin and reparations for Ukraine require Russia's defeat. Any compromise that helps Putin stay in power must be rejected. The interests of law and human rights require that war crimes and criminals be punished.

What Does China Owe Its Peoples?

What happened to the harmony of Yin and Yang and the humane side of Confucianism? They have vanished in storms of aggrandizing power. Xi has not killed millions, but he has intensified Sinification of Tibet and Central Asia with policies that amount to cultural genocide. More than one million Uyghurs have languished in indoctrination camps while others have been forcibly relocated—without their spouses—to far parts of the empire. Even the Han people of Guangdong and Hong Kong are being forced to use Mandarin and let their own language and culture wither. Having bullied all the nations bordering the South China Sea, Xi claims nearly the entire body of water and its resources for China. He threatens to take Taiwan by force no matter what its people want.

Far from implementing a Mandate from Heaven, China's Communist leaders have brutalized their subjects—Han Chinese as well as Tibetans and other minorities forced to accept Beijing's rule. China's Communist rulers consistently edit history to underline their achievements and mask their failures and abuses.[33] Still, memoirs and once-hidden documents reveal a long record of human rights violations including both physical and cultural genocide. Put side by side with the records of Russia, North Korea, Vietnam, and Cuba, they present a powerful indictment of Communist dictatorships no less evil than Hitler's—aggravated by their claims to be all-knowing and dedicated to public weal.

As in dealing with the law of the sea, so also in regards to human rights: China works to rewrite existing rules while relying on its brute strength to win support and avoid punishment.[34]

The crackdown on China's already beleaguered human rights field intensified in 2015, half-way through Xi Jinping's first term. More than 300 lawyers, legal assistants and activists were questioned in Xi's "war on law." Some were given long jail terms; some awaited sentencing; at least one disappeared.

Like others targeted by the campaign, Xie Yanyi, spent much of his legal career representing clients involved in sensitive cases—victims of official corruption, police violence, or religious persecution. Harassment and abuse were part of the job. He was also a bold advocate for peaceful democratic reform, once having filed a

---

33 Xin Fan, *World History and National Identity in China: The Twentieth Century* (Cambridge, UK: Cambridge University Press, 2021).

34 The conservative majority on the U.S. Supreme Court does the same thing. Capturing maximum flexibility in 2nd Amendment cases, Judge Clarence Thomas declared that for any contemporary gun regulation to be constitutional, the government would have to identify an "historical analogue" to it from the nation's founding. Since relevant precedents are rare, lower courts are striking down a wide range of modest restrictions. Paul Waldman, "What a new 2nd Amendment could look like," *The Washington Post*, March 20. 2023.

lawsuit against the former Chinese leader Jiang Zemin for refusing to step down from the Central Military Commission at the end of his presidency.

Released on bail after 18 months in detention, Xie told the BBC he did not see sunlight for six months. He was kept in a stress position, crouched on a stool from 6 in the morning until 10 at night. After 15 days like this, his legs went numb, and he had difficulty urinating. At times he was denied food and interrogated for hours at a time. He was beaten and then watched while he slept, with guards insisting he keep the same position all night. Even harder to bear than all of this, Xie said, was solitary confinement. "I was kept alone in a small room and saw no daylight for half a year. I had nothing to read, nothing to do but to sit on that low stool.... People could go mad in that situation. I was isolated from the world. This is torture—the isolation is more painful than being beaten."

Xie's account tallied with other reports of the suffering endured under the so-called "war on law," launched during the Xi Jinping's first years in office. Shortly after Xi Jinping came to power in 2012, a leaked document circulated online that outlined seven key ideological concepts said to threaten Communist Party rule and forbade the promotion of them in China's universities or in the media. Issued by an office close to the Communist leadership, the forbidden ideologies included "Western constitutional democracy," "universal values," and "civil society." Xi proceeded to curtail the room for public discussion, add restrictions on foreign organizations and charities, clamp down on the internet, and punish human rights lawyers.[35]

Censorship applies also to public health, as seen in the life and death of Jiang Yanyong. Known to many Chinese as a skilled and brave hero doctor, he was vilified, exiled, ostracized, and turned into a non-person by the CCP. Dr. Jiang was a prominent military surgeon who became a national hero for exposing the Chinese government's cover-up of the SARS epidemic in 2003 but was later punished for denouncing the 1989 Tiananmen Square crackdown. In 2023, he died at 91 without public notice except in Hong Kong. A

---

35 John Sudworth, "China lawyer recounts torture under Xi's 'war on law,'" BBC, 10/26/2017 at https://www.bbc.com/news/blogs-china-blog-41661862

7. What Do Putin and Xi Owe Their Victims?

source close to Jiang's family said that he tested positive for Covid in January, soon after zero-Covid restrictions were lifted.[36]

Born into a Shanghai banker's family in 1931, Jiang was inspired to become a military physician by Norman Bethune, a Canadian doctor who died on the front lines of the Communist resistance to the Japanese occupation in 1939. Having graduated from one of China's leading medical academies, Jiang enlisted in the People's Liberation Army and specialized in surgery. In 1957, he was assigned to No. 301 Hospital in Beijing.

During the Cultural Revolution that began in 1966, Dr. Jiang was branded a counterrevolutionary. He was imprisoned, beaten, and later sent to a prison farm for five years in the remote deserts of Qinghai Province, away from his wife and children. Rehabilitated in the early 1970s, he returned to No. 301 Hospital, where he became chief of surgery.

In 2003, alarmed to hear health officials playing down the threat of severe acute respiratory syndrome, or SARS, Dr. Jiang sent a letter to several news organizations refuting the official story. His revelations prompted China's top leaders to acknowledge that they had provided false information about the epidemic and to begin a nationwide effort to battle it, thereby saving many lives. Top leaders fired the health minister and the mayor of Beijing. For a brief period, Dr. Jiang received nationwide acclaim. One local magazine called him the "honest doctor."

Emboldened by his new political capital, Jiang in 2004 wrote a letter to top Chinese leaders, calling on them to acknowledge that the 1989 crackdown on the Tiananmen Square pro-democracy protests had been wrong, and that the student movement had in fact been a "patriotic movement." Treating victims of the shooting at No. 301 Hospital, Jiang recalled, "My brain buzzed and I almost passed out. Lying before me this time were our own people, killed by children of the Chinese people, with weapons given to them by the people."

---

36 Josephine Ma, "Chinese military surgeon who blew the whistle on Sars cover-up dies at 91," *South China Morning Post*, March 13, 2023; Amy Qin, "Jiang Yanyong, Who Helped Expose China's SARS Crisis, Dies at 91," *The New York Times*, March 14, 2023.

Soon after the letter became public, Dr. Jiang and his wife were detained. For seven weeks he was forced to undergo lengthy interrogation and indoctrination sessions. For years he was barred from leaving China and periodically subjected to monitoring, harassment, and house arrest. Though a CCP member with a military rank equivalent to major general, he all but disappeared from public view.

Not long after the SARS epidemic, the Chinese authorities would virtually repeat the cover-up with the outbreak of Covid-19. In late 2019, when a new coronavirus was emerging in China. Dr. Li Wenliang in Wuhan posted a warning to fellow physicians about the still-unidentified disease, which he said resembled the SARS virus. The government reprimanded Dr. Li and forced him to renounce his warning. As the epidemic grew, government officials continued to underplay the coronavirus's threat, delaying efforts to contain it, with global ramifications. When Dr. Li himself died of Covid, he was mourned across China as someone who had spoken truth to power—as Dr. Jiang had done for years.

Like others who challenged Communist Party policy, Jiang was largely erased from the official record, and sometimes painted as a wrongdoer for having spoken out. A multiple-choice question posed by a test-prep school in 2017 asked about the doctor's decision to come forward about SARS. The "correct" answer was B: doing so was wrong because it harmed the interests of the nation, the society and the community, and the doctor should be subject to legal punishment.

For young Chinese, the lesson: If you see Communist evil, cover it up.

China's history of human rights abuse, like Russia's, includes crimes against its own ethnic majority as well as ethnic minorities subjected to imperial repression. Here are some major events and estimated death tolls (mostly Han):

Collectivization and purges after 1949………..1 million

Great Leap Forward starvation ………………38.5 million

Opponents of the Great Leap executed ………..1.5 million

Cultural Revolution.............................. 2 million

Tiananmen and other repression since 1989...... 1 million.[37]

CULTURAL AND PHYSICAL GENOCIDE

To these numbers we should add the deaths of Tibetans, Mongolians. Kazakhs, Uyghurs, and other ethnic minorities killed for opposing Communist policies or who died deaths of despair brought on by those policies. Reliable body counts are difficult if not impossible to obtain, but the total could easily reach 5 million—bringing the total number to some 50 million human victims of Communist rule since 1949. This total omits the millions killed in Communist-Nationalist civil war or "volunteers" killed in the Korean War. Though the numbers are high, China's totals are much smaller on a *per capita* basis than the victims of Soviet rule since 1917. On a per capita basis, they are also less than the 12 million or more Africans killed under the imperial rule of Belgian King Leopold II and the 10 million or more Native Americans killed by U.S. and Canadian military action, forced relocations, and disease.

Besides human life, governments, and other agents (such as missionaries and business operations) damage cultures. Soviets killed many priests and mullahs; burned sacred texts; and forced Central Asians to use Cyrillic.[38] They made Russian the language of empire. Chinese carried out similar outrages in Tibet and Central Asia. Han settlers became the majority ethnic group in Tibet, Mongolia, and Xinjiang.[39] Pressures mounted to forgo traditional

---

37 Ian Johnson, "Who Killed More: Hitler, Stalin or Mao?" *The New York Review of Books*, February 5, 2018.

38 See the works reviewed in my "Review Essay: Enlightenment Lost?" *NETSOL* 6/2 (Fall 2021): 14-19 at https://doi.org/10.24819/netsol2021.10

39 The Han people are the largest ethnic group in mainland China. In 2010, 91.5% of the population were classified as Han (~1.2 billion). There were 55 other ethnic groups—totaling approximately 105 million people (8%). The largest groups were Zhuang) 16.9 million), Hui (10.5 million), Manchu (10.3 million), Uyghur (10 million), Miao (9.4 million), Yi (8.7 million), Tujia (8.3 million), Tibetan (6.2 million), Mongolian (5.9 million), Dong (2.8 million), Buyei (2.8 million), Yao (2.7 million), Bai (1.9 million), Korean (1.8 million), Hani (1.6 million), Li (1.4 million), Kazakh (1.4 million) and Dai (1.2

ways and languages and adopt the "Thought" of Mao Zedong and, later, of Xi Jinping.

Starting in 2017, Chinese authorities incarcerated one or two million Uyghurs (from a total of some 10 million) in hundreds of reeducation barracks and subjected others to intensive surveillance, religious restrictions, forced labor, and forced sterilization—crimes against humanity and probably the Genocide Convention.[40] Former inmates said they were forced to swear loyalty to the CCP; renounce Islam and praise Communism; learn Mandarin; endure surveillance by cameras and microphones. Guards were trained shot to kill. Family separations led to falling birth rates—well below the (low) Chinese average.

Some Han Chinese also experienced cultural genocide. Speakers of Cantonese and dialects, as in Fujian, were pressured to learn and use Mandarin. Hong Kongers and other Chinese were compelled to renounce free speech and other civil rights and liberties, that is, their civic and intellectual culture.

How to put price tag on China's treatment of ethnic and cultural minorities? Canada recognizes it has done great harm to its First Nations over the centuries and has proposed five major settlements since 2006—$31 billion in 2020 in compensation to several hundred tribes for indigenous children and families harmed by the on-reserve child welfare system and, in 2022, another $2 billion to settle lawsuits seeking reparations for the harm done by mandatory residential schools that a national commission termed "cultural genocide." By these standards, China should be offering its minorities, 100 times more than Canada's $33 billion, because China's ethnic minorities number about 115,000,000 compared to Canada's 1,100,000 Indians.

What if China compensated its minorities at just one-tenth the Canadian rate? That would amount to $330 billion. What if Beijing

---

    million). There were also about 730,000 people in unrecognized ethnic groups such as Chuanqing people.

40 https://www.ohchr.org/sites/default/files/documents/countries/2022-08-31/22-08-31-final-assesment.pdf; https://www.xinjiangpolicefiles.org/; also https://www.cfr.org/backgrounder/china-xinjiang-uyghurs-muslims-repression-genocide-human-rights

decided to pay its Han majority $3,000 each for bodily harm done to their families since 1949 and deprivation of political and cultural rights? That would amount to more than $3 trillion—bringing total reparation payments to some $3,330,000,000. If China were to compensate other littoral states on the South China Sea for damage to their fish and other seabed resources, the bill for restitution could easily reach $4 trillion. That is surely a large sum, but not if paid out over five or ten years from a GDP approaching $20 trillion. This would be a bargain price to reboot China with a clean slate and a cleaner conscience. As in Russia, China would need a new government and public education to recognize and act on its debts.

Instead of admitting to past and present injustices, Beijing works to mask them. On October 6, 2022, the UN Human Rights Council rejected a resolution to hold a debate on China's violations of human rights in Xinjiang. The vote was spurred by a detailed report by the Office of the High Commissioner for Human Rights (OHCHR), which documented Chinese state-directed persecution of Uyghurs and other Turkic Muslim minorities that "may constitute crimes against humanity."

The resolution—which failed by 19 votes to 17, with 11 abstentions—represented the first formal attempt to hold China accountable for its massive and ongoing human rights abuses at the Human Rights Council since the body's inception in 2006. According to the OHCHR report, Chinese violations in Xinjian included mass arbitrary detention, widespread torture, sexual violence, coercive birth suppression, family separation, forced labor, and repression of religious and cultural practices.

According to Kelley E. Currie, a veteran human rights lawyer, the council's failure to carry out its most basic function as the UN's premier venue for the promotion and protection of human rights is an indictment of the council itself and the human rights system it purports to anchor. It also demonstrates the deep success of China's decades-long project to rewire the normative framework of international human rights and replace it with the idea that human rights are negotiable and subject to the prerogatives of states.

China's campaign to subvert the existing human rights paradigm has made headway thanks to the acquiescence of many countries that purport to defend human rights. Consider the Human Rights Council vote in March 2018 to adopt China's proposed resolution on "Promoting Mutually Beneficial Cooperation in the Field of Human Rights." The resolution sublimated individual rights to both collective rights (such as the "right" to development) and to state sovereignty. Only the U.S. delegation voted against it. Despite lobbying by the United States and human rights organizations, thirteen delegations *abstained*—including Australia, Belgium, Germany, Japan, Switzerland, and the United Kingdom. Some claimed the resolution provided an entry point for human rights engagement with China.

By enshrining fawning references to "Xi Jinping Thought" into the UN's human rights lexicon, the 2018 resolution represented a step forward in China's efforts to reshape the UN human rights system. Beijing's ability to handpick the report-writing team meant the final report required framed "mutually beneficial cooperation"—an undefined term in the human rights vocabulary—just as Xi does by privileging sovereignty and noninterference in internal affairs, and by delegitimizing approaches to human rights protection that involve criticism of a regime's abuses.[41] These values undergird Xi's claims for civilizational relativism—let each political system do what it wants.[42]

The governments of Russia and China have prioritized the power and material perks of their leaders over the wellbeing of their subjects. When state power was at issue, each government ran roughshod over the material and spiritual values of its peoples—the majority as well as minority ethnic groups. Russia has also invaded neighboring countries and tried to bring them back into its former imperial domain. Except in Tibet, China has maintained its pre-Communist empire with coercion but without full-scale war. Its claim to the South China Sea, however, has been buttressed by PLA forces on several islands, a huge navy and coast guard.

Xi Jinping in 2022–2023 drew China much closer to Putin's

---

41 Kelley E. Currie. "How to Stop China Killing Human Rights at the U.N.," *Foreign Policy*, 11/09/22 at https://foreignpolicy.com/2022/11/09/china-human-rights-un-xinjiang-resolution-international-system/

42 "Global Civilization Initiative injects fresh energy into human development," 3/19/23 at http://english.scio.gov.cn/topnews/2023-03/19/content_85177312htm

Russia and away from the United States and Europe—the very countries whose welcome into the World Trade Organization opened the way to technology transfers and investments crucial to China's material growth. Failing to make a clear choice in the Russian-Ukrainian war, Xi added to China's isolation as multinational companies moved some or all their supply chains away from China. Japan and some European countries joined the United States in blocking transfers of advanced technology to China. Xi's crackdowns on human rights also ensure that people in Taiwan resist any prospect of integration with China.[43]

Apart from the debts owed to their own peoples, the Putin and Xi Jinping regimes owe a great deal to humans everywhere. They have created a model of ruthless authoritarianism that says, "might makes right" and that evil will triumph over good.

Xi's support for civilizational relativism is bad history and morality. Today's China does not inherit thousands of years of continuous civilization. China has been shaped by many centuries of Mongolian and, later, Manchurian rule. The strongest alien influence, however, has been Marxism-Leninism-Stalinism. What remains embodies little of traditional Confucianism or Taoism.

The best indicator of societal fitness is the UN Human Development Index ranks the factors that enhance individual choice. In 2021–2022 all the top places were occupied by Western or Westernized countries, while Russia ranked 52nd and China 79th.[44] This was another indicator of how Putin and Xi neglected the real needs of their subjects.

Meanwhile, an unrepentant Russian soldier scrawled on the wall of a bar in a Ukrainian village: "It doesn't count as a war crime if you had fun." Another wrote: "With a happy smile I burn foreign villages." (Thomas Gibbon-Neff in *The New York Times*, June 15, 2023).

---

43 These views have also been expressed by Chinese academics unable to express them publicly. See Li Yuan, "Under Xi, China Is Distancing Itself From Nations That Helped It Rise," *The New York Times*, March 25, 2023.

44 Hong Kong, 4th; Japan, 19th; South Korea, 20th; USA, 21st; and Israel, 22nd. See hdr2021-022overviewenglishpdf_1.pdf

CHAPTER 8
CAN—SHOULD—PUTIN AND XI REMAIN IN POWER?

Both presidents—Vladimir Putin and Xi Jinping—make big claims for themselves and their countries. However, the main achievement of each has been to manipulate his political system to allow him a third term at the pinnacle of power. Apart from that win, each has wasted his country's assets; voided its cultural and spiritual achievements; and made life everywhere on earth more precarious. Neither Putin nor Xi deserves to stay on his throne. Rising storms threaten to unseat each of them, but each controls multiple tools to subdue any opposition.

BLUNDERS AT THE TOP

Should these two dictators, Putin and Xi, stay in power? Can they? Each is making major blunders as he holds on—possibly a function of age plus swelling self-confidence from years at the top.

Having done almost nothing to energize Russia's economy or culture for more than two decades, Putin degrades them both in his unprovoked war that harms Russia as well as Ukraine. Putin's special military operation should put him and other Russians in the dock for war crimes. Meanwhile, he degraded Russia's future as well as its present by driving away hundreds of thousands of young talents and souring the context for honest, well-motivated, and creative behavior. Even Russian athletics has been polluted by sophisticated masking of banned substances. Putin has also degraded Russia's past by propagandistic rendering of a "Russian World" where all ways of life converge with the values of Ivan III and Peter I as updated by Putin and his Patriarch Kirill.

While Putin for years was a "spin dictator" relying mainly on deception, after 2014 he turned increasingly to terror—within Russia and beyond. Defeated or stalemated in Ukraine, Putin may become more desperate. Unlike Khrushchev or Brezhnev at the height of the Cold War, Putin has no way to climb down or return to a pre-war status quo. He might well step up asymmetric warfare just short of any Western red line—cyber hacking; assassination, sabotage of pipelines, LSG terminals, satellites, fiber cables; challenges to election credibility, disinformation about everything. Increasingly frustrated, he flirts with nuclear saber rattling.

Any Mechanisms for Change? *Nyet*

The Russian Federation Constitution of 1993 is hopeful but vague. Article 3 provides:

1. The bearer of sovereignty and the sole source of power in the Russian Federation shall be its multinational people.

2. The people shall exercise its power directly, as well as through State government bodies and local self-government bodies.

3. The supreme direct expression of the power of the people shall be referendum and free elections.

4. Nobody may usurp power in the Russian Federation. The seizure of power or usurpation of State authority shall be prosecuted under federal law.

Since the powers-that-be rig the elections, the Russian constitution's assurances mean nothing. Public demonstrations also seem destined to fail. Either the powers-that-be ignore protests or crush them. Little has changed since Bloody Sunday in 1905 when the tsar's forces shot and killed more than 100 marchers and wounded hundreds more. Strikes and protests emerged in many parts of the tsarist empire.

A year later the revolution was suppressed or coopted. Yes, in 1906 the tsar established a parliament, the Duma. But he kept a veto over its actions, which he used. He prorogued the first Duna after 75 days, The fourth Duma, elected in 1912, was shut down in March 1917. After the tsar's abdication, the Provisional Government conducted elections for a Constituent Assembly in late 1917. Having won less than one-fourth of the vote, the Bolsheviks were displeased. In January 1918, Bolshevik soldiers let the assembly

8. CAN—SHOULD—PUTIN AND XI REMAIN IN POWER?

talk for twelve hours and then dispersed it, never to return. For most of Russian history, legislatures have done little except rubber-stamp edicts by the current dictator.

Elections? Communist rule meant that Russians and other Soviet citizens had no free and fair elections for over 70 years. In 1990, however, voters in the Russian Republic freely chose Boris Yeltsin as their president—even while Mikhail Gorbachev remained president of the USSR. After the Soviet Union imploded, Yeltsin moved into the Kremlin. He spoke of democracy, but felt compelled to rule by presidential decrees. Opposition led by Vice President Aleksandr Rutskoy and Chairman of the Supreme Soviet Ruslan Khasbulatov blocked many of Yeltsin's initiatives and led to a paralysis of governing. In October 1993 Yeltsin ordered tanks and airborne troops to shell and storm the "White House," the Russian Parliament building, to suppress the opposition trying to remove him. The Bill Clinton administration said Yeltsin had little choice and backed his actions. A new constitution strengthened presidential powers. So Russia again experienced the overwhelming preponderance of executive power. October 1993 proved to be a crucial turning point towards renewed autocracy.

Six years of chaos ensued. Yeltsin used all his powers to designate a successor who would not prosecute him or his family for graft and corruption. In August 1999, he named Vladimir Putin the country's prime minister. On December 31, Yeltsin resigned and named Putin Russia's acting president, a base from which he could mobilize support in an election several months later. Thus, ostensible democrat Yeltsin established a new dictator. He handed the country's top job on a platter to a former agent in the KGB.

Putin served two terms as president; one term as prime minister; and then was elected to a third term as president. Could he win a fourth election in March 2024? As of 2023 his major rivals had been assassinated, imprisoned, or so intimidated they moved abroad. The political parties in the Duma were aligned with Putin or, despite some ostensible disagreements, exaggerated their differences to show the vigor of Russian democracy. The liberal Yabloko party had representation only in four regional parliaments, but some of its members were jailed for criticizing the Ukraine special operation.

Self-rule? Unlike China, Russia has experienced times and traditions of self-rule—bottom-up by popular assemblies or by a privileged upper class whose views had to be considered by number one. For several centuries, Pskov and Novgorod were governed by popular assemblies known as *Veche* that gathered in front of the local cathedral at the ringing of church bells. When Muscovy's Grand Prince Ivan III conquered Novgorod in 1471, he removed its bells to show that his rule was absolute. He also arrested boyar clans opposed to his dominion.

In Kyivan Rus during the 10th–12th centuries. The boyars constituted the senior group in the prince's retinue (*druzhina*) and occupied the higher posts in the armed forces and in the civil administration.[1] They also formed a boyar council, or duma, which advised the prince on important matters of state. In the 13th and 14th centuries, in the northeastern Russian principalities, the boyars were a privileged class of rich landowners; who served the prince as his aides and councilors. From the 15th to the 17th century, the boyars of Muscovy formed a closed aristocratic class that surrounded the throne of the grand prince and ruled the country together with him. Below the boyars was the group of okolnichy, courtiers of the second class, many of whom did administrative work, while boyars led military forces. Together these two strata helped the tsar direct the internal and foreign affairs of the state. In the 16th century, however, boyar clans fought each other and fomented a "Time of Troubles" that precipitated a new dynasty, the Romanov, in 1613. A century later Peter the Great abolished the rank and title of boyar and made state service the exclusive means of attaining a high position in the bureaucratic hierarchy.

Could populist pressures change anything? Some 19th century intellectuals, the *Narodniki* (narod = people), wanted to "go to the country" where most peasants still lived on a commune (the *mir*), and get them to rise up against the tsar and bourgeois landowners who virtually owned many of them, even after serfdom ended in 1861. Within a decade or two, the Narodniki found that the peasants did not like them. Instead, peasants trusted and revered the tsar.

---

1 The term *druzhina* probably derives from the Slavic word *drug*, meaning "friend"; the term *okolnichy* from *okolo*—near, as in near to the throne.

8. Can—Should—Putin and Xi Remain in Power?

Repressed by the tsarist regime, the Narodniki gave up on the peasantry, still so illiterate they could not read political pamphlets. Russia's first organized political party, *Narodnaya Volya*, (the People's Will) stepped in and used terror to show the tsar's frailty. When they killed Aleksandr II in 1881, this did not inspire the peasantry but horrified them. The party fell apart when its leaders (including Lenin's elder brother) were executed for attempting to assassinate Aleksandr III, but some of its ideas nourished the revolutions of 1905–1906 and 1917–1918. However, these flickers were extinguished by the Bolsheviks who did not trust the peasantry and claimed instead to lead a dictatorship of the proletariat.

The Soviet regime, like all Communist systems that emerged elsewhere, purported to work for and guide the people. The ruling Communist parties referred to their regimes as "people's republics." Whatever a Communist Party did—by definition—was supposed to be democratic. Kim Il Sung employed all the high-falutin terms and called his state the "Democratic People's Republic of Korea."

Could Putin be ousted by a boyars' revolt? In Putin's Russia there was no equivalent to a *veche* or to boyars. There was no longer a Communist Party Presidium to approve or vote against a top leader, as happened to Khrushchev. Those close to Putin got there in an ad hoc manner. Early in his presidency Putin surrounded himself with *siloviki*—"strong men" from the secret services and other power ministries. Putin also collaborated with oligarchs who had become rich in Yeltsin's 1990s. One of the wealthiest, Mikhail Khodorkovsky, pushed for political reforms as Putin began his reign. Accused of fraud, Khodorkovsky was siberianized for nearly a decade. Other oligarchs got the message: "Don't challenge the boss." Once freed, Khodorkovsky joined other oligarchs seeking refuge abroad.

At the height of Covid-19, an increasingly isolated President Putin sat at the end of a very long table where, occasionally, he met with guests and advisers. The individual closest to Putin in 2022–23 appeared to be a ruthless entrepreneur, Evgeny Prigozhin (b. 1961), known as "Putin's chef," because he owned restaurants and catering companies providing services for the Kremlin. Once a convict in the former Soviet Union, Prigozhin emerged from prison in 1990 and gradually rose to control a network of influential companies including the mercenary Wagner Group and three companies accused of interfering in U.S. elections. According to investigations by Bellingcat, *The Insider*, and *Der Spiegel*, Prigozhin's activities in 2022 were tightly integrated with Russia's Defense Ministry and its intelligence arm, the GRU. His private army, the Wagner Group, fought in Syria and several African countries as well as in Ukraine. In 2023, however, Prigozhin and his mercenaries appeared to rival or even oppose regular government forces. Prigozhinc complained the Defense Ministry starved his mercenaries of ammunition.

Military intervention? In 2023, three private armed forces operated in Russia. Each received both public and private funding; each was linked to leaders with serious political ambitions. (1) Prigozhin's Wagner Group had 10,000 to 20,000 well-trained and well-armed mercenaries who led some assaults in the Donbas, plus 40,000 former convicts who joined Wagner in late 2022 to escape jail but were often used as cannon fodder. (2) Chechen strongman Ramzan Kadyrov had an army of 12,000 Chechen fighters—more than 1,000 deployed in Ukraine. (3) Defense Minister Sergei Shoigu had his own "Patriot" private military company, also deployed in the Donbas, where it tried to outperform Wagner.

Without a clearly defined legal status, each existed as a private army that could undermine the Russian state's monopoly of violence. Competing—perhaps fighting—with each other, they could return Russia to another "Time of Troubles." Troubles came to a head on June 24, 2023, when Prigozhin led his forces to Rostov-on-Don and then toward Moscow. Putin called this treachery but agreed to a deal mediated by President Aleksandr Lukashenko of Belarus. Prigozhin would reverse his advance and himself take refuge in Belarus. No charges would be brought against Prigozhin or his troops, who could now sign contracts with Russia's Defense Ministry. Many key details were unspecified, Progozhin's future and Putin's authority were in doubt.[2]

Putin appeared to have succumbed to the sunk-cost fallacy of war. He committed ever more troops and resources in a vain attempt

---

2 Alexander J. Motyl, "As Russia weakens, whoever has soldiers and guns will survive," *The Hill*, 1/18/23 at https://thehill.com/opinion/international/3811547-as-russia-weakens-whoever-has-soldiers-and-guns-will-survive/

to make the previous losses mean something or take on a larger purpose. Leaders locked in armed struggle must convince their citizens that those sacrifices are part of a journey that ultimately leads to a better outcome.³ Even the parents of Wagnerite convicts butchered in Ukraine wanted their sons to be honored as war heroes.

Here was a paradox: Putin claimed to lead a "Russian world," but the Russian word for "world" is *mir*, which has two other meanings: "peace" and peasant "commune." Communist Russia claimed to bring peace to the world—*mir miru*, Putin estranged Russia from the world and destroyed its peace, while peasant communes disappeared long ago. To get rid of Putin, Russia might need to suffer complete defeat in Ukraine.

CAN XI JINPING'S TYRANNY BE TRANSFORMED?

Xi Jinping became number one in the Chinese Communist Party and the military in 2012 and the government in 2013. He helped a somewhat unreal economy to flourish. Colossal foreign trade earnings permitted colossal investments not only in infrastructure but also in huge apartment buildings never completed or without tenants. Xi's determination to shut out all dissent terminated free speech across the country—even in Hong Kong. Censorship diminished the free flow of information needed for science, business, and the arts. Xi produced a pressure cooker primed to explode.

Global risk analysts Ian Brenner and Charles Kupchan underscored the dangers: "Having stacked the Communist Party's Politburo Standing Committee with his closest allies, Xi was virtually unfettered in his ability to pursue his statist and nationalist policy agenda. But with few checks and balances left to constrain him and no dissenting voices to challenge his views, Xi's ability to make big mistakes expanded. Arbitrary decisions, policy volatility, and elevated uncertainty could become endemic in Xi's China—a danger to world peace and prosperity given the unprecedented reality of a state capitalist dictatorship with an outsized role in the global economy."⁴

---

3   David V. Gioe. "Putin Is Trapped in the Sunk-Cost Fallacy of War," *Foreign Policy*, 3/14/ 23 at https://foreignpolicy.com/author/david-v-gioe/
4   Eurasia Group, "Top Risks 2023," 1/3/23 at https://www.eurasiagroup.net/live-

The costs of monopolizing information and decision making were manifest in China's responses to the corona virus: first, denial; second, cover-up; third failure to conduct mass vaccination campaigns—not even among the elderly—with Chinese-made vaccines and refusal to import superior foreign vaccines; fourth, protracted lock-downs; fifth, a sudden reopening, with little immunity buildup from previous exposure. The dangers of this approach even at high levels of society were manifest in December 2022-January 2023 when the death rate of distinguished but elderly Chinese academics skyrocketed.[5] All these policies harmed public health and lowered public confidence in government.[6]

Xi's actions abroad probably encouraged nationalistic pride, but needlessly antagonized outsiders. The Belt and Road campaign boosted economic development in some countries, but left many, such as Sri Lanka, in unsustainable debt—bad for them and bad for China if they could not pay up. Many Chinese aid programs looked like thinly veiled ways to grab cobalt, oil, and other natural resources in Africa and South America regardless their environmental and societal consequences.

China's claim to most of the South China Sea was a naked grab for power and wealth. Rejecting an international tribunal's finding that this claim has no historical or legal foundation, China occupied several islands and built up several more, turning some into military bases. Chinse fishing fleets scraped the seabed near these islands and ravaged the coastal waters of other littoral nations—the Philippines, Vietnam, and Indonesia. Dredging to make artificial islands, Chinese pulverized coral beds home to multiple forms of ocean life. Fishing and overfishing by Chinese fleets damaged fish stocks all the way to Ecuador and South Africa.

---

post/top-risks-2023-2-Maximum-Xi

5 At the Harbin Institute of Technology, for example, the average death rate jumped from two deaths per month to 29. See Pablo Robles. Vivien Wong, Joy Dong, "In China's Covid Fog, Deaths of Scholars Offer a Clue," *The New York Times,* February 16, 2023.

6 Still, the rates of Chinese deaths from the virus were lower than in the United States, where the whims of an aspiring dictator wreaked a public health catastrophe. If a million Chinese died from the virus, that would still be a much lower per capita toll than in the United States.

8. CAN—SHOULD—PUTIN AND XI REMAIN IN POWER?

Completely indifferent to what residents of Taiwan might want, Xi's air, land, and sea forces acted like they were preparing to take Taiwan by force regardless the cost. PLA threats to Taiwan, along with China's actions in the South and East China Seas, push neighboring countries—from Japan to Vietnam to Australia—together and into deeper ties with the U.S. military. On another Chinese frontier, India also looked for support from Australia, Japan, and the United States. Like Putin's aggressions, Xi's military and economic expansions generated walls of resistance—stiffened by the fiery rhetoric of Xi's "wolf warrior" diplomacy.

One of Xi's greatest follies was to pledge unconditional solidarity with Putin. Surely Chinese intelligence must have seen Russia's buildup to invade Ukraine. Why tie China to such a dangerous loser? Granted that China (along with India) can now purchase all the carbons it wants at discount prices, China could have enjoyed this perk without offering exorbitant assurances of friendship. If Xi ever seeks Putin's help to conquer Taiwan, the outcome will probably be no more substantial than in 1958, when Khrushchev blustered his support only *after* the crisis had unwound.

Ronald Linden has noted the many ways that China's policies have stirred worry and resistance in much of the world. In 2022 NATO formally declared the Indo-Pacific a part of its "shared security interests." The EU adopted the strategic aim of insuring an "open and rule-based" South China Sea—a rejection of China's unilateral claims. Italy, once quite open to Chinese investment, has announced the deployment of one of its two aircraft carriers to the region. Italy has confirmed a tripartite deal with Japan and the UK to develop and produce a new generation fighter plane. In Japan, the defense budget increases. After a visit to Ukraine, Japanese prime minister Fumio Kishida warned that "Ukraine today could be East Asia tomorrow."[7]

The balloon incidents in February 2023 showed that Xi's grip on policy was either unwise or incomplete. One balloon, 200-feet high, carried its surveillance devices across the United States just

---

7 For more, see Ronald H. Linden, "Is the Chinese Dream Turning into a Chinese Nightmare for Beijing?" *National Interest*, 4/3/23 at https://nationalinterest.org/feature/chinese-dream-turning-chinese-nightmare-beijing-206374

as Secretary of State Anthony Blinken prepared to fly to Beijing for talks meant to reduce or at least control tensions—a goal probably shared by both sides. Like the American U-2 flight over Russia in 1960, the balloon could be spotted and shot down—spoiling any efforts at better relations. Like Ike in 1960, Chinese called their espionage device a tool for studying the weather—another blow to credibility. The vitriolic style of Chinse denials recalled Hitler's devotion to the Big Lie (*grosse Lűge*) because the putative weather balloon contained tons of listening devices—risky chutzpah at the highest level. The evidence showed that Chinese spacecraft had intruded the air space of 40 countries across five continents. Xi Jinping's government and his vaunted security apparatus appeared less coherent or less functional than the image he so confidently projected. The momentum of bureaucratic routine or political rivalries could have undermined any attempt to mount a monolithic policy.

The last time a Chinese leader had this much power to pursue such a misguided policy agenda was in 1958–1962 and 1966–1976 when the Great Leap Forward and Cultural Revolution, brought on widespread famine, economic ruin, and death. Today's educated urban middle classes may try to prevent a return to such policies but have few tools to do so.

Any Mechanisms for Change?

The avenues for political change in Xi's China appear to be even more limited than in Russia. China had no *veche* to resurrect; no boyar council; no parliament subject to imperial veto; no constituent assembly as in 1917; no free and fair presidential election as in 1990. For better or worse, Xi's China had no private armies competing with official forces, as in Putin's Russia.

A People's Republic? While there were signs of populist sentiment in old Russia, like the Narodniki in the 1860s and 1870s, the dominant motif in China was kow-towing respect for the emperor, seen as *pater familias* of the empire, in accord with Confucian principles. To be sure, in 1895 the exiled writer Liang Qichao called for popular rule to replace the Qing dynasty. He had read Thomas Hobbes and other European theorists, but nonetheless taught that individual and state interests were the same. At about the same time, Sun Yat-sen saw shadows of democracy in Hawaii and came to organize his "three principles" around people [*minzū*]—nationalism (independence from foreigners), rights of the people (democracy), and people's livelihood (welfare). Before this worldview could shape Chinese politics, however, Sun Yat-sen died in 1925, and his principles were devoured by the top-down authoritarianisms of Chiang Kai-shek and his bitter opponent Mao Zedong—each of them supported by the one-party clique controlling the Soviet Union.

Mao's Communists won supreme power on the mainland in 1949 and called their state the *People's* Republic of China. Since the people did not know what was best, the leaders of the Communist Party would set out the most appropriate policies for the time and place. In 1957 Mao said he wanted "a thousand flowers to bloom." But when challenges emerged to his rule, he launched an "Anti-Rightist" campaign that persecuted more than a million voices and shut down all dissent. A similar cycle took place later under Deng Xiaoping. Deng believed that the nation's progress required a well-educated population. As part of the reform process, he sanctioned more open debate and discussion. Throughout the 1980s, students demonstrated publicly, newspapers and radio shows began to discuss social problems openly, and it became possible once again to travel and study abroad. The documentary "River Elegy" (*Heshang*) was broadcast on national Chinese television in 1988, arguing that China had been led astray by Mao, the false "peasant emperor," and that the country needed to return to the message of the 1919 May Fourth Movement for "science and democracy." As dissent became stronger in 1959, Deng authorized the PLA to crush protestors on Tiananmen Square.

Consultative democracy? Rebounding from this event, some Chinese leaders in the 1990s and early 2000s advocated consultative democracy to improve the government's capability to satisfy citizens' demands. One tool for this campaign was the "Mayor's Mailbox," which appeared in the early 2000s in a nationwide "government online" campaign. The mailbox permitted anyone to submit questions, complaints, and suggestions to local leaders. By 2014, 98 percent of China's 336 prefectural level governments provided this service. Research showed that the Mayor's Mailbox delivered helpful information in response to 43 percent of the requests. Still, nothing changed unless authorized from on high.[8]

After Xi Jinping came to power in 2012, the Party weakened the infrastructure of consultative democracy. The CCP came to see its institutions not as sources of resiliency but as threats to regime stability. Mass arrests, such as the 2015 arrests of lawyers, aimed to eliminate or intimidate all human rights activists and their families. Crackdowns suffocated the operations of NGOs in China and their ability to cooperate with foreign counterparts. Online whistleblowing met with charges of "spreading rumors."

As Xi Jinping began his second decade at the top, there was no way to remove him and institute a new leader. No way to institute a political system less arbitrary and more representative. China did not have a dictatorship of the proletariat or a people's democracy but the dictatorship of one man abetted by a coterie of his selected helpers. The top leaders were not chosen in popular elections but by Communists deemed reliable by Xi.

Could prosperity nurture democracy? It did not. The affluent middle and upper classes that emerged since the 1990s lacked political clout. If they harbored deviant opinions, they had no venue to express them. If their wealth or actions could challenge Xi, their businesses were shut down or they were forced to resign. Many business people resented the government's heavy hand in commerce—arresting bosses of major corporations. Many Chinese showed their displeasure with Xi's covid lockdown, which he ended precipitously with few precautions. Some Chinese called for an end to dictatorial mind-control. Many government officials tasked to implement Xi's policies at home or abroad probably saw them as "hare-brained," the charge for which Khrushchev was ousted. But their feelings altered nothing.

Batons and guns proved mightier than banners, pens, or Virtual Private Networks. Millions of protestors in Hong Kong challenged Xi's efforts to curb their liberties and political rights. In two or three

---

8 Zhuoran Li, "The Rise and Fall of Democracy with Chinese Characteristics," *Diplomatic Brief*, 2/05/22.

years, however, the former free-spirited city-state became another cog in a strong police-state. Many leading dissenters fled or were jailed.

Military coup? In Xi's China there could be no parallel to 1971 when Defense Minister Lin Biao was accused of planning a coup against Mao.[9] Today's commanders of the People's Liberation Army are well fed and equipped. They are probably happy to demonstrate their new planes and ships in threats to Taiwan and the patriotic vigor of their soldiers as they push into India. The PLA has no need to recruit convicts to get the necessary numbers, as in Russia. So long as China is not engaged in a major war, there is no danger of a catastrophic defeat like that facing Putin in Ukraine. Nor does China risk the chaos inherent in the three private armies fighting in Ukraine and portending a possible civil war, as in Russia.

Minority secession? China's ethnic minorities posed no threat of secession. Tibetans and Uyghurs were enveloped by Han Chinese and had no organized military, as did Chechens in Russia. China's ethnic minorities never had a platform to rebel as did the popular fronts in Estonia, Latvia, and Lithuania permitted by Gorbachev in the late 1980s.

THE CUBAN EXAMPLE

The dictatorships in Russia and, even more so, in China looked nearly impregnable in 2023. If in doubt, consider Cuba and its one-party system. Huge numbers of the Cuban public disliked the regime—many of them for decades. Many hungered for food as well as freedom. Many thousands fled and thousands kept trying to flee—often in rickety ships on dangerous seas. Cuban athletes and some artists made it big in the United States, where a substantial Cuban diaspora opposed the regime in Havana. The United States tried since 1960 to undermine Communist rule in Cuba, but the regime held on even after its legendary founders passed on. *Fidelismo* still stood—though much weaker than the regimes of Putin and Xi Jinping. In Cuba, as in Russia and China, totalitarian controls worked—for decades if not forever.

---

9 Some outsiders doubt that he aimed at a coup. In any case, he did not get far. His escape plane crashed in Mongolia near the Soviet border.

CHAPTER 9
TRIANGULAR DIPLOMACY IN THE AGE OF PUTIN, XI, AND BIDEN

Who Is Playing Whom?

Putin was the first leader whom Xi visited after becoming China's president in 2012. Since then, the two have held at least forty one-on-one meetings—twice as many times as either met with any other world leader. Putin calls Xi his "best and bosom friend," who, as Putin noted in 2018, is the only world leader with whom he has celebrated his birthday. But when Xi Jinping arrived in Moscow in March 2023, "he was standing tall, both literally—towering over Putin by five inches (12.7 centimeters)—and figuratively. Yes, he celebrated the strength of the bilateral relationship. But, wearing his habitual enigmatic smile, he carried himself with an air of superiority, whereas Putin's expressions appeared strained. As desperate as Putin may be to project an image of strength, he knows that he cannot risk alienating China, and he treated Xi as Mao had wished to be treated by Nikita Khrushchev in the 1950s.[1]

The United States has been the world's most powerful country since the 1940s. The former Soviet Union, centered in Russia, rose to parity with the U.S. militarily but never economically or in other forms of power and influence. In the 1950s it appeared that China joined with the USSR against the USA, but by 1959–1960 their alliance turned into mutual hostility, President Nixon's Special Assistant for National Security, Henry Kissinger, sought to use "triangular diplomacy" to leverage Sino-Soviet tensions to U.S. advantage. Kissinger and his successor, Zbigniew Brzezinski (under President Carter) brought the United States closer to China than to the USSR, but presidents Reagan and George H.W. Bush developed good working relations with Gorbachev's USSR that seemed to end the Cold War in the late 1980s and early 1990s. Moving in fits and

---

1 Nina Khrushcheva, "Xi's the Boss." Project Syndicate, March 29, 2023.

starts, China joined trade and other forms of cooperation with the West. The yuan overtook the dollar as the most traded currency on the Moscow Exchange for the first time ever, representing almost 40 percent of total trading volume.

Absolutism and Aggression

Starting with the ascendancy of Vladimir Putin in the 2000s and Xi Jinping after 2012, the West's relations with both Moscow and Beijing became fraught along many dimensions. Both Russia and China became more dictatorial at home and more aggressive abroad. The Kremlin's brutal actions against Chechens, Moldovans, Georgians, and Ukrainians—as well as Russians—created new debts to the Kremlin's victims. China's repression of its Han majority and minorities such as Tibetans, Kazakhs, Uyghurs, and Mongolians intensified, adding to Beijing's debts.

All this confronted the United States and its partners with profound challenges. Coping with global problems such as climate change and nuclear weapons need positive teamwork by all nations, but especially the most powerful. Granted that the United States and most Western nations committed multiple crimes against humanity in the past, how could they cooperate with leaders in Moscow and Beijing committing serious crimes *now*? Not only were Putin and Xi Jinping abusing their own subjects and neighbors, but they were building military and espionage capabilities that threatened Western security and could provoke a nuclear Armageddon.

Dan Coats, then the Director of National Intelligence, stated in January 2019 that "China and Russia are more aligned than at any point since the mid-1950s." Chinese media agreed that relations with Russia were at "their best in history." When Russian President Vladimir Putin visited Beijing in April 2019, Xi Jinping stressed that both China and Russia remained committed to their respective national development programs and face the same tasks and challenges. "We should always regard each other as important development opportunities, support each other and draw on each other's strengths to achieve revitalization together and jointly build a community with a shared future for mankind." Visiting Moscow

9. Triangular Diplomacy in the Age of Putin, Xi, and Biden

in June 2019, Xi noted, "Russia is the country that I have visited the most times, and President Putin is my best friend and colleague." What lay beneath this ostensible solidarity?

On February 4, 2022, Chinese President Xi Jinping welcomed his Russian counterpart to Beijing with great fanfare. Putin was the only head of state Xi had met in two years. The two leaders inked a flurry of trade and energy deals, lunched together, and posed before their nations' flags. In the evening, Xi feted the Russian leader at the opening ceremony of the 2022 Winter Olympic Games. A sweeping joint statement issued at the end of the summit proclaimed that the friendship between Russian and China "has no limits." The joint statement pledged the two countries would have "no 'forbidden' areas of cooperation."

China joined Russia in denouncing NATO as a Cold War relic and blamed Washington for expanding the alliance and aggravating Russian security concerns. President Xi vowed to work together with Russia in areas ranging from trade to aerospace. Xi called "Russia an important partner in co-building the Belt and Road Initiative" and said that the "two countries should strengthen international co-operation and adhere to multilateralism." Putin offered his support for the Beijing-led initiative, saying Xi had "built an important platform for expanding international co-operation." Putin added that "Russia is willing to strengthen exchanges and cooperation, and work with China in energy, connectivity, and other major projects."[2]

Xi visited Putin in Moscow for three days in March 2023. Analysts debated whether this meant an even stronger Sino-Russian entente against the United States or proof of Russia's subservience to Chinese dominion. Some said Putin had become Xi's vassal. Did the summit show that Xi Jinping was a brilliant practitioner of Realpolitik with Chinese characteristics? Or a blind fool to align with a big-time loser while ringing alarm bells across the West and Asia? No matter which interpretations s were more valid, senior

---

[2] Jonathan E. Hillman, *The Emperor's New Road: China and the Project of the Century* (New Haven: Yale University Press, 2020), reviewed by Clemens on 10/29/20 at https://www.nyjournalofbooks.com/book-review/emperor%E2%80%99s-new-road

officials in democratic countries worried that the ostensible entente signaled that Beijing and Moscow were joining forces to reshape the global order closer to their authoritarian vision.

UKRAINE AS CRUCIBLE

The divergent impulses of China's foreign policy were reflected in Beijing's shifting diplomatic rhetoric regarding Russia and Ukraine.[3] Sources within the Xi Jinping regime complained that Putin did not warn the Chinese leader in early 2022 that he planned to invade Ukraine in the very near future—surely a burden on a friendship with "no limits." On the other hand, how could Beijing not be aware of a planned invasion that a retired Russian general (see Chapter 1) as well as U.S. intelligence warned was imminent? Perhaps Xi, like Putin, thought the fighting would end quickly without major tremors on the world scene.

Seeking to avoid U.S. sanctions, China seemed to deliver only dual-use goods to Russia—no weapons of war. In 2022, however, the state-owned Poly Technologies company sent tons of smokeless gunpowder to Russia's Bernal Cartridge Plant—the lethal aid Washington tried to ban.

On key UN votes, China abstained-—not joining UN majorities in condemning the invasion. China in September 2022 joined Russian forces on land and at sea for a week of joint exercises in Russia's Far East. But even that event could be read differently. The chief of the Russian general staff, Gen Valery Gerasimov, oversaw the drills. But was all this just for show? Russia claimed it was sending 50,000 troops but only 15,000 appeared[4]—along with just 2,000 from China. They were joined by units from Belarus, India, Mongolia, Laos, Nicaragua, and Syria.

---

3 Clay Chandler, "Putin's and Xi's 'no limits' friendship is put to the test in Ukraine," *Fortune* (February 25, 2022) at https://fortune. https://fortune.com/2022/02/25/ukraine-invasion-china-xi-jinping-russia-vladimir-putin-relationship-foreign-policy/

4 Mia Jankowicz, "Russia is using a fraction of soldiers it claimed for military exercises with China and India, UK intel says," *Business Insider*, 9/2/22 at https://www.businessinsider.com/vostok-22-will-be-fraction-of-the-size-uk-intelligence-2022-9.

In February 2023, Chinese and Russian ships exercised for ten days with South Africa vessels off the coast of South Africa. "South Africa is going to play the Russia and China cards and try to achieve more bargaining chips when dealing with the United States," which failed to obtain South Africa's support over the Russia-Ukraine war, said Ni Lexiong, a political science professor at Shanghai University of political science and law.[5] The naval exercises were a show of diplomatic independence for South Africa and its alignment with Brazil, Russia, India, and China—known as BRICS. South Africa was among three dozen countries that abstained in 2022 in votes at the United Nations condemning Russian aggression. BRICS may not be a military alliance like NATO, but it is still presenting itself as a "countervailing force to the West." Since 2011, however, South Africa conducted joint military drills with the United States four times, most recently in July 2022.

China's biggest contribution to Putin's special military operation was to sharply increase its purchases of Russian oil and gas—albeit at bargain prices as global demand shrank. No matter the sympathies of Beijing elites, China's purchases of Russian carbons in 2002-2003 kept the Kremlin financially afloat. China's imports from Russia (mostly oil and natural gas) rose by 43 percent in 2022. By 2023, however, China's energy imports from Russia seemed to have reached a plateau. To have a diverse mix of energy suppliers, China generally caps oil imports at around 2 million barrels per day from any one country—a number that Russia probably hit by October 2022. In addition, few Chinese refineries can work with Urals crude, which contains high levels of mercury. The picture is similar to gas. Shipments through Power of Siberia, the main gas pipeline between Russia and China, cannot grow by much until upgrades to the pipeline are completed. Moscow has asked China to help fund a second pipeline, but Beijing has said *nyet*.[6] China is

---

5 Minnie Chan, "South Africa 'plays China and Russia' card against U.S. with joint naval exercise," *South China Morning Post*, January 22, 2023.

6 Agathe Demarais, "Russia Sanctions: 10 Lessons and Questions for What Comes Next," *Foreign Policy*, 2/24/23 at https://foreignpolicy.com/2023/02/24/russia-sanctions-war-ukraine-lessons; also Christina Lu, "Russia Has the Hydrocarbons, but China Has the Cash," *Foreign Policy.* 3/23/23 at https://foreignpolicy.com/2023/03/23/xi-putin-russia-china-energy-gas-pipeline-

happy to buy carbons at a discount to world prices but is reluctant to invest in a long-term dependency. Russia needs China more than China needs Russia.

Still, the Putin-Xi summit in 2023 produced a new accord affirming that Russia would permit its professors to share advanced information technology with Chinese students. This was a breakthrough the Chinese had aspired to for decades Unlike the United States until the late Trump years, Russia had long denied Chinese students access to advanced engineering and IT research. However, in July 2022 the Bauman Moscow State Technical University agreed to participate in a joint venture in Shenzhen already underway with Moscow State University. Bauman is the best engineering university in the country and heavily involved in military and security research—missiles, tanks, surveillance technologies. "We decided to . . . establish cooperation with Bauman University so that students would study according to the highest Russian standards," explained Sergei Shakhrai, Vice President of MSU in Shenzhen. Learning with Russians in China would not be the same as in Russia. Still, some analysts said the Russian concessions showed that Moscow was playing little brother to Xi's regime.[7]

In 2022, Western sanctions mostly targeted Russia's ability to import high-tech products, such as top-notch semiconductors and parts for aircraft and cars. For Moscow, locating alternative suppliers was a priority. But Chinese firms did rush to fill the gap left by Western businesses. China's exports to Russia grew by 13 percent in 2022—a rate on par with Beijing's other key trade partners. Russia absorbed only 2 percent of China's exports, hardly a solid trade relationship. These data points did not capture smuggling, but illicit trade was unlikely to provide Russia with enough high-tech components for its vast economy and war machine.

As of mid-2023 the United States and EU had not exhausted all the options in their arsenal. Western sanctions against Russia were *not* the most robust ever imposed: the sanctions against Iran between

---

economy/?utm_source=

7 Andrei Soldatov and Irina Borogan, "China Finally Enters Russia's Technological Treasure House," *Europe's Edge*, 3/23/23 at https://cepa.org/article/china-finally-enters-russias-technological-treasure-house/

2012 and 2015 were far more stringent. Western countries wanted to keep some sanctions firepower in reserve to deter Moscow from escalating the war even further. Keeping some powder dry would also give Western countries leverage if peace negotiations ever took place.

China noted that the United States had not yet imposed secondary sanctions on Russia. Such measures would force businesses everywhere to choose between the U.S. and Russian markets—a scenario in which most firms would certainly ditch Russia. In 2023, Washington concluded it could not force a global decoupling from Russia so long as Europe needed Russian energy. Another obstacle was that secondary sanctions could disrupt global commodity markets and give credence to Russia's claims that sanctions hurt energy and food insecurity globally.

The tightrope act facing Beijing was how to mitigate the widespread perception that it sided with Moscow against the West. While international pressure motivated Beijing to distance itself from Russia, the majority of Chinese foreign policy and security experts were genuinely sympathetic to Russian perspectives, according to Tong Zhao, a senior fellow at the Carnegie Endowment's Tsinghua Center for Global Policy in Beijing.[8] As China braced itself for a world in chaos, Xi Jinping focused on "filling the gap to win the hearts and minds of the Global South," as evidenced by his Global Security Initiative which aimed to "uphold the idea of indivisible security."

The U.S. National Intelligence global threat assessment in 2023 expected that China would continue cooperating with Russia as part of Beijing's campaign to replace the United States as the preeminent power in East Asia and to push aside the rules-based order cultivated by the West in favor of an order hospitable to authoritarianism.[9]

---

8 https://carnegieendowment.org/2022/04/12/how-china-has-handled-its-strategic-dilemma-over-russia-s-invasion-pub-86875

9 *Annual Threat Assessment of the U.S. Intelligence Community*, 2/6/23 at https://www.dni.gov/files/ODNI/documents/assessments/ATA-2023-Unclassified-Report.pdf

China's Interests in Ukraine

As regards Ukraine, China's interests and Russia's were not aligned at home or worldwide. As Ronald Linden and Emilia Zankina remind us, Thucydides quoted the Athenian general who warned Melians that the strong do what they *can* and the weak suffer what they *must*. But Thucydides did not claim that the strong do whatever they *want*. For China, Russia's invasion of its neighbor and Europe's second largest country puts them squarely within this paradox. As the Athenians learned, (and the Russians might still apprehend), there are limits on the strong and their friends, even when they profess none. [10]

In January 2022, on the eve of Putin's war, Xi formally congratulated Ukrainian President Volodymyr Zelenskyy on the 30th anniversary of diplomatic relations between the two countries. "China-Ukraine relations have always maintained a sound and stable development momentum," Xi told Zelenskyy, according to China's Ministry of Foreign Affairs. "The two sides enjoy deepening political mutual trust, fruitful cooperation in various fields, and even closer people-to-people and cultural exchanges, which have improved the well-being of the two peoples." Putin's decision to attack his Western neighbor created new headaches for Xi and highlighted the complex and contradictory nature of China's foreign policy. "Beijing's global aspirations are now clashing with its desire to remain selectively ambiguous and aloof." China's refusal to condemn Russia's attack on a smaller neighbor recognized as sovereign and independent by the rest of the world called into question Beijing's oft-stated assertion that it follows a principle of noninterference in its foreign policy. Some analysts argued that turning a blind eye to Russia's Ukraine invasion jeopardized China's own long-term interests. Two experts cautioned: "Although Chinese leaders may not recognize it, their country's closer alignment with Russia is far from prudent."[11] Ukraine is—or was—an important trade partner

---

10 Ronald H. Linden and Emilia Zankina, "No Limits? China, Russia, and Ukraine," *Eurozine*, 5/4/22 at https://www.eurozine.com/no-limits-china-russia-and-ukraine/

11 Jude Blanchette and Bonny Lin, "China's Ukraine Crisis: What Xi Gains—and Loses—From Backing Putin," *Foreign Affairs* (February 21, 2022) at https://

for China with trade between the two nations—including iron ore, corn, and sunflower oil from Ukraine and consumer goods and machinery from China—totaling $19 billion in 2021. Ukraine was an enthusiastic supporter of the Belt and Road Initiative, Xi's policy to create a network of new trade and transit links between China and Europe. But Xi's tilt toward Moscow threatened its relationship with Kyiv.

History's March

Russia, China, and the United States in the early 21st century remained the world's three greatest military powers. While Russia stagnated economically for decades, China steadily grew in material terms and matched or exceeded the U.S. GDP. If Russia and China worked together, their combined assets—military, geopolitical, technological, financial—could produce mighty tools to use against the United States and its allies. Graham Allison wrote that the undeclared alliance that Xi has built with Putin has become much more consequential than most of Washington's official alliances. As Russia's trade with China increased in 2022, the yuan overtook the dollar as the most traded currency on the Moscow Exchange in 2023.[12]

On the other hand, Allison also recalls what former U.S. Defense Secretary James Mattis noted in 2018: Moscow and Beijing have a "natural nonconvergence of interests." Geography, history, culture, and economics give both nations many reasons to be adversaries. Large swaths of what was once Chinese territory are now within Russia's borders—including Moscow's key naval base Vladivostok, on Chinese military maps still labeled by its Chinese name, *Haishenwai*. Russia was a prime antagonist in China's "century of humiliation," joining Western imperialists against the Boxer Rebellion and forcing China to sign eight "unequal treaties." The 2,500-mile border between the two nations has repeatedly seen violent clashes, most recently in 1969. Siberia is full of natural

---

www.foreignaffairs.com/articles/china/2022-02-21/chinas-ukraine-crisis

12 Graham Allison, "Xi and Putin Have the Most Consequential Undeclared Alliance in the World," *Foreign Policy*, 3/23/23 at https://foreignpolicy.com/2023/03/23/xi-putin-meeting-china-russia-undeclared-alliance/

resources but has a population of just 32 million people, while in China millions of people live with few natural resources. In recent decades, the status inversion resulting in Russia's decline from its position as the second superpower combined with China's meteoric rise, must cause Putin some consternation.

Separated by an ocean, China and the United States have had fewer occasions for conflict than Beijing and Moscow. During the Second World War, the USA was allied with the USSR against Adolf Hitler and with Chiang Kai-shek's China against Japan. In 1949, however, Mao Zedong's troops forced Chiang Kai-shek to withdraw to Taiwan. Stalin and Mao signed an alliance on Valentine's Day 1950 that led Americans to imagine that a "monolithic" Communism threatened the "Free World." In 1950 Stalin reluctantly gave a go-ahead to Kim Il Sung's attack on the South but pressed a reluctant Mao Zedong to fight with the North if needed. Soon the United States was de facto at war with Mao's China as well as Stalin's Soviet Union, which supplied arms to North Korea and pilots to fight U.S. bombers.

U.S. leaders did not know how tenuous the Sino-Soviet alliance was and how bitter were the resentments Mao felt toward Stalin and later toward Soviet Party leader Nikita S. Khrushchev. Washington did not know that Khrushchev in October 1957 had promised a sample atomic bomb to Mao in exchange for his declaration that "the USSR is the leader of the Communist movement"—only to slowly backtrack and finally suspend all aid programs to China in 1959–1960. (This process was described in my book *The Arms Race and Sino-Soviet Relations* [1968] and confirmed in the memoir of Nie Rong Zhen, head of China's nuclear and missile programs, 1958–1970.) Despite Moscow's duplicitous double-game, China persisted and tested its first atomic bomb in October 1964—the same month that Khrushchev's comrades ousted him for "hare-brained" policies. China's nuclear development, however, led Washington and Moscow in 1963 to consider some kind of intervention to stop it. As late as 1970, the Kremlin contemplated a surgical strike to destroy China's nuclear facilities.

By the time that Richard Nixon became president in 1969, there was no longer a meaningful Sino-Soviet alliance. Nixon's

National Security Assistant and later Secretary of State, Henry Kissinger, espoused a triangular diplomacy to pit Beijing and Moscow against each other to bolster U.S. objectives. Washington's goals included ending the Indo-China War on terms acceptable to Washington and capping the U.S. nuclear arms race with the USSR. But neither Beijing nor Moscow had much influence in Indochina and Washington finally withdrew from Saigon in disgrace. Kissinger and Nixon did establish a sort of entente with Beijing in 1971–72, but Kissinger's effort to leverage China did not contribute to the Nixon's arms accords with Leonid Brezhnev's Kremlin in 1972. These agreements took shape because they satisfied the strategic needs of both Washington and Moscow. Kissinger's triangular diplomacy was not needed for Washington to have more normal relations with Beijing or for arms controls with Moscow.

In the late 1970s, President Jimmy Carter sought to inject more idealism and concern for human rights into U.S. policies, but his National Security Assistant Zbigniew Brzezinski favored a tough Realpolitik. He deemed détente with Moscow a chimera and worked for a real entente with Beijing. Washington in 1979 shifted diplomatic "recognition" from the Republic of China based in Taiwan to the People's Republic of China in Beijing. When the Soviets invaded Afghanistan in December 1979, this brought new intensity to U.S.-Soviet hostility, reinforced by Chinese opposition to Moscow's Afghan intervention. Washington's relationship with Moscow remained very tense as President Ronald Regan, elected in 1980, faced off against an ailing Leonid Brezhnev followed by two other sclerotic general secretaries.[13] When Mikhail Gorbachev became the paramount Soviet leader in 1985, however, he and Reagan became partners in reversing the arms race and trying to end the Cold War. Gorbachev also sought to restore good relations with China, but the Tiananmen massacre in 1989 set back China's ties with Moscow as well as with the United States.

---

13 Ronald Reagan's election victory in 1980 may have been helped by John B. Connally, Jr. who visited the Middle East that summer and suggested to Arab leaders they advise Iranians not to surrender their U.S. hostages while Carter was president because they could get a better deal with Reagan. Peter Baker, "43-Year Secret of Sabotage: Mission to Subvert Carter Is Revealed," *The New York Times*, March 19, 2023.

What is known as Deng Xiaoping's "24-Character Strategy" first emerged in 1990 in response both to the global backlash from the 1989 Tiananmen Square crackdown and to the Chinese Communist Party's sense of alarm following the collapse of the Communist regimes in Eastern Europe. Deng advised his comrades: "Observe calmly; secure our position; cope with affairs calmly; hide our capacities and bide our time; be good at maintaining a low profile; and never claim leadership. Keep a cool head and maintain a low profile. Never take the lead — but aim to do something big." On the other hand, Deng also declared: "China is not a superpower, nor will she ever seek to be one .... If one day China should change her color and turn into a superpower, if she too should play the tyrant in the world, and everywhere subject others to her bullying, aggression and exploitation, the people of the world should identify her as social-imperialist, expose it, oppose it and work together with the Chinese people to overthrow it."[14]

Beijing blamed Gorbachev's reformist line for the collapse of the Soviet empire in 1989–1991, but Deng also courted the United States. Washington welcomed signs that China was ready to join the club of nations and helped China join the World Trade Organization. But dedication to keeping a low profile changed when Xi Jinping became Communist Party general secretary in 2012. The country's policies became even tougher at home and abroad after Xi became president in 2013. In October 2017, he said: "It is time for us to take center stage in the world and to make a greater contribution to humankind." China was "standing tall and firm in the east." A "flourishing" economic model of socialism with Chinese characteristics offered a "new choice" for the developing world.

Ties between Beijing and Moscow developed further after 2017 as each encountered a tense, unpredictable and potentially antagonistic relationship with President Donald Trump. Still, the scale of Sino-Russian trade remained limited. Chinese investment in Russia declined even though trade between the two countries in 2018 rose 24.5 percent to a record US $108 billion — due largely to

---

14 Speech by Chairman of the Delegation of the People's Republic of China, Deng Xiaoping, at the Special Session of the UN General Assembly, 4/10/74, https://www.marxists.org/reference/archive/deng-xiaoping/1974/04/10.htm

greater Russian oil and gas exports, making it China's largest energy supplier. Under the Belt and Road Initiative, China invested 2.58 billion yuan (US $370 million) in building its part of the Khabarovsk bridge over the Amur River to link Heihe in Heilongjiang Province and the Russian city of Blagoveshchensk, which could facilitate transport of agricultural products from Russia to China. In 2021, the bridge opened for business.

In response to Trump's trade war, China significantly reduced its imports of liquefied natural gas from the United States in 2019. Only two vessels in early 2019 made the trip from the United States to China—one in January and one in February—compared to fourteen during the first four months of 2018, before the trade war accelerated. Meanwhile, U.S. trade with Russia, never very substantial, also declined.

Looking Ahead

For Chinese leaders, the three-way geopolitical dynamic between Beijing, Moscow and Washington was anticipated in China's classic tale, *Romance of the Three Kingdoms*.[15] In this 14th-century epic, Luo Guanzhong tells a story of warfare and deceit among three competing fiefdoms some 2,000 years ago. After the fall of the Han dynasty, the kingdoms of Shu, Wu, and Wei battled and circled one another in a dance of alliance, betrayal, enmity, and realignment. This tale of human ambition and ruthlessness describes each king's personality traits and traditional battlefield tactics that still pop up in Chinese diplomacy, corporate negotiations, and popular internet games. The ominous opening lines from the revised 1679 edition of the *Romance* cannot be far from Xi's mind: "The Empire, long divided, must unite; long united, must divide. Thus, it has ever been." Neither unity nor division is permanent; they are forever feeding and promoting each other.

The Putin-Xi flirtation could be fleeting. The greater likelihood is that each party will keep its options open. Vladimir Putin welcomes

---

15 Melinda Liu, "Xi Jinping Has Embraced Vladimir Putin—for Now," *Foreign Policy* (October 3, 2019) at https://foreignpolicy.com/2019/10/03/xi-jinping-has-embraced-vladimir-putin-for-now/

Chinese actions that weaken U.S. influence, but the Kremlin must also worry about the growth of Chinese power. Chinese expansion into Central Asia may eventually threaten Russian interests. For now, however, Moscow sees China's rise more as opportunity than as menace. In a world of zero-sum politics, the Kremlin's view may prove naïve—as happened in the late 1950s as the Sino-Soviet honeymoon collapsed.[16] Beijing in the 1960s claimed that Khrushchev did nothing to back China against Taiwan and the United States in 1958 until the Quemoy (Kinmen) islands crisis had ended.

From either perspective—political realism or idealism—there is little reason for the United States to try and play off the two bad guys against each other. It is more likely that Beijing and Moscow will pull each other down than they will join effectively against Western democracies. Neither China, Russia, nor the United States needs more hard power to improve the quality of life for its people.

With the fall of the Soviet Union, the weight of each factor in the dynamic changed, but never really went away. A triangular relationship among the three countries remained.[17] Each of the big three could profit from equitable trade and collaboration on common problems such as climate change.[18] Mutual gain—not exploitation—should be their guiding principle. But enlightened self-interest often drowns in world affairs. As Mephistopheles informed *der Alte* in *Faust*, "Humans call it reason, but use it only to be more beastly than any beast."

The future? Given their negative experiences with each other in the past—reinforced by their asymmetrical material assets, diverse ambitions, and security interests—it is unlikely that China and Russia will collaborate long-term in any deep sense against

---

16 Chris Miller, "U.S.-China Competition in the Post-Soviet Space," *Strategic Asia 2020: U.S.-China Competition for Global Influence*, eds. Ashley J. Tellis, Alison Szalwinski, and Michael Wills (Seattle and Washington: National Bureau of Asian Research, 2020) at https://www.nbr.org/publication/strategic-asia-2020-u-s-china-competition-for-global-influence/

17 Alexander Korolev, "Beyond the Putin-Xi Relationship: China, Russia, and Great Power Politics," *The Diplomat,* Issue 99 (February 2023).

18 Mel Gurtov, *Engaging China: Rebuilding Sino-American Relations* (Lanham MD: Rowman & Littlefield, 2022), reviewed at https://www.globalasia.org/v17no4/book/the-urgent-need-to-build-bridges_walter-c-clemens-jr

the Western democracies. But the United States and its partners do face serious threats from both Beijing and Moscow here and now as each aggressively expands. Both Xi and Putin insist on keeping and, where possible, enlarging their domains, often ignoring the wishes of their subject peoples and their uneasy neighbors. Beijing's repression of Uyghurs and other ethnic minorities adds another cancer to world affairs. Ditto Russian repression of Dagestan and the other "republics" in the Russian "Federation." But the greatest threat to world security comes from each country's outward expansion—Beijing's claim to most of the South China Sea and its militarization of several islands, along with the Kremlin's occupation of Transdniestria, South Ossetia, Abkhazia, and Crimea, and other parts of Ukraine.

HAVING TIED ONE ARM BEHIND THEIR BACKS, WASHINGTON AND MANILA STRUGGLE

Today there is some external resistance to China in the South China and East China Seas, but it is sporadic and not coordinated. Washington and its allies have sanctioned Russia and have aided Ukraine in many ways, but they have done little to penalize China for its attempted take-over of the South China Sea and its threats to Taiwan. The U.S. and other Western navies (including Australia's) on occasion send warships close to Chinese occupied islands in the South China Sea and through the Taiwan Straits to demonstrate that those waters remain "international." But none of these countermeasures is sufficiently strong to compel Beijing to pull back.[19] None begins to match the strong measures mandated by the UN Security Council against North Korea for its weapons tests.

America's interest in the South China Sea goes back to the 19th century. Concerned for its ability to buy and sell goods around the world—from the "shores of Tripoli" to Edo to Guangdong—the United States has long asserted its right to enjoy freedom of the seas. A latecomer to imperial expansion, Washington gradually built naval forces that permitted it to compete with British and other European powers. During the Cold War, the Soviet navy was far inferior to the

---

19 Gregory B. Poling, *On Dangerous Ground: America's Century in the South China Sea* (New York: Oxford University Press, 2022).

American. Now U.S. naval superiority is challenged by a China that leads in quantity though not in quality of ships at sea.

Beijing showed little interest in the South China Sea until after World War II. Now it claims virtually the entire body of water and its resources. Under Xi Jinping China has erected military facilities on several islands, including several rocks built into man-made islands by dredging up adjoining sand and coral. China's fishing fleets ravage the coasts of the Philippines, Vietnam, and Indonesia (not to mention Ecuador and Africa). China's navy and coast guard challenge U.S. and European ships when they sail close to the islands claimed by Beijing.

In theory the world community benefits from the rules-based maritime order, where international law, as reflected in the 1982 UN Law of the Sea Convention (UNCLOS), sets out the legal framework for all activities in the oceans and seas. This body of international law, ratified by more than 160 UN member-states including China, but not the USA, sets out rules for national, regional, and global action and cooperation in the maritime sector and is vital to ensuring the free flow of global commerce.

China prioritizes its sovereign rights over freedom of navigation. Its neighbors such as Vietnam and Indonesia often concur with this orientation, but China is inconsistent. For Beijing, might makes right. It values its own rights in offshore waters but not those of its neighbors such as Vietnam. Indeed, Beijing acts as though its territorial waters extend far beyond any existing definition.[20] It also rejects third-party mechanisms for dispute resolution. By far the strongest local power, it prefers to "resolve" disputes in bilateral negotiations where it can bully

---

20 President Harry Truman initiated unilateral deviations from existing rules in 1945 when he declared that all resources on the continental shelf contiguous to the United States belonged to the U.S. Unlike China's policy in the South China Sea, the U.S. proclamation did not affect other nations' rights of free and unimpeded navigation of waters above the shelf, and the limit of U.S. territorial waters remained three miles seaward from the coast. A second proclamation provided for the establishment of conservation zones for the protection of fisheries in certain areas of the high seas contiguous to the United States. Many other nations quickly made their own claims. Argentina claimed both its continental shelf and the epicontinental sea above it, while Chile and El Salvador asserted sovereignty over a 200-mile zone.

each weaker neighbor into submission.[21]

UNCLOS provided an Arbitration Tribunal to rule on disputes. The Philippines asked the Tribunal to rule on China's activities in the South China Sea. The People's Republic of China asserted the court had no right to rule on matters affecting PRC sovereignty. But the court sided with the Philippines. In 2016, the Tribunal delivered a unanimous decision firmly rejecting China's expansive South China Sea maritime claims as having no basis in international law. The Tribunal stated that the PRC has no lawful claim to the area determined by the Arbitral Tribunal to be part of the Philippines' exclusive economic zone and continental shelf. The PRC and the Philippines, pursuant to their treaty obligations under the Law of the Sea Convention, are legally bound to comply with this decision.

Despite its legal victory, a new administration in Manila, that of Rodrigo Duterte, tried to align with Beijing to obtain development aid. It did nothing to pursue the court's ruling. Vietnam and other members of the ASEAN (Association of Southeast Asian Nations) could benefit from the court ruling but, fearing Beijing's wrath, also did little to act on it. Neither did the United States, except to insist on its right to enjoy freedom of the seas.

After having downplayed the victory that it won in the South China Sea arbitration, Manila gradually came to confirm the value of the Award. Addressing the UN General Assembly in September 2020, President Duterte stated that "the Award is now part of international law, beyond compromise and beyond the reach of passing governments to dilute, diminish or abandon."

Isolated on the world stage, China held onto its "Four No's" policy in the South China Sea: no acceptance, no participation, no recognition, and no implementation of the South China Sea arbitration. One year after the Award, the Chinese Society of International Law published a 500-page treatise entitled *The South China Sea Arbitration Awards: A Critical Study* which argued that the ruling rendered by the South China Sea Arbitral Tribunal was erroneous.

---

21 Isaac B. Kardon, *China's Law of the Sea: The New Rules of Maritime Order* (New Haven: Yale University Press, 2023).

U.S. Secretary of State Anthony Blinken addressed these issues in 2021. He said that the rules-based maritime order was in jeopardy in the South China Sea. China continued to coerce and intimidate Southeast Asian coastal states, threatening freedom of navigation in this critical global throughway. The United States reaffirmed its policy regarding maritime claims in the South China Sea. It also reaffirmed that an armed attack on Philippine armed forces, public vessels, or aircraft in the South China Sea would invoke U.S. mutual defense commitments under Article IV of the 1951 U.S.-Philippines Mutual Defense Treaty. Washington called on China to abide by its obligations under international law, cease its provocative behavior, and take steps to reassure the international community that it is committed to the rules-based maritime order that respects the rights of all countries, big and small.

Despite these brave words, the U.S. Departments of State, Defense, and Commerce approach these issues with one arm tied behind their backs. The UN Convention on the Law of the Sea spells out the rights and duties of sea-faring and littoral nations. The Clinton administration helped negotiate this treaty, but a group of senators has blocked its ratification, fearing it would constrict U.S. ability to mine the seabed.

Ferdinand Marcos Jr., elected Philippines president in 2022, took a much harder stance on the South China Sea than did Duterte. In February 2023, Marcos summoned China's ambassador to protest the use of a military-grade laser by the Chinese coast guard that briefly blinded some of the crew of a Philippine patrol vessel in the South China Sea. This was one of over 200 diplomatic protests Manila has filed against Beijing's actions in the disputed waterway since 2022. For its part, China accused the Philippines of intruding into its territory and said its coast guard used a harmless laser to track the Philippine vessel. After decades of combating Muslim and communist insurgencies, Marcos told his armed forces their first priority is now external defense—defending the country's sea borders. Under a 2014 defense pact with the United States, Marcos approved a wider U.S. military presence in the Philippines by allowing rotating batches of American forces to stay in four more

Philippine military camps.[22]

THE THUCYDIDES TRAP BECKONS

What Graham Allison termed the "Thucydides trap" is the danger that a rising, revisionist power will fight with a status quo or declining power. A rising China may act in ways that provoke the United States to try to stop this upstart before it is too late. Alarmed by threats to its hegemony, Washington is trying to stop delivery of the most advanced semiconductors to China—an expression of just how serious their competition is.

What Deng Xiaoping said of the Soviet Union and United States in 1974 may apply to China and the USA today: "Since the two superpowers are contending for world hegemony, the contradiction between them is irreconcilable; either one overpowers the other or is overpowered. Their compromise and collusion can only be partial, temporary and relative, while their contention is all-embracing, permanent and absolute." There can be no "balance" or "limitation" of forces. "They may reach certain agreements, but their agreements are only a facade and a deception. At bottom, they are aiming at greater and fiercer contention. The contention between the superpowers extends over the entire globe."[23]

Each of the three great powers faces the same hard choices as the players in game theory's Prisoner's Dilemma. Should they cooperate or be tough with each of the other actors? President Joe Biden generally wanted cooperation with all nations. Putin and Xi Jinping, however, behaved like the hardline players who "defect" from any common cause and seek total victory—as if politics is nothing but zero-sum struggle. Sooner or later, in the *game* they lose when cooperation would have netted consistent if moderate gains. But if one player counts on cooperation and others defect, it will have harmed its own basic interests. This is a real dilemma.

---

22 Jim Gomez, AP News, 2/28/23 at https://apnews.com/article/politics-philippines-government-united-states-ferdinand-marcos-jr-beijing-fb1479b04bc3279ad0344c0f4d4b5b52
23 Speech to UN General Assembly on April 10, 1974.

CHAPTER 10
CONFRONTING EVIL

LIGHT AND DARKNESS

Ever since Cain killed his brother Abel, both violence and virtue have persisted among humans. *Genesis* tells us that when God saw that man had done much evil and that man's thoughts and inclinations were toward evil, he decided to wipe out all life with a flood. But when God spotted Noah, a righteous and blameless man, He relented and saved Noah and two of every kind from the flood. When the waters abated, God pledged never again to destroy all life, no matter how evil some humans became.

Both good and evil have coexisted throughout the ages in what both Zoroaster and Spinoza saw as the struggle of light against darkness. Many Enlightenment thinkers trusted in light. Some believed humans are good by nature but can be corrupted by dark forces around them.

These persistent dilemmas do not go away. How should leaders of today's democracies deal with evil both within and without their societies? Given the life-and-death issues at stake, how should they cope with the evil manifest at the top in Russia and in China? Climate change and other global problems challenge all societies, but how to address them with dictators so ruthless as Vladimir Putin and Xi Jinping?

Western leaders should avoid self-righteous airs. Their policies have often strayed from virtue and failed to appreciate the harm they do to others. Now, however, is a time when they must cope with powerful, uncompromising evil. Both Putin and Xi are descendants of tyrants whose evil far outreached whatever good they did for Russia and China.

Taken together, the brutalities of Lenin and Stalin (including the war he started *with* Hitler) killed nearly 100 million Soviet citizens—Russians as well as Ukrainians, Kazakhs, and other peoples of the Soviet Union. Consider again the questions raised in

Chapter 6: What happened to the deep humanity of Russian cultural figures such as Anton Chekhov? To the human rights work of physicist and Nobel Peace laureate Andrei Sakharov? His Memorial Foundation, remembering the victims of Stalinism, was shut down by Putin in 2021—only to share in the 2022 Nobel Peace award with other human rights defenders in Ukraine and Belarus.

Putin's invasion of Ukraine and its brutal conduct exemplify the evil of his policies and that of the villains who execute them, Stalin made some effort to hide his crimes. Not Putin. His major political rival was shot not far from the Kremlin. Two other challengers, having survived lethal poisons, have been locked away for years. Thousands who shouted "no war" have been jailed—some for 15 years. When Putin's armed forces, corrupt and poorly led, get nowhere in Ukraine, Putin replies with his ace—brute force against playgrounds, schools, hospitals, apartment buildings, power plants, and at least one major dam.

What can stop these atrocities? The veto power of both Russia and China can block Security Council decisions against them. The "Uniting for Peace" Resolution 377 (V) adopted November 3, 1950, empowers the General Assembly to *recommend* action when the Security Council is deadlocked. It has been used a dozen times since 1951 (the last in in 1997), to establish UN peacekeeping or to demand withdrawal of military forces.[1]

Today, many UN member-states fear the wrath of Beijing and Moscow—the more so as Putin threatens nuclear escalation. Still, October 12, 2022, saw 143 UN members vote for General Assembly Resolution ES-11/4 that condemned Russia's "illegal so-called referendums" in four regions within internationally-recognized borders, and demanded that Russia reverse its annexation declaration. Five of the usual suspects voted against the

---

1 In 1951 it was used to continue collective security in Korea. The March 27, 2022 action marked the first time in 40 years the Security Council referred a crisis to the General Assembly and only the 11th time an emergency session of the General Assembly was called since North Korea invaded the South in 1950. The 1950 "Uniting for Peace" resolution authorizes global threats to be referred to the General Assembly "if the Security Council, because of lack of unanimity of the permanent members, fails to exercise its primary responsibility to act as required to maintain international peace and security."

resolution—Russia, Belarus, North Korea, Syria, and Nicaragua. Thirty-five delegations abstained—including China, India, Cuba, Vietnam, Mongolia, Armenia, Pakistan, Kazakhstan Uzbekistan, Tajikistan, Kyrgyzstan, and many African countries that need food from Russia or Ukraine. Several countries did not vote—among them, Afghanistan, Azerbaijan, Iran, Turkmenistan, and Venezuela. Saudi Arabia, accused of aligning with Russia on oil issues, and Iraq were among those voting to condemn.

Russia's strategy clearly violates the U.N.'s foundational document, according to U.N. Secretary-General António Guterres. "The Charter is clear," he said. "Any annexation of a State's territory by another State resulting from the threat or use of force is a violation of the Principles of the UN Charter and international law."

Ignoring the United Nations, Russia resumed bombing civilian targets and energy infrastructure in Ukraine. The United States and most NATO members pledged more military equipment but held back from actions that could trigger war with China or Russia.

All measures short of all-out war were needed to drive Putin's motley forces from Ukraine—more weapons for Ukrainians; more pressure on enablers such as Iran and India; stronger trade and other sanctions; intensified ostracism. Not needed were diplomatic suggestions for compromise that could weaken Ukrainians and others struggling to resist powerful dictators.

Can—Should—Ukraine Hit Back?

Russia gives itself the right to invade sovereign neighbors, while denying their right to retaliate. The base basics are that Russia has launched a brutal war on Ukraine in violation of its pledges in 1928 (the Litvinov Protocol and Kellogg-Briand Peace Pact) and 1945 (the United Nations Charter) never to fight except in self-defense. Putin's wars also violate Moscow's pledge in the 1994 Budapest Memorandum to respect Ukraine's independence and borders after Kyiv transferred its nuclear arsenal to Russia. Washington also looked past its implicit obligation in the memorandum to assist Ukraine if its sovereignty is violated, as happened already in 2014.

Pursuing its "special military operation," Putin's war also

violates international laws on the required treatment of civilians and prisoners of war. Russia bombs nurseries, schools, and hospitals as well as apartment buildings. It starves, tortures, mutilates, and kills prisoners of war. A Russian diplomat called for some POWs to be executed by hanging. Individual Russian soldiers steal what they can from private homes while the larger Russian machine loots museums, purloins grain, impedes grain shipments needed to prevent starvation in the Middle East and Africa. Meanwhile, Ukrainians mobilize to drive back the invaders. Their own pluck is bolstered by U.S. and other Western weapons. Russia complains about this foreign assistance even as it seeks military and economic help from China, Belarus, Chechnya, Iran, Syria, and Africa.

Mindful that no Western country wants the Ukrainian war to spread, Ukraine agreed not to use NATO-supplied weapons to strike targets in Russia. The effect was uneven. Russians did whatever they wished inside Ukraine, but Ukrainians could do little or nothing inside Russia, Innocents were murdered while war criminals went unpunished.

Could Ukraine receive UN authorization to hit back? On February 25, 2022, the day after the war began, Russia vetoed a UN Security Council resolution demanding that Moscow immediately stop its attack on Ukraine and withdraw all troops. This veto pushed Ukraine's allies on the Council to refer the matter to the General Assembly.

On March 2, 2022 the UN General Assembly voted overwhelmingly for a resolution deploring Russia's invasion of Ukraine and calling for the immediate withdrawal of its forces. In an emergency session of the UN General Assembly, 141 of the 193 member states voted for the resolution, 35 abstained, and five voted against. This expression of global outrage highlighted Russia's isolation. The only countries to vote against the resolution in support of Moscow were Belarus, North Korea, Eritrea, and Syria. Long-standing Kremlin comrades Cuba and Nicaragua joined China in abstaining.

Only hours before the Russian-Ukrainian war entered its second year, the UN General Assembly on February 23, 2023, resuming its eleventh emergency special session, adopted a new resolution calling for an end to the war in Ukraine. By the terms of the 11-paragraph resolution, the Assembly reiterated its demand that Russia "immediately, completely and unconditionally withdraw all of its military forces from the territory of Ukraine and called for a cessation of hostilities." The resolution reaffirmed the Assembly's commitment to the sovereignty, independence, unity, and territorial integrity of Ukraine within its internationally recognized borders, extending to its territorial waters. For the full text of Assembly resolution—a virtual catalog of Russia's crimes, see the appendix to this chapter.

The Assembly resolution also emphasized the need to ensure accountability for the most serious crimes under international law committed in Ukraine through independent national or international investigations and prosecutions to ensure justice for all victims and the prevention of future crimes.

Results: 141 member states voted *for* the resolution and seven *against*: Belarus, DPRK, Eritrea, Mali, Nicaragua, Russia, and Syria (each rated "Not Free" by Freedom House). Among the 32 abstentions were China, India, Pakistan, Cuba, Iran, Ethiopia, El Salvador, and the former Soviet republics of Central Asia. Eleven countries did not vote, including Azerbaijan and Lebanon.

Even without explicit UN approval, the UN Charter permits Ukraine to hit targets inside Russia. Article 51 provides: "Nothing in the present Charter shall impair the inherent right of individual or collective self-defense if an armed attack occurs against a Member of the United Nations, until the Security Council has taken measures necessary to maintain international peace and security."

A serious danger, as the Kremlin constantly warns, is that Russia might escalate—perhaps even using nuclear weapons against Ukraine or its backers. The possibility of escalation is intimidating, but Putin is an egotist concerned for his own survival even more than for his macho image. If he remained a calculating schemer, he would not risk a response in kind by NATO.

As for Ukraine, it has already displayed through drone attacks on targets in Russia and sabotage behind the lines that it understands its right to self-defense. The United States and other actors concerned for world order have every legal right, and possibly a moral obligation, to supply the powerful weaponry that would make a real difference. If other countries assist Russia's aggression—Belarus, Iran, North Korea, China—shouldn't they also be punished?

True Grit?

Today's great power realities make it difficult to implement one of the most effective tools of conflict resolution developed to tame the Cold War—"Graduated Reciprocation in Tension-Reduction" or GRIT. The idea, articulated by psychologist Charles Osgood in 1962, was to begin small and—if the other side showed a willingness to reciprocate—proceed to more far-reaching actions to reduce tensions.[2] Thus, after pulling back from the brink of war over Cuba, JFK on June 10, 1963 uttered a few gracious words about the wartime sacrifices of the Soviet people.[3] Soon FDR's wartime ambassador to Stalin, W. Averell Harriman was flying back to Moscow to be hugged by Khrushchev and negotiate a limited test ban treaty, By December 1963, Khrushchev was calling for "disarmament by mutual example."

There were ups and downs, but this kind of graduated reciprocation helped pave the way for Nixon and Brezhnev to approve SALT I and the ABM Treaty in 1972 and for Gorbachev's arms accords with Reagan and Bush in 1987–1991.[4]

A similar pattern worked with China. In 1970–1971, official Washington began to speak of the "People's Republic of China" instead of Red China. After a few such gestures, there were signs that Mao Zedong and Zhou Enlai got the message and were trying to reciprocate, Soon, Kissinger was in Beijing on a secret mission (secret in case he was rebuffed). Nixon came the next year and relations began to normalize.

---

2 Osgood, *An Alternative to War or Surrender* (Urbana: University of Illinois Press, 1962).

3 For Kennedy's American University speech on June 10, 1963, and comments by experienced observers, see Clemens, ed., *Toward a Strategy of Peace*, Foreword by Robert F. Kennedy (Chicago: Rand McNally, 1965).

4 For details of the Soviet and Chinese cases, see Clemens, *Dynamics of International Relations: Conflict and Mutual Gain in an Era of Global Interdependence* (Lanham MD: Rowman & Littlefield, 1998, 2004).

Donald Trump tried to do something similar with North Korea, but it did not fructify because he refused to offer anything substantial to Kim Jong until the North disarmed. For GRIT to work, the two sides have to make concessions in tandem. Each side must truly seek less tension and more cooperation. Each party must accept the risk that its moves toward peace may get nowhere or even backfire.

The danger is that if one side smiles and offers a concession, the other may pocket the concession and do nothing to reciprocate. The would-be initiator of GRIT will have been suckered—turned into a martyr by a cynical practitioner of power politics. French President Emmanuel Macron risked being used and abused in this way when he talked for hours with Putin about possible steps to stop the fighting in Ukraine. The key concessions would have been by Ukraine. What would Kyiv pay to get Putin to stop his invasion? The scene resembled the meeting in 1938 when leaders of Britain, France, and Italy offered Germany a valuable part of Czechoslovakia to appease Hitler. In dealing with the likely aggressors in the 1930s, GRIT would have been futile and self-destructive. A rapid and effective arms buildup and mobilization would have been the wiser course. Tragic though this prescription may appear, it seems appropriate now as humanity faces the likelihood of continued aggression by Russia and China and severe abuse of human rights wherever they rule.

Wiser to Err on the Side of Soft or Hard Measures?

Confronting bad guys, is it wiser to hope for the best or prepare for the worst? Unless the bad actors prove that they have changed, it is prudent to err on the side of caution. Just look at America's record. The United States was caught unprepared for its own Civil War, World War I, World War II, the Cold War, the Korean War, and the 9/11/2001 attacks. It survived each challenge thanks to favorable geography and huge reservoirs of material, industrial, and human resources. These advantages may not suffice for all future contingencies and must be steadily replenished. Besides its own requirements, the United States needs the means to assist friends and allies as they deal with bad guys. True, most Europeans should be doing far more to help themselves. Still, shared interests as well as shared values require that the United States help its friends and allies to rebuff the challenges to their independence and well-being. All this is a big order—one that requires unity on the home front, For the present, the most pressing challenges to the United States come not from Moscow or Beijing but from within—from Mar-a-Lago and all those Americans who reject the norms and institutions of democracy.[5]

How acute are the dilemmas in forging a constructive policy to China is suggested by the discord between two experts published in *Foreign Affairs*. Jessica Chen Weiss recognized the dangers to China and the world posed by Xi Jinping, but she argued the perilous logic of zero-sum competition. If the Biden administration seeks a better world order, it should not try to out-China China. On the other hand, Cai Xia, a former professor at the Central Party School in Beijing until 2020, when he was expelled from the Party for criticizing Xi, warns of chaos inside China. He knew the Communist Party from the inside and deemed it an unscrupulous, mafia-type organization.[6]

Cai Xia witnessed wide and deep elite displeasure with Xi's imperious behavior and unwise policies toward Covid, Taiwan, and the United States. But how to get rid of the tyrant? What could bring down Xi? Defeat in war? Emperors and empires do not last forever. The Qing dynasty's empire under Qianlong (1735–1796) expanded and consolidated border regions, but at a cost that eroded the foundations of power.

Should Biden try to achieve better rapport with a bully disliked by his own colleagues? This question applies not only to Xi Jinping but to Putin and Kim Jong Un as well.

Even if no open hostilities break out between China and the United States, rapprochement between them will be thwarted by

---

5 Walter C. Clemens, Jr., *The Republican War on America: Dangers of Trump and Trumpism* (Washington DC: Westphalia, 2023).

6 Jessica Chen Weiss, The China Trap," *Foreign Affairs* 101, 5 (September-October 2022): 40-84; Cai Xia, "The Weakness of Xi Jinping," ibid., pp. 85-107. For an effort to skirt Scylla and Charybdis, see also Dani Rodrik and Stephen Walt, "How to Build a Better Order: Limiting Great Power Rivalry in an Anarchic World," ibid., pp, 142-155; also, Mel Gurtov, *Engaging China: Rebuilding Sino-American Relations* (Lanham MD: Rowman & Littlefield, 2022).

the unresolved status of Taiwan and by competing ambitions to dominate world affairs. The danger will linger they can stumble into a Thucydides trap.

Reward Putin for Halting Aggression?

With Russia engaged in a multifaceted imperial war, there seems little room for cooperation with the United States until that war ends—with Russia's defeat. If Russia triumphed and Putin remained at the helm, how could any U.S. administration even think about cooperation with this monster? If "good guys" somehow took control of the Kremlin, the United States and other democracies would probably be happy to resume cooperation, as they did with West Germany after 1945. Students of conflict resolution say that to get an agreement, you need to offer the other side an inducement. To persuade Vladimir Putin to stop the war in Ukraine, he must obtain some sort of gain. Without some tangible benefit, Russians will see Putin's special military operation as a serious waste of resources. He will lose face and maybe his job. Faced with this danger, Putin might resort to extreme measures—even to nuclear war.

This argument surfaces not only in Paris and Berlin, but also in Washington. The Biden administration asserts that Kyiv will have the final say on any peace deal, but some Republicans demand only that Ukraine get back its pre-invasion borders of February 23, 2022. Peace on those terms would mean that Russia retains Crimea, which it annexed in 2014, plus large slices of Donbas, which Russia occupied and then recognized as independent just before its February 24 attack.

By this reasoning, the victim of Russia's aggressions must surrender territory to induce the aggressor to cut short its aggression. To cinch the deal, Ukraine may also have to forgo its sovereign right to join whatever international affiliation it chooses, such as NATO and the European Union.

A similar deal could have been offered to Hitler in 1943. By then his Third Reich was clearly losing. German troops were being pushed back from Soviet territory and southern Europe. To terminate the bloodshed and destruction, why not offer Hitler an inducement, for example, pull out of Russia and most of Poland, but let Germany keep the German-speaking Austria, Sudetenland, and Danzig it took in 1938–1939. Austria, Czechoslovakia, and Poland would lose something, but this would be a small price for halting the carnage of world war.

Such terms could also appeal to Tokyo. By 1943, Japan was losing the Pacific war but might still hold out for years. Why not let Japan keep Korea and Manchuria but retreat from the rest of China and the other parts of Asia and the Pacific it occupied? Koreans and Chinese would pay a price, but millions of lives would be spared.

Neither scenario took place. Savage fighting continued until 1945 when Nazi Germany and Japan were defeated and occupied. Their wartime leaders were tried by international tribunals. Some were found guilty, and some executed. Many—probably most—German and Japanese citizens came to understand that their countries had done evil and needed to change their ways.

Germany and Japan changed for the better. Could a similar future await Russia?

To offer Putin large chunks of Ukraine to halt his aggression would obviously be unfair to Ukraine—analogous to giving part of Czechoslovakia to Hitler in 1938 to secure "peace in our time." It also would destroy any confidence in international laws against war and war crimes. The 1928 Kellogg-Briand Pact banning all aggressive war (endorsed by the protocol of Stalin's foreign commissar Maksim Litvinov) is still the law of nations. Most members of the League of Nations backed the 1932 Stimson Doctrine of the U.S. Secretary of State refusing to recognize any territorial or political change accomplished by force. All members of the United Nations have signed the UN Charter outlawing all war except in self-defense.

Putin's war also violates the Helsinki Accords signed by thirty-five states in 1975. Moscow embraced the agreement because it affirmed the inviolability of Europe's borders and banned interference in any country's internal affairs. While not legally binding, Brezhnev approved the Helsinki accords because they seemed to prop up Soviet controls in Eastern Europe.

The Budapest Memorandum signed by Russia, Great Britain,

and the United States in 1994 prohibited them from threatening or using military force or economic coercion against Ukraine, Belarus, and Kazakhstan "except in self-defense or otherwise in accordance with the Charter of the United Nations." In return, Ukraine, Belarus, and Kazakhstan gave up their nuclear weapons. In 2009, Russia and the United States declared they would respect the Budapest security assurances even after their START I treaty expired. After Russia seized Crimea in 2014, the G8 suspended Russian participation for its violations of the Budapest Memorandum commitment.

If Putin faces defeat in Ukraine, might he resort to nuclear weapons? He had already risked nuclear contamination by military actions near Ukraine's nuclear reactors. Russia retained far more tactical nukes than the West. Putin bragged he had strategic weapons unlike anything in NATO arsenals. His disdain for human life was evident in his use of poorly equipped soldiers as cannon fodder—200,000 dead or wounded in one year.

The Biden administration moved cautiously to avoid crossing any red line that could provoke direct hostilities with Putin's forces. Even before the war began, however, Washington supplied valuable intelligence to Kyiv. In 2023, it sent Patriot defense systems and tanks but no aircraft except F-16's provided by U.S. allies.

It was not clear if Putin had any red lines. He talked loosely about using nukes (as Nikita Khrushchev did on many occasions). But U.S. intelligence saw no preparations to do so. How credible were Putin's threats? Not very. Strategic missile attacks on NATO countries could trigger Armageddon. Even if Putin cared nothing for others' lives, Putin surely cared for his own.

Even tactical nuclear explosions in Ukraine could blow back on Russian troops and Russia proper. A tactical nuclear weapon would cause all the horrors of Hiroshima, though possibly on a smaller scale. It would produce a fireball, shock waves, and deadly radiation that would cause long-term health damage in survivors. As U.S. Defense Secretary James Mattis warned in 2018: There is no such thing as a tactical nuclear weapon. "Any nuclear weapon used any time is a strategic game changer."[7]

---

7 Quoted in Nina Tannenwald, "'Limited' Tactical Nuclear Weapons Would Be

More Western aid to Ukraine presents a risk of escalation but letting Putin continue his attacks on Ukraine unchecked or trying to appease him, as Chamberlain did Hitler, would generate huge risks. The safest approach for the West was to help Ukraine defeat Russia and drive its forces from what was Ukrainian territory before 2014.

One expert cautioned: "Urging the Ukrainians to make peace with Russia today is like urging a rape victim to make peace with her rapist. Peace will be possible only if the rapist is arrested or flees the country."[8]

If pressed to choose between a conciliatory stance and firmness, the United States and its partners should remember Munich 1938. Appeasement of evil does not pay.

To let Russia win anything by its unprovoked war and abundant war crimes would make a mockery of law and morality and undermine U.S. interests. Russia's leaders need to be brought to justice and the country compelled to pay reparations. Purgation before resurrection—as in Germany and Japan after their crimes were recognized and partially expiated following the World War.

Which Nobel Laureate Gave the Best Advice—Sakharov or Solzhenitsyn?

Aleksandr Solzhenitsyn won the Nobel Prize for Literature in 1970 "for the ethical force with which he has pursued the indispensable traditions of Russian literature." The Secretary of the Swedish Academy observed that Solzhenitsyn's narratives focused "on the only human element in existence, the human individual, with equal status among equals, one destiny among millions and a million destinies in one. This is the whole of humanism in a nutshell, for the kernel is love of mankind. This year's Nobel Prize for Literature has been awarded to the proclaimer of such a humanism."

Andrei Sakharov won the Nobel Prize for Peace in 1975 "for his struggle for human rights in the Soviet Union, for disarmament and cooperation between all nations."

Catastrophic," *Scientific American*, March 10, 2022.

8   Alexander J. Motyl, "When it comes to peace talks, the problem is Russia, not Ukraine," *The Hill*, March 13, 2023.

10. Confronting Evil

Each Nobel laureate knew first-hand the cruelties of the Soviet regime, but disagreed about how the West should cope with the issue. Solzhenitsyn warned the West not to hope for a deep accommodation with the Kremlin.[9] Outsiders could not expect to be treated better than the subjects of Soviet power, seriously abused since 1917. Sakharov, an architect of the Soviet H-bomb, knew the horrors of nuclear weapons and argued for negotiation.[10]

The words and deeds of Communist regimes violate the laws of nations and human rights, but who is entitled to throw the first stone? No individual and no group of people is beyond reproach. Darkness as well as light colors most human behavior. Germans in the 21st century recalled that their ancestors committed genocide in South-West Africa in 1904–1908. Better late than never, many Americans acknowledged the genocidal policies of U.S. authorities toward indigenous peoples. Many, but not all, believed that Black Lives Matter. Some Americans observed but most ignored the centenary of the Tulsa, Oklahoma race massacre in 1921. Guantánamo and Abu Ghraib symbolized other abuses. Many Americans accepted that former president Trump was guilty of multiple crimes—some bordering on democide (high death rates from the corona virus) as well as treason and tax evasion. Others denied Trump did anything wrong.

Every continent is burdened with dictators who exploited others to enrich themselves. Still, the track record and current policies of Communist regimes set them apart from all other violators of human rights. All seven Communist-legacy states are judged "not free" by Freedom House. The same is true for most former Soviet republics such as Uzbekistan and Azerbaijan.

Collaboration on arms control and other global concerns offers potential benefits to all parties but could be counterproductive if any side cheats. The West needs the cooperation of Beijing and Moscow to deal with global problems, but how can any responsible

---

9 Aleksandr Solzhenitsyn, *Warning to the West* (New York: Farrar, Straus and Giroux, 1976).

10 Andrei D. Sakharov, *Alarm & Hope: The World-Renowned Nobel Laureate and Political Dissident Speaks on Human Rights, Disarmament, and Détente* (New York: Alfred A. Knopf, 1978).

government negotiate with persistent violators of law and human rights?

Sakharov's answer is irrefutable: Survival is the *sine qua non* for any human or other planetary value. Communist as well as Western governments share this interest. Each actor—governmental and non-governmental, Communist and non-Communist, affluent or impoverished—needs to cooperate with others to limit the danger of human extinction.[11]

U.S. adversaries have reason to distrust Washington. The American record is replete with many examples of bad faith as well as poor judgment. Starting with his Strategic Defense Initiative in 1983, Reagan wanted to nullify the 1972 Nixon-Brezhnev anti-ballistic missile treaty, and George W. Bush actually did so in 2002. The Barack Obama White House signed the Iran nuclear accord (Joint Comprehensive Plan of Action) in 2015, but the Trump administration withdrew from it and piled more sanctions onto Iran. What the Biden administration says and does could be reversed by its successor. *Caveat emptor*—any buyer must be cautious.

Both Solzhenitsyn and Sakharov were correct. The history of Communist policies at home and abroad gives strong reason for other actors to approach any potential deal with profound caution. Still, with the fate of humankind at stake, non-Communist actors must strive for accords with Communist and other adversaries such as Iran to contain the arms race and stabilize peace.[12] If agreements

---

11 The risk of human extinction has risen from 1 in 100 in the 20th century to 1 in 6 in the 21st--similar to Russian roulette, according to Toby Ord, *The Precipice: Existential Risk and the Future of Humanity* (New York: Hachette Books, 2020), Table 6. See also William Macaskill, "The Beginning of History: Surviving the Era of Catastrophic Risk," *Foreign Affairs* 101, 5 (September-October 2022): 10-24.

12 Should the United States negotiate with a regime whose president is noted not only as a tough guy but also as an executioner of thousands? See Reuel Marc Gerecht and Ray Takeyh, "In Ebrahim Raisi, Iran's clerics have groomed and promoted their ruthless enforcer," *The Washington Post,* June 25, 2021. The leader of nuclear-armed India, a sometime partner of the United States, helped sustain Putin's economy against sanctions by large purchases of Russian oil. His anti-Muslim policies invalidated India's claim to be the world's largest democracy. Modi seemed indifferent to the dangers of Covid. See Kunal Kamra, "Thanks to Modi, India Had a 'State Orchestrated Covid Massacre,'" *The New York Times,* June

can be reached on non-military issues such as public health and the environment, perhaps grounds for mutual trust could be strengthened. At best, however, this would be a drawn-out process while the danger of Armageddon in 30 minutes persists. The responsibilities of each nuclear-armed actor are enormous, and the grounds for mutual trust are not becoming any firmer. A charismatic and persuasive leader— another Gorbachev or JFK—might sever the Gordian knots that bind the great powers, but no such leader is visible in the shadows of today's high and mighty.

Instead, as the Slavophile diplomat poet Fyodor Tyutchev noted in "Vision" (1829):

The night thickens, like chaos on the waters.

Forgetfulness [bezpamiatsvo], *like Atlas, grips the earth.*

A LIBERAL PEACE?

The only way to get Russia and China to pay off their debts—to their own peoples, to their neighbors, and to some more distant—would be to have a new regime in Moscow and Beijing. Like Germany and Japan after 1945, Russia and China need to start afresh. They need to join the nations that have enjoyed a liberal peace and slowly growing prosperity since 1945.

Russia and China are in a bind. The only way they do big things is from the top-down. To acquire greater societal fitness, they need to rely more on self-organization and what the Russian zoologist Petr Kropotkin called mutual aid.[13] They need to develop all five ingredients for a good life as outlined by Immanuel Kant in his 1795 booklet *Toward Perpetual Peace.*[14] The conditions are

---

23, 2021. Of course, charges of reckless indifference to the pandemic apply also to Donald J. Trump, Xi Jinping, Vladimir Putin, Jair Bolsonaro, and other top leaders.

13 On societal fitness, see my *Complexity Science and World Affairs* (Lexington: University Press of Kentucky, 2013); for some of Kropotkin's views, see his *Mutual Aid: A Factor in Evolution* (New York: McClure, Philipps, 1902) and Project Gutenberg.

14 *Zum ewigen Frieden.* For an English translation, London: George Allen & Unwin, 1903 and Project Gutenberg.

representative government, participation in a federal association of nations, respect for international law, a spirit of trade, and the growth of a common, enlightened culture.

The key ingredient is representative government.[15] Why? Where "the consent of the citizenry is required ... to determine whether there will be war, it is natural that they consider all its calamities before they enter so risky a game." By contrast, authoritarian rulers can simply declare war and leave it to sophists to concoct justifications—as Putin has done repeatedly.

The second ingredient emerges because free, self-governing peoples will tend to form federations to preserve peace and their rights. If an enlightened people forms a representative government, "it will provide a focal point for a federal association among other nations that will join it in order to guarantee a state of peace among nations ... and through several associations of this sort such a federation can extend further and further."

Third, since these representative governments will not accept any other government *over* them, they will accept an enlarged body of international law that will "finally include all the people of the earth." As community prevails among the earth's peoples, "a transgression in one place in the world is felt everywhere"— as happens now in Ukraine. China, we have seen, also ignores international law, or tries unilaterally to rewrite it.

Fourth, representative government and law are linked with commerce. The "spirit of trade cannot coexist with war, and sooner or later this spirit dominates every people."[16] Those with the most to lose economically will exert every effort to head off war by

---

15 Kant referrred to representative government as a "republic" to distinguish it from the direct democracy convulsing France as he wrote. The only republics in 1795 were the Swiss cantons and the recently formed United States, with very limited suffrage, Kant lived in the former Hanseatic city-state Königsberg, ruled in Kant's time by the King of Prussia. Since 1946 it has been called Kaliningrad and ruled from Moscow.

16 Kant did not treat commerce as a cure for war. He avoided the simplistic view of the "Manchester School" economists who, in the 19th century, promised that "the free flow of goods across national boundaries" would erase misunderstandings and ensure peace. Unlike them, Kant insisted that peace depended upon a combination of factors, beginning with representative government.

mediation. Top-down regimes, however, as in Moscow and Beijing, often put politics above profit, conducing to counterproductuve decisions.

Fifth, common institutions should lead to mutual respect. Language and religion divide men, but "the growth of culture and men's gradual progress toward greater agreement regarding their [common] principles lead to mutual understanding and peace." The "right to visit, to associate [with other peoples], belongs to all men by virtue of their common ownership of the earth's surface...."

Perceptions are crucial. Peoples that perceive one another as democratic have not fought each other. Indeed, they tend to band together against authoritarians. They have have repeatedly fought—even preemptively—regimes perceived as non-democraric. As Britain became more democratic in the late 19th century, tensions between London and Washington diminished. In the late 19th century the U.S. and Britain committed themselves to third-party arbitration of disputes they could not resolve bilaterally. Instead of struggle between the imperial hegemon and the challenger, a "special relationship" developed between them. The United States has intervened in and even invaded many countries—from Cental America to Vietnam to Iraq and Syria—believing them to be dangerous dictatorships. Lacking mutual respect and ruled sometimes by dictators, NATO members Greece and Turkey have experienced many "close calls."

Western democracies (including Japan, South Korea, and Taiwan) have met the essential conditions for "perpetual peace" as set out by Kant. Their combined effects—their synegy—leads them never to fight each other and to settle their disputes by negotiation or accommodation. *Neither Russia nor China any other Communist or post-Communist state has met the five conditions,*

No liberal democracies have ever fought each other. Soviet and post-Soviet Russia, by contrast, has invaded its own allies, client states, and neighbors—East Germany, Hungary, Czechoslovakia, Afghanistan, Moldova, Chechnya, Georgia, Ukraine, and threatened the world with nuclear weapons. Soviet Russia even came to blows with China. China and its Communist neighbor Vietnam have also fought each other. Neither Moscow nor Beijing has fought with North Korea, but their support is grudging at best.

Kant expected that as the number of representative governments expands, the bases for peace will become global and perpetual. There must be justice and peace among states for these virtues to be strong within a single state. Civil society cannot flourish in fear of external attack. Kant urged governments to remember that if their policies attempt to do what is morally right, peace and other good results will follow. If each state behaves morally, the space between them can become an extension of the rational political community or "civil society" achieved within each state. The international arena then could be dominated not by amoral anarchy but by "pure practical reason and its righteousness."

Kant also realized that the system he outlined would be vulnerable to the wild streak in human nature that could tear down the rule of reason. He cautioned that "from the crooked timber of humanity no straight thing can ever be made." But he hoped that each human, reaching upward like a tree for air and sun, would grow straight under the canopy of civil society. Kant's views might seem naïve, but the most *honest* states in the world—Finland and its Scandianvian neighbors—also rank among the most content.

Taken together, Kant's five points read like a description of the European Union and, by extension, the "security community" that links Europe, Canada, the U.S., and their Asian partners. These factors interact to form a "social field"—an exchange society with a habit of problem-solving by negotiation and accommodation.[17]

Could Russia and China ever join this community? As governed by Putin and Xi, a truly democratic future for Russia and

---

17 Kant's vision may also explain the long peace and proesperity enjoyed by the league of Hanseatic city-states such as Lübeck, Riga, and Königsberg, each governed by a twenty-person town council elected from merchant guilds. These towns took shape in the 12th and 13th centuries and flourished for four to five hundred years. The German-speaking Hansas lived in peace with each other and prospered from trading along routes that extended from Novgorod to London and Lisbon. The Hansas' values were so similar that lesser towns simply copied the laws of Lübeck. When challenged by Denmark, the Hansas put together a navy and replaced the Danish king. In the 17th century, however, the Hanseatic city-states were absorbed by expanding nation-states such as Prussia and Poland.

China seems an impossible dream. Still, we have the examples of Germany and Japan that gradually became democratic after defeat in a world war. Portugal and Spain quickly embraced democracy—with no military defeat—after their dictators died in 1970 and 1975. After Chiang Ching-kuo ended nartial law in 1987, a year before his death, Taiwan rapidly shifted from dictatorship to a vibrant democracy—also without defeat in war.[18]

Taiwan's transformation benefited from education. Chiang's successor as president, Lee Teng-hui, earned a Ph.D. from Cornell in agriculural economics in 1968. Many of his cabinet appointees also held advanced degrees from U.S. universities. They were not alone. In 1990, a student group known as "Wild Lilly" organized a sit-in by over 300,000 students in Taipei. They demanded direct elections of the national president and vice president and a new election for all legislative seats. Lee welcomed some of the students to the presidential building and expressed his support for their goals and pledged his commitment to full democracy. Tsai Ing-wen, president since 2016, holds a law degree from Cornell and a Ph.D. ftom the London School of Economics. The very idea that the people if Taiwan could ever be ruled by a dictatorshp in Beijing is anathema in the Republic of China.

Education, democracy, and prospertity advanced together. When I visited Taiwan, South Korea, and Hong Kong in 1970, many people slept rough on sidewalks, even in the rain. Some students sold cigarettes, one at a time, to fund their education. When I lectured, only senior professors could pose questions. By 1992, professors were drowned out by students and had to struggle to say anything. What once looked in Taipei like a hopelessly modest startup later became the world's major producer of semi-conductors.

Democratic societies have created for their members the highest living standards in history. They are geared to mutual gain and value creation rather than toward exploitation, at least within their borders. Except for Singapore, most of the top thirty countries

---

18 See Clemens and Jun Zhan, "Chiang Ching-kuo's Role in the ROC-PRC Reconciliation," *American Asian Review* 12, 1 (Spring 1994): 140-163.

on the UN Human Development Index have been democracies.[19]

    The ultimate reason to reject authoritarianism is that it endangers life. Authoritarian regimes tend to be exploitative. They seek power and/or wealth for the rulers and the "state" rather than for most of the body politic. Today, as in Soviet times, Russia is more fit for war than for peace. Most Communist dictators have lived in luxury while their subjects scraped by and sometimes starved. Exploitation of the many by the few can benefit the regime for years, but tends to boomerang over time. How quickly this can happen in Russia and China is unkown. Nor is there any way to know when Russia and China will honor their blood debts. So free peoples face a clear and present danger.

---

19 Whether Hong Kong without self-rule can remain high on the HDI is doubtful.

Appendix 10

Principles of the Charter of the United Nations underlying a comprehensive, just and lasting peace in Ukraine

UN General Assembly A/ES- 11/L.7   23 February 2023

The General Assembly, Recalling the purposes and principles enshrined in the Charter of the United Nations,

Recalling also the obligation of all States under Article 2 of the Charter of the United Nations to refrain in their international relations from the threat or use of force against the territorial integrity or political independence of any State, or in any other manner inconsistent with the purposes of the United Nations, and to settle their international disputes by peaceful means,

Reaffirming that no territorial acquisition resulting from the threat or use of force shall be recognized as legal,

Recalling its relevant resolutions adopted at its eleventh emergency special session and its resolution 68/262 of 27 March 2014 [which condemned the Russian takeover of Crimea and underscored "that the referendum held in the Autonomous Republic of Crimea and the city of Sevastopol on 16 March 2014, having no validity, cannot form the basis for any alteration of the status of the Autonomous Republic of Crimea or of the city of Sevastopol"],

Stressing, one year into the full-scale invasion of Ukraine, that the achievement of a comprehensive, just and lasting peace would constitute a significant contribution to strengthening international peace and security,

Recalling the order of the International Court of Justice of 16 March 2022 [that "Ukraine has a plausible right not to be subjected to military operations by the Russian Federation for the purpose of preventing and punishing an alleged genocide in the territory of Ukraine," where Putin claimed millions are at risk of genocide].

Deploring the dire human rights and humanitarian consequences of the aggression by the Russian Federation against Ukraine, including the continuous attacks against critical infrastructure across

Ukraine with devastating consequences for civilians, and expressing grave concern at the high number of civilian casualties, including women and children, the number of internally displaced persons and refugees in need of humanitarian assistance, and violations and abuses committed against children,

Noting with deep concern the adverse impact of the war on global food security, energy, nuclear security and safety and the environment,

1. *Underscores* the need to reach, as soon as possible, a comprehensive, just and lasting peace in Ukraine in line with the principles of the Charter of the United Nations;

2. *Welcomes and expresses strong support* for the efforts of the Secretary-General and Member States to promote a comprehensive, just and lasting peace in Ukraine, consistent with the Charter, including the principles of sovereign equality and territorial integrity of States;

3. *Calls upon* Member States and international organizations to redouble support for diplomatic efforts to achieve a comprehensive, just and lasting peace in Ukraine, consistent with the Charter;

4. *Reaffirms its commitment* to the sovereignty, independence, unity and territorial integrity of Ukraine within its internationally recognized borders, extending to its territorial waters;

5. *Reiterates its demand* that the Russian Federation immediately, completely and unconditionally withdraw all of its military forces from the territory of Ukraine within its internationally recognized borders, and calls for a cessation of hostilities;

6. *Demands* that the treatment by the parties to the armed conflict of all prisoners of war be in accordance with the provisions of the Geneva Convention relative to the Treatment of Prisoners of War of 12 August 1949 (2) and Additional Protocol I to the Geneva Conventions of 1949, 3 and calls for the complete exchange of prisoners of war, the release of all unlawfully detained persons and the return of all internees and of civilians forcibly transferred and deported, including children;

10. Confronting Evil

7. *Calls for full* adherence by the parties to the armed conflict to their obligations under international humanitarian law to take constant care to spare the civilian population and civilian objects, to ensure safe and unhindered humanitarian access to those in need, and to refrain from attacking, destroying, removing or rendering useless objects indispensable to the survival of the civilian population;

8. *Also calls for* an immediate cessation of the attacks on the critical infrastructure of Ukraine and any deliberate attacks on civilian objects, including those that are residences, schools and hospitals;

9. *Emphasizes* the need to ensure accountability for the most serious crimes under international law committed on the territory of Ukraine through appropriate, fair and independent investigations and prosecutions at the national or international level, and ensure justice for all victims and the prevention of future crimes;

10, *Urges* all Member States to cooperate in the spirit of solidarity to address the global impacts of the war on food security, energy, finance, the environment and nuclear security and safety, underscores that arrangements for a comprehensive, just and lasting peace in Ukraine should take into account these factors, and calls upon Member States to support the Secretary-General in his efforts to address these impacts;

11. *Decides* to adjourn the eleventh emergency special session of the General Assembly temporarily and to authorize the President of the General Assembly to resume its. meetings upon request from Member States.

CHAPTER 11
WE VERSUS US: TOTALITARIAN TRENDS IN RUSSIA, CHINA, AND THE USA

An inspiration for George Orwell's *1984*, Yevgeny Zamyatin's dystopian novel *WE*, written in the first years of Bolshevik rule in Soviet Russia, anticipated many features of the totalitarian dictatorships that emerged under Mussolini, Stalin, and Hitler and have reemerged in Communist China and Putin's Russia, and may be taking root in the United States and other Western countries where modern technologies bolster government capacities to watch and control one their subjects and other targets. Science fiction in Russia, China, and the United States illustrates the perils facing all life.

The Setting

It has been one century since a New York publisher received the smuggled manuscript of Zamyatin's *WE (МЫ)*— one of the greatest dystopias ever written and a vivid warning of where humanity may be heading. Written during the first years of Leninist rule in Russia, *WE* in 1921 became the first book manuscript banned by Soviet censors. *WE* was translated by Columbia medical student and future psychiatrist Gregory Zilboorg and published by E. P. Dutton in 1924. It was reissued in 2021 in a sparkling translation by Bela Shayevich (the version quoted here).[1]

Not until 1988, the era of Gorbachev's "openness," was *WE* published in the Soviet Union. In February 2022, however, the magazine *GQ Rossiia* listed *WE* as one of eight books "everyone"— or at least cultivated young men—should read, adding that these works were not banned without cause.[2] A film version of the novel

---
1 *WE: A Novel* (New York: Ecco, 2021).
2 Dmitrii Petros'iants, "8 controversial and banned books everyone should read," *GQ Rossiia*, February 3, 2022 at https://www.gq.ru/entertainment/8-spornyh-i-

WE, directed by Hamlet Dulyan (born in Armenia) was scheduled for release in 2023.³

Why reflect on *WE* now? Zamyatin anticipated the crushing of individual freedom by top-down manipulators of an indoctrinated collective. Not only did *WE* forecast many features of Fascism, Stalinism, Nazism, Maoism, and Castroism; it also previewed totalitarian rule in Vladimir Putin's Russia and Xi Jinping's China. *WE* also suggests a possible trajectory of politics in the United States as Americans absorb the Big Lies of power-hungry politicians and their media partners manipulating the anxieties of whites who feel they are losing.⁴

What Happens in *WE*?

Set several centuries into the future, *WE* portrays life in the ONE STATE, a society ruled by the great BENEFACTOR and on the verge of launching a mission into outer space. Authorities advise the spaceship's crew they will encounter unfamiliar beings on alien planets living in savage states of freedom who will be subjugated to the beneficent yoke of reason. ONE STATE (always in caps) instructs: "IF THEY DON'T UNDERSTAND THAT WHAT WE BRING THEM IS MATHEMATICALLY INFALLIBLE HAPPINESS, WE WILL BE IMPELLED TO FORCE THEM TO BE HAPPY" (pp. 11-12).

WE is the diary of D-503, a mathematician and master builder of the spaceship *INTEGRAL*. He intends to share his journal with whoever occupies the distant planets. D-503 says he feels like a square—an entity that would not think to talk about its corners and

---

zapreshennyh-knig-kotorye-stoit-prochitat-kazhdomu. The other recommended books, summarized below, include Kornei Chukovsky, *The Monster Cockroach* [*Tarakanishche*], Ayn Rand, *Fountainhead*; Vladimir Nabokov, *Lolita*; Kurt Vonnegut, *Slaughterhouse-Five*; Lois Lowry, *The Giver*; and Bret Easton Ellis, *American Psycho*; and Eduard Limonov, *Eta ya—Edichka* [*That's me—Eddie*].

3   However, most of the film production was completed and a trailer posted in 2021. Since the novel and book can be seen as attacks on Putin's ONE STATE, outsiders must wonder whether Russian authorities will permit the film to be shown or whether the authors have been censoring their own creation.

4   See my *The Republican War Against America: Dangers of Trump and Trumpism* (Washington D.C.: Westphalia, 2023).

other dimensions (p. 31). He feels it odd to be informing ETs about life in the ONE STATE such as the pink tickets that authorize pairs of numbers to copulate.

The BENEFACTOR's subjects have no names but are identified as "numbers" or "unifs" (for the uniforms they all wear) (p. 16). All their activities are planned according to the theories of Frederick W. Taylor (1856–1915) (p. 45), the American inventor of scientific management and a strong influence on the early Soviet administration.

To make people happy, the ONE STATE had to conquer Love and Hunger. Master builder D-503 concedes that a high price was paid to conquer these impulses. The city had to wage the Great Two Hundred Years' War to defeat the countryside, where the peasants (like their Russian ancestors in 1919 and again in 1928) held onto their "bread" as tenaciously as their religious superstitions (pp. 22, 31). Only 0.2 percent of the world's population survived the great war. But now the face of the earth is bright and shining. People now subsist on petroleum-based food. "They taste bliss from inside the walls of the ONE STATE."

The master builder opens the *ONE STATE GAZETTE* and reads that the great BENEFACTOR has addressed "all numbers of the ONE STATE." All numbers able to produce treatises, epic poems, or odes celebrating the glories of the ONE STATE must do so. These writings will be the *INTEGRAL*'s first cargo into space. One of D's friends is indeed a poet, R-13, repeatedly described as having large, "African" lips—a likely reference to the poet Aleksandr Pushkin (1799–1837), whose great grandfather, enslaved as a child in Africa was adopted and later employed by Tsar Peter the Great. D himself also bears an unusual trait. His hands are covered with fur, a relic of savage times before the new order.

At scheduled times D-503 walks or couples with one of two females. The first is designated O-90. She is shorter, rounder, and more sentimental than the second, I-330, whose body and mind are more angular. One day, as O-90 walks into his hangar, D-503 is reflecting on the mechanical ballet of his machines. Why is this dance beautiful? Because the movements are unfree. D-503 tried to explain to O-90 the flywheel logic whirling inside him, but she merely replies, "Spring." D thinks, "There she goes again ... women."

It is the afternoon Personal Hour which they use for extra walking. D-503 and O-90 step outside the hangar and hear the Music Factory pipes playing the March of the ONE STATE. Thousands of numbers exuberantly step to the beat in orderly rows of four. D-503 and O-90 join two other numbers. One is I-330—slender, sharp, supple, and stubborn, like a whip—with whom D eventually falls in love. She is totally different from O, who is all curves with plump, childlike wrists (p. 18). At the outer edge of the foursome is a male number, his body doubly bent, like the letter S. He turns out to be a watcher for the Guardians (p. 25). His badge says S-4711.

On another occasion this femme fatale, I-330, laughs when she sees how intent D looks as he recalls a painting from the 20th century showing a riot of people, wheels, animals, trees, and colors. This chaotic freedom strikes him as unbelievable, so he laughs. I-330 reads his mind and says, "Yes... alas!" Her comment could be regarded as inappropriate, but D-503 responds by defending things as they have become. "Nothing to 'alas' about. Science marches on and clearly...." Anticipating his direction, she says that science will soon give every number the same shaped nose. For now, however, she regards the nose of D-503 as what "the Ancients would have called 'classical.'" When O sees I looking at D up and down, she "cheerfully, rosily" opens her mouth to say: "He's registered to me today." She means that she has a pink ticket authorizing her to copulate with D. At an appointed time, they will go to his glass-lined space (what people used to call an apartment) and—for one hour—are permitted to lower the shades and do their thing.

Later, as D and I become acquainted, she invites him to join her at the House of Antiquity, a museum with artifacts of how people once lived (p.36). It emerges that she wants him to stay there with her and miss the mandatory lecture at 17 hours. She can get him an excuse written by a doctor friend, but D flees the scene and dutifully arrives at the lecture just before it starts. Still, D worries that he should report I's proposal—her Deviationism--to the Guardians. He puts off ratting on her for the next day, but then encounters the

11. *WE* versus Us: Totalitarian Trends in Russia, China, and the USA

Guardian S-4711 and starts to confess. As if to draw him out, S praises I as a "very interesting, talented woman" and volunteers that the House of Antiquity "often "provides material for drawing very instructive conclusions." With a double smile, S nods goodbye.

Gradually we learn that I-330 smokes cigarettes, drinks vodka, and shamelessly flirts with D-503 instead of applying for a pink ticket sex visit. All these activities are highly illegal according to the laws of ONE STATE.

D now has a deeper problem. He has passed up a chance to report I's Deviation. She expected this outcome and smiles: "Now you're all mine. Any number who fails to report to the Bureau within forty-eight hours is considered...." She stands up and lazily stretches before pressing the button. "With a slight rattle, the blinds came down ... I was cut off from the world, alone with her."

D calls her "darling" and begins to strip off his unif. But she shows him a clock. It is just five minutes before 22:30—the required time to be home for sleep-eye. "All of my madness went out . . . I was myself again," he says. Frustrated, he mutters, "I hate her!" He dashes home just in time. Deeply worried, he can't sleep. Not sleeping is itself a crime, because sleep is essential for work. "I'm dying," he concludes— "incapable of fulfilling my duties to the ONE STATE...I...."

Next day D opens his gazette and is shocked to read: "There is new evidence of an elusive organization striving for liberation from the beneficent yoke of the State." Self-righteous for the ONE STATE, D reflects that freedom and crime are linked. "The only way to eradicate crime is to eradicate freedom."

How does the regime hold on? Against extremists, we learn, it uses torture and execution; for everyone else, it requires surgery to remove both the soul and imagination.

Still determined to report I's Deviationism, D leaves his job at 16 hours and plans to report to the Bureau of the Guardians. But he runs into O on the corner. She is "filled with pink glee at this chance encounter and urges him to walk with her. No, he refuses and tells her his planned destination. To his surprise, her lips slump into a pink crescent moon, its horns down. "You're off to see the spies—

yuck! And to think I got you a sprig of lilies of the valley from the Botanical Museum...."

"To *think*," he replies, "so typically feminine." D goes into a tirade contrasting the smells of lilies and henbane—one odor good and one bad. Every state has spies, he says. The "spies of the ancient state were like henbane while ours are like lilies of the valley!"

D is nothing if not conflicted with multiple cognitive dissonances. O convinces D he is sick and should go to the Medical Bureau instead of to the Guardians. He does so and she visits him that evening. They pour over problems in an ancient math book. He "felt good inside, simple, precise...." After she leaves, he turns in for the night, but finds something unpleasant in bed—a sprig of lilies of the valley. So utterly tactless of her, he thinks. But she was right. He was sick—so nothing is his fault.

Though O and D do not share the same vibes, she schemes to conceive a baby by him. She does so even though she is not authorized to do so because she is so short and that illegitimate conceptions are punishable with death. Aware of her likely fate, she nonetheless is ecstatic to feel the baby growing within her.

Meanwhile, I-330 reveals to D-503 that she and her doctor friend are members of MEPHI, an organization of rebels against the ONE STATE. I-330 takes D-503 through secret tunnels to the untamed wilderness outside the Green Wall, which surrounds the city-state. There, D-503 meets human inhabitants the ONE STATE claims no longer exist. They are hunter gatherers whose bodies are covered with animal fur. The aims of MEPHI are to topple the ONE STATE, destroy the Green Wall, and reunite the people of the city with those living in freedom.

The Guardians and the great BENEFACTOR learn who is doing what and arrest all the guilty parties. Enemies of the state are dispatched by a great machine operated by the heavy hands of the BENEFACTOR himself in a public spectacle while poets sing his praise (pp. 59-61). D is spared from execution because he is master builder of the *INTEGRAL*. To make him function, however, specialists remove both his soul and his imagination (pp. 104-106). His insides purged; he watches calmly as his lover I-330 is tortured (pp. 142, 161). Nearly vaporized three times, she refuses to confess. The book ends without saying if she too, like other insurgents, will be zapped by the BENEFACTOR into a few drops of liquid.

Despite its tragic ending, *We* still carries a note of hope. Despite the rout of the rebellion, "there is still fighting in the western parts of the city." Many "numbers" have escaped beyond the Wall.[5]

Utopias and Dystopias

Dreams of a better world and fears of a worse one go back millennia.[6] Visons of utopia have often overlapped with counter-utopias—dystopias. Plato's *Republic* with its Guardians, social classes, Big Lies, and eugenics can be seen as a model for totalitarian dictatorship. Some dystopian scenarios purport to be set in the future but often depict worrisome features of present realities. This, we shall see, is the case with much science fiction in contemporary Russia and China.

WE "is the best single work of science fiction yet written," according to the American novelist Ursula K. Le Guin, whose comments in the 1970s are appended to the 2002 translation.

Depicting a self-proclaimed utopia as a dystopia, *WE* unites some classic features of Plato's *Republic* and Thomas More's *Utopia* with futures shaped by modern technology such as H. G. Wells, *War of the Worlds* (1899), E.M. Forster's *The Machine Stops* (1909), Alexander Bogdanov's *Red Star* (1912); Aldous Huxley's *Brave New World* (1932), and George Orwell's *Nineteen Eighty-Four* (1949). Like the *Lorax* of Universal Pictures (2012), *WE* warns of environmental destruction as well as social-political-economic absolutism. Like the ever-reborn reincarnations of *Star Wars*, *WE* suggests that absolute dictatorships can bounce back and survive attacks by good guys.

One leitmotif in these modern dystopias is the domination of humans by machines and the masterminds who control them. A

---

[5] Mirra Ginsburg's introduction to her translation of *WE*. (New York: Avon Books, 1967).

[6] Douwe Fokkema, *Perfect Worlds: Utopian Fiction in China and the West* (Amsterdam: Amsterdam University Press, 2011).

second theme is that, as Dostoevsky's Grand Inquisitor informed Christ, most people prefer bread to freedom.

Translated versions of *WE* in English and French may have inspired Huxley's *Brave New World* and, by his own reckoning, Orwell's *Nineteen Eighty-Four*. A Czech translation of *WE* smuggled back into Russia in the 1920s infuriated Stalin. Still, perhaps because the young Zamyatin had been an ardent Bolshevik, whose request to emigrate was backed by Maxim Gorky, Stalin permitted Zamyatin and his wife to depart Soviet Russia in 1928. The impoverished dystopian died in Paris in 1936 or 1937.

Born in provincial Russia in 1884, son of an Orthodox priest, Zamyatin was a polymath. In school he excelled in humanities but chose to study naval engineering. Joining the Bolsheviks as a young man, he was arrested by tsarist police and jailed for joining the 1905 revolution. Still, he completed his studies and, two years into world war, the tsarist government sent him to England where he oversaw production of what became the world's largest icebreaker. He returned to Russia in 1917 shortly after the October Revolution. What Zamyatin witnessed during the first two years of Bolshevik rule led him to revolt again—this time drawing a horrifying portrait of an all-powerful and all-knowing ONE STATE claiming to provide a perfect life for its inhabitants and for denizens of other planets.

As noted here in previous chapters, Zamyatin became the first of many Soviet writers, musicians, artists, and scientific innovators silenced, condemned, exiled, gulaged, or expelled. "Like Bulgakov and like Babel, Zamyatin gives us a glimpse of what post-revolutionary Russian literature might have become had independence, daring, and individuality been prized and not been stamped out ruthlessly by the dictatorship."[7]

Outsiders can only weep at the way that Communist and former Communist politicians have dried up or pushed into exile the artistic fountains that burst forth throughout the 19th and 20th centuries—from Pushkin to Brodsky; Vrubel to Chagall; Glinka to Stravinsky; and Pavlova to Baryshnikov and Osipova.

---

[7] Anatoly Kuznetsov, cited above, page 71, note 7.

Dystopia in Today's Russia

Apart from *What Is to Be Done?* (1863) written by Nikolai Chernyshevsky while imprisoned in St. Petersburg's Peter and Paul Fortress, and *Red Star* (1912) by Alexander Bogdanov, plus Andrei Platonov's, *Chevengur* (1928–29), relatively few Russians published dystopian works before or after Zamyatin's *WE*—until the end of Soviet Communism. However, in the first decades after the fall of the USSR, dystopian novels poured forth. Though set in the future, many offered a very dim appraisal of Russia today and tomorrow. Many suggested a cycle in which an authoritarian Russia keeps devouring itself.[8] Here are some examples, available now in English as well as Russian:

- *Rabbits and Boa Constrictors* (Ardis, 1989) by Fazil Iskander resembles *Animal Farm* by George Orwell. The allegory dissects the psychology and mechanics of a dictatorship, "Their hypnosis is our fear," one of the rabbits realizes.[9]

- Victor Pelevin's *The Yellow Arrow* (New Directions, 1997) describes an express train, perhaps a metaphor for Russia, heading towards a collapsed bridge. The train moves on robotically as passengers give birth and die, do their business and go bankrupt, fall in love and start families. The main character, Andrei, is a passenger who begins to despair over the train's ultimate destination and tries to jump out.

- Tatyana Tolstaya's *The Slynx* (Houghton Mifflin Harcourt, 2000) presents the world after a nuclear apocalypse. Most technology, culture and language have been wiped out. In post-nuclear Russia villagers live like animals—and often look like them, some with horns and tails. There is also the Slynx, a forest-dwelling monster—a metaphor for fear of

---

8 Sergey Toymentsev, "Retro-Future in Post-Soviet Dystopia," *CLCWeb: Comparative Literature and Culture* 21,4 (June 2019) at http://docs.lib.purdue.edu/clcweb/vol21/iss4/4

9 Iskander lived in Abkhazia, then part of Georgia, until age 18, but wrote in Russian and died in Peredelkino in 2016, where Pasternak and other cultural luminaries lived.

the unknown. The few books found after the Explosion are taken from people and stored in a book depository. There, the main protagonist, Benedict, works. He reads books randomly—from children's stories to specialized technical guides and copies them by hand to preserve them. But Benedict is unable to educate himself enough to take in the world around him. Despite being obsessed with books, he still lives like a caveman.

- Dmitry Glukhovsky's *Metro 2033* (2007) posits a post-nuclear Earth with the remaining survivors lurking in subterranean tunnels. The biggest is the Moscow Metro, where all the stations are like mini-countries and chaos reigns in the dark tunnels themselves. The dictator, who fears losing power, conceals the news that the world above has not in fact been utterly destroyed.

  In 2022 Glukhovsky told *GQ Rossiia*, "Now my readers in Kharkiv and Kyiv send me photos on Instagram from the tunnels of metro stations. I feel nothing but horror from this. We are all hostages on board a plane that has been hijacked by a madman—and he's about to fly it into a cliff face." A Russian film adaptation of the sequel *Metro 2034* was planned for 2024, but Glukhovsky says that's now all over: "Over the next year only pseudo-patriotic films will be made in Russia—or mindless comedies that will turn off people's brains completely." On June 7, 2922, Glukhovsky was added to Russia's federal wanted list for discrediting the army. He is now abroad in an undisclosed location.[10]

- *The Day of the Oprichnik* (Farrar, Straus & Giroux, 2012) by Vladimir Sorokin, portrays Russia in 2027, a country that has become a twisted, military dictatorship in the style of Ivan the Terrible where the population is terrorized by the Oprichniki, the medieval secret police. The new Russia's futuristic technology works in synch with the draconian codes of Ivan the Terrible. The Oprichnik Andrei Komiaga

---

10 Vadim Smyslov at https://www.gq.com › story › russia-cultural-brain-drain, June 13, 2022.

attends extravagant parties, partakes in brutal executions, and consumes an arsenal of drugs. He will rape and pillage, but also shed tears listening to the sweet songs of his homeland. The Russian state holds on, little changed. Russians have lived under tyrants for at least thirteen centuries—Varangian princes, Mongols, tsars, party secretaries, and—since late 1999—a tyrannical prime minister/president.

UPDATE 2022: WHAT EVERY STYLISH YOUNG RUSSIAN MUST READ

On the eve of Russia's invasion of Ukraine, the gentlemen's quarterly magazine *GQ Rossiia* in February 2022 ran a flashy essay "The Eight Controversial and Forbidden Books Everyone Should Read—No Wonder They Were Banned."[11] Only two were written in Russia—just over one century ago. The first book listed is Zamyatin's *WE*.[12]

The second work recommended by GQ was also completed in 1921—*The Monster Cockroach [Tarakanishche]* by Kornei Chukovsky. A series of verses for children to enjoy, *The Monster Cockroach* describes the reign of a bullying dictator over other insects until he is pecked apart by a sparrow.[13] Like *WE*, the cockroach verses prefigured terrible things to come. Though criticized by Nadezhda Krupskaya, Lenin's wife, Chukovsky became a much-honored author of children's stories in the USSR. Under President Yeltsin, in 1993 the Monster Cockroach was captured on a postage stamp. In 2020–2021, Belarusian dissidents called their President Aleksandr Lukashenko the "Monster Cockroach." The businessman and blogger Sergei Tikhanovsky initiated an "Anti-Cockroach

---

11 Dmitrii Petros'iants, *GQ Rossiia,* February 3, 2022, at https://www.gq.ru/entertainment/8-spornyh-i-zapreshennyh-knig-kotorye-stoit-prochitat-kazhdomu

12 Russian authorities did not want *GQ* readers to access Scott Anderson's report on the mysterious apartment building bombings as Putin took the helm in 1999. Condé Nast, owner of *GQ Rossiya*, made sure the story did not reach Russia in any format and muffled it in the United States, See David Folkenflik, "Why 'GQ' Doesn't Want Russians To Read Its Story" at https://www.npr.org/2009/09/04/112530364/why-gq-doesnt-want-russians-to-read-its-story.

13 To read the text and hear the author read the verses, go to https://www.chukfamily.ru/kornei/tales

Revolution" that called for smashing the cockroach with a slipper. Accused of fomenting public disorder, in 2021 (one century since publication of Chukovsky's verses), Tikhanovsky was jailed for eighteen years. His wife, having lost a rigged presidential election to Lukashenko, fled with their children to Lithuania.

Three of the eight *GQ* recommended books were written by Russians in the United States. Strictly speaking, none is a dystopia, but each comes close. *The Fountainhead* (1943) was by Ayn Rand—born as Alisa Rosenbaum in Tsarist Russia. She studied in a renowned girl's academy in St. Petersburg with her best friend, Vladimir Nabokov's younger sister, Olga. Rand found the school boring and began writing screenplays at age eight and novels at age ten. After the Bolshevik revolution, the Rosenbaums moved to White army-occupied Crimea and then back to Petrograd. In 1925 Rand, her adopted pen name, escaped to New York, met film director Cecil B. DeMille, and got a job in Hollywood. She wrote several screenplays and short stories but did not enjoy major commercial success until *The Fountainhead.* It tells of a young architect who concludes that a creative person must be an egotist. Only a self-seeker can develop the energy to do great things. The novel presents a dystopian future in which totalitarian collectivism goes so far that the word "I" disappears and is replaced by "we." What *GQ* calls collectivists disparaged her book but two years after its publication in Russia (as *Istochnik),* it became a best seller. Her subsequent novel *Atlas Shrugged (*1957*)* and her philosophy of rational self-interest known as Objectivism have inspired conservatives everywhere.

Lolita by Vladimir Nabokov details the intimate relationship between middle-aged professor Humbert and his twelve-year old stepdaughter, leading some critics to condemn Humbert as a child rapist. Nabokov completed the manuscript in 1953. Since no U.S. publisher would print it, the author had it published in Paris in 1955. After some strong endorsements, G. P. Putnam's Sons published it in 1958. For many years *Lolita* was banned not only in the USSR but in many countries—from France to Argentina to New Zealand. Translated into Russian by Nabokov in 1967, *Lolita* was not published in the USSR until 1989 (like *We,* in the Gorbachev era). Having experienced much controversy, *Lolita* has been converted into an opera as well as several movies. *Time* Magazine and many critics have judged *Lolita* a literary classic. Among Nabokov's students at Cornell University, where he taught literature, sat the future U.S. Supreme Court Justice Ruth Bader Ginsburg, who later identified her professor as a major influence on her own development as a writer.

GQ treats as a "classic" Eduard Limonov's dystopian memoir of New York, *Eta ya—Edichka* [*It's Me—Eddy*], published in France in 1979 and Russia in 1991 but not in the United States. Limonov belonged to a different and less cultivated generation than Nabokov and Rand. Born in Russia in 1943, he grew up in Ukraine, in Kharkhiv (recently flattened by Putin's forces). Limonov moved to New York in 1974 and lived there and in Paris until the fall of Soviet Communism. In Soviet times *Eta ya* was banned for its unusual lexicon as well as its vulgarity and pornographic features. Nonetheless Grove in 1987 published another Limonov novel-memoir, *His Butler's Story,* inspired by the author's experiences working for a wealthy Manhattanite. Reviewing the book, Maggie Paley wrote that the author "hates the underclass for being weak and stupid and the ruling class for being insensitive. He hates women—whom he describes in terms of female sex organs—for using men. He considers the other Russians in New York to be snobs or boors. He has no use for political systems, Communist or capitalist. He believes in revolution as a "phenomenon of nature."[14] Returned to Russia from New York and Paris, Limonov founded the anti-liberal National Bolshevik Party in 1993, later banned in 2007. Limonov did not like Putin but endorsed his seizure of Crimea in 2014. Limonov died in 2020.

The three other mandatory readings are by authors born in the United States. *American Psychopath* by Brett Easton Ellis describes a Manhattan investment banker addicted to serial murdering and to careful grooming. Condemned in the United States for its detailed depictions of sex and violence, including toward women, the book's publication was delayed several times. Despite continuing objections, *American Psychopath* was published in 1991. A decade later it evolved into a film starring Christian Bale.

---

14 Maggie Paley, "Sneering His Way to the Top," *The New York Times*, July 5, 1987.

The anti-war novel *Slaughterhouse-Five* (1999) by Kurt Vonnegut was based in part on his own experiences as a German prisoner-of-war at a time when Allied planes fire-bombed Dresden. The Russian edition is entitled *War Number Five*, a misreading of the English title, which derived from the empty slaughterhouse called *Schlachthof-fünf* where German guards kept some prisoners and joined them during the bombings. After 1945 the story's central figure suffers from posttraumatic stress and other encounters with violence including the Vietnam War. In the United States critics tried to ban or expunge *Slaughterhouse-Five* for its irreverent tone, obscenity (soldiers swear!!!), depictions of sex, perceived heresy, and factual reporting that Germans killed male homosexuals ("fairies") in the Holocaust.

Slightly more hopeful than the other books recommended, *The Giver* by Lois Lowry (1993) depicts another dystopia, like *WE*, masked as utopia. The society has taken away pain and strife by converting to "Sameness." Its basic feature is conformism. Each citizen has no will. Elders decide what role each person will play in society and with whom they will interact. There is no war, no poverty, no hunger, or other misfortune. There is also no emotion, joy, or love. One Elder, called the Giver, is authorized to read books and remember the past. He trains a twelve-year old boy, Jonas, to do the same. Enlightened, Jonas flees the commune with a baby destined to be "released" into oblivion (killed) because he is sickly. Lowry describes their future in follow-on novels. *The Giver* was banned in parts of the United States because it mentions euthanasia and suicide. In 2012, however, *The Giver* was ranked number four among all-time children's novels in a survey published by *School Library Journal*. Reviewing the book for the *Washington Post* (May 9, 1993). Natalie Babbitt wrote that "*The Giver* has things to say that cannot be said too often, and I hope there will be many, many young people who will be willing to listen."

Outsiders may question whether the *GQ* recommendations represent the best literature of the past century. *GQ* passes over other authors including the five Russians and twelve Americans who have won the Nobel Prize in Literature. None of the *GQ* endorsements is pro-Soviet, pro-Russian, or pro-American. Each paints a dark picture of human affairs. The most positive selection, *The Giver*, tells how one boy managed to escape from a collectivist hell.

It is doubtful that any of the recommended books would encourage a young Russian to join an attack on Ukraine. Indeed, *Slaughterhouse-Five* casts a plague on all war anywhere.

The good life pictured in *GQ Rossiya* is not that mandated by the Great Benefactor. Ads in *GQ* urged young men to buy their girlfriends Dior perfumes for February 23, 2022—"Defenders of the Fatherland Day," celebrating the founding of the Red Army in 1918. (This holiday continued to be celebrated in Kazakhstan as well as Russia but was terminated in Ukraine in 1992—except among some Russian-speakers.)

GQ also endorses Calvin Klein perfume, assuring young men its odors will make each feel "unique"—ignoring that the label claims the perfume is for "everyone." *GQ* readers, presumably quite "woke," are assured that the product uses a "vegetarian formula" with "naturally derived alcohol" and that the "packaging is recyclable." *GQ* also urges readers to acquire a fashionable cardigan (1950s style, I would say). For looks, *GQ* advises readers to copy the gold encrusted sunglasses worn by Disney Channel star Cole Sprouse. They can also learn from Rafael Nadal his nine favorite things, besides his tennis racket, such as his Apple laptop. If still in need, *GQ* points patrons to "twenty basic things you can now buy at a big discount." If readers seek diversion, *GQ* points them to five films about the porn-industry." If any young sophisticate, is slowing down, *GQ* also explains how to find the energy to work.

If young Russian men read the eight recommended books and absorb the *GQ* advice for consumers, some of the rising generation may need counseling on how to cope with cognitive dissonance.

Utopia and Dystopia in China

Chinese fiction is booming, but authors cannot escape the regime's tightening grip. Mo Yan won the Nobel Prize for Literature in 2012. Salman Rushdie, along with some Chinese intellectuals, deemed Mo a patsy of the regime. Megan Walsh offers a broader view. Her *Subplot* explains that "modern Chinese fiction is a mixture of staggering invention, bravery and humanity, as well as soul-crushing submission and pragmatism—a confusing and intricate tapestry that offers a beguiling impression of Chinese society itself." Science fiction permits some writers to portray unpleasant realities *verboten* in nonfiction. The stories of Liu Cixin, for example, are politically ambiguous. They could be interpreted as a critique of communism, a swan song of democracy, or as a parable for the dog-eat-dog world of e-commerce.[15]

Chinese utopian writers often posit a secluded world difficult to access and hence protected against outside influences. Utopia may be projected into a distant, little-known past or a completely imaginary fairyland. Such a location resides in the foundational text of the Chinese literary utopian tradition. "The Story of Peach Blossom Spring" by Tao Yuanming (*ca.* 421 CE) tells of a fisherman who, wandering down a stream and through a grotto, finds a forest of peach blossoms where people love life and are at ease, with no demons, no rules, no war, no exploitation. They know nothing of the chaos beyond their idyllic existence. The fisherman departs after a few days and no other outsider has ever discovered this paradise. Tao wrote the story while living in the Eastern Jin kingdom as it collapsed amid violence and corruption.

What one expert calls the "most eminent and significant dystopian novel in the history of Chinese literature" *Cat Country: A Dystopian Satire*, was published in 1933 by Lao She (1899–1966). The book's pessimistic outlook caused the author to be demoted from "people's writer" to "counter-revolutionary writer" as the Cultural Revolution began.[16]

Marx and Engels had their utopian visions of a classless society and the withering away of the state, and so did Mao Zedong. But Mao's utopianism was different, in that it was embedded in Chinese tradition, eschewed economic problems, and demanded voluntarist action. Some of Mao's poems and many of his policies radiated

---

15 Megan Walsh, *The Subplot What China Is Reading and Why It Matters* (New York: Columbia Global Reports, 2022); *also* Katie Stallard, "Literature under Xi Jinping," *The New Statesman*. March 23, 2022.

16 Koon-Ki Tommy Ho, "Cat Country: A Dystopian Satire," *Modern Chinese Literature* 3, 1/2 (Spring/Fall 1987): 71-89 (published by Edinburgh University Press and available at JSTOR.org/stable/41492507).

utopian optimism.[17] Mao's Great Leap Forward (1958–1962), for example, assumed that the Chinese people were like blanks that could be mobilized to do great things in a hurry.[18] As it happened, however, the Great Leap led to mass starvation—costing 25 to 40 million deaths. A few years later, the Cultural Revolution (1966–1976) also killed millions and set back education and science by at least a decade.[19]

Ideas of historical cyclicalism, of utopia, and utopia lost are ancient—and recurring—worldwide. Cruelty in history appears to many recent Chinese novelists to be intermittent—even cyclical. They see flaws in human nature as a constant. "Dystopia is eternal rather than futuristic."[20]

Many historical novels in today's China seem to attack Chairman Mao but reduce the danger of political criticism by putting their stories in a timeless context. They deploy avant-garde narrative techniques adapted from Latin American and Euro-American modernists to re-present the overthrow of the monarchy in the early 20th century, the ensuing chaos of revolution and war, the miseries of class warfare under Mao Zedong, and the social dislocations caused by China's industrialization and rise as a global power.[21] Recent science fiction in China reveals a surprisingly "un-Chinese" dystopian vision and critical view of human culture and ethics. Two dystopian syndromes appear and reappear: the stifling

---

17 Mao's short-lived appeal in 1957 to "let a hundred flowers bloom" may have referenced the 7th century CE Tang dynasty novel *Flowers in the Mirror* in which Empress Wu in defiance of the Flowers Fairy ordered all flowers to bloom at the same time. Like some free-wheeling writers in 1957, the flower-spirits were punished for acting too freely. Equally ironic, the Empress Wu—like Mao—let the power she acquired go to her head.

18 Mao claimed that the People's Communes established during the Great Leap contained "sprouts of communism." Their large common dining halls partially realized the utopian dreams of Thomas More and Edward Bellamy. The prospect of free food, however, did not encourage productivity.

19 On different forms of idealism in the eras of Mao Zedong, Deng Xiaoping, and Xidan Democracy Wallposters, see Mah Huang, *Intellectuals, Utopian Dreams, and the Question of Human Rights in China* (Newcastle upon Tyne, UK: 2022).

20 Jeffrey Kinkley, *Visions of Dystopia in China's New Historical Novels* (New York: Columbia University Press, 2014), pp. x-xiv.

21 Ibid.

of individualism under totalitarianism and terror under anarchy. The optimism towards science that underlay much of Chinese science fiction in the late 20th century almost vanished in the early 21st. Recent writing in China reflects deep anxiety about technological progress. The futures portrayed in these works are dark and uncertain. Even if a bright future appears occasionally, it arrives only after much suffering and a tortuous path.

Official Chinese policy discouraged science fiction in the 1980s. In the 1990s, however, the Party line changed. "What if memories could be transplanted?" This was the final question on China's national college entrance exam in 1999. This was the moment when Chen Quifan, later published in the West as Stanley Chen, says was the moment that modern Chinese science fiction was born. It inspired a new generation of sci-fi authors whose work became popular in China and around the world. Western sci-fi looks parochial next to the expansive ideas in Chinese. For example, engines the size of mountains stop the Earth from spinning in *The Wandering Earth* by Liu Cixin and the planet escapes the solar system as the sun explodes.[22]

Chinese sci-fi has become a global phenomenon thanks to a trilogy by Liu Cixin. Its first volume, *The Three-Body Problem*, was published in China in 2008 and in English in 2014. Fans of the series have included Barack Obama and Mark Zuckerberg. The story opens in 1967 during a Cultural Revolution "struggle session" in which an eminent physicist is beaten to death by four Red Guards. In the crowd, the man's teenage daughter watches him die. The daughter, also a physicist, is sent to a remote military base, where she makes a discovery that allows her to take revenge on the human race. In the third volume, *Death's End*, Liu annihilates not only civilizations but the physical dimensions in which they exist—an image that may reflect widespread fears in modern China. Some characters look forward to an apocalypse that ends "human tyranny" over nature. The anxiety Chen Quifan describes and its connection to the slow-motion apocalypse of the anthropocene era can be found in much modern Chinese sci-fi.

---

22 Will Dunn, "How Chinese novelists are reimagining science fiction, *New Statesman*, February 13, 2019 at https://www.newstatesman.com/culture/2019/02/chinese-science-fiction-dystopia-liu-cixin-triology

11. *WE* VERSUS US: TOTALITARIAN TRENDS IN RUSSIA, CHINA, AND THE USA

The Fat Years by Chan Koonchung (2009) lays out a trajectory like Zamyatin's *WE*. Published in Hong Kong and Taiwan but never in mainland China, the book is set in 2013. It describes how, responding to challenges to Communist Party legitimacy, the Beijing leadership takes up an "Action Plan for Ruling the Nation and Pacifying the World." Widespread upheaval and rumor mongering are suppressed by the People's Liberation Army and police. The restoration of order and ensuing crackdown cements in the public mind the necessity of Communist rule—reinforced by adding to public drinking water and bottled drinks a drug that induces the kind of contentment fabricated in *Brave New World*.

Rubbish is at the heart of Hao Jingfang's story "Folding Beijing." Its protagonist is one of millions of waste workers permitted to occupy the Chinese capital for eight hours on every other night. For the rest of the time they are sedated, their buildings fold themselves into the ground, and the city reorganizes itself for the rich. The only contact the waste workers have with those on the city's other side is by sorting their trash.

Another of the stories collected with "Folding Beijing" in the *Invisible Planets* anthology is "The City of Silence" by Ma Boyong.[23] It describes a brutal regime that monitors and controls everything its subjects write or say. The protagonist is a lonely computer programmer who watches as word after word is erased from the list of permitted speech.

The sci-fi film *Wandering Earth*, based on the 2000 short story by Liu Cixin, was a surprise box-office hit in China in 2019. It fused the science fiction of Liu Cixin with the *Wuxia* tradition of actor Wu Jing. Available on Netflix, *Wandering Earth* gained a global audience. A sequel appeared in 2023. One website criticized *Wandering Earth* for combining the cyber-nationalism of Wu Jing with those who, like Liu Cixin, put their faith in technology and

---

23 Ken Liu, ed. *Invisible Planets: Contemporary Chinese Science Fiction in Translation* (Amazon, 2016 and later editions). The collections include works by Chen Qiufan, Xia Jia, Ma Boyong, Hao Jingfang, Tang Fei, Cheng Jingbo, Liu Cixin, and Ken Liu. A concluding chapter by Cixin Liu and Ken Liu was in *Tor-Com*, October 20, 2014, at https://www.tor.com/2014/10/30/repost-the-worst-of-all-possible-universes-and-the-best-of-all-possible-earths-three-body-and-chinese-science-fiction/

educated elites. Combining these groups spawned the fantasy figure of a heroic, knight-errant serving the broad masses. But he is actually saving all humanity—if necessary, acting against the masses who are depicted as huddled underground or sacrificed *en route*. The Australian environmentalist John Hartley complains that using a fantasy hero to "save" humanity allows the movie to ignore the crisis from which humans must be saved. Instead, it naturalizes nationalistic populism and rule by technological elites.[24]

REALITY OVERTAKES FICTION IN CHINA

Xi's all-seeing Chinese state is even closer to Zamyatin's *WE* than Putin's. Cameras and computer monitoring are everywhere. All newspapers and media are under state control—now, even in Hong Kong. Any symbols that recall how the state has crushed any challenge (as at Tiananmen Square 1989) are being removed. The standard language used in Beijing is being imposed everywhere—not just where other languages such as Tibetan and Mongolian have been used for centuries but also where other forms of Chinese are traditional, as in Hong Kong.

While Orwell's *Nineteen Eighty-four* (in 1949) predicted technological totalitarianism in the future, for Ma Boyong this -ism is now—in everyday life. In today's China the app WeChat automatically blocks any message containing any banned word or phrase suggesting discontent with the regime, support for religious groups, or knowledge of the state's human rights abuses. Among 1.4 billion people, no one is allowed to mention Winnie the Pooh, to avoid offending President Xi (who, some say, looks like the cartoon character).

The stories being written in China feel significant because they are emerging from a real dystopia that becomes stranger and more futuristic by the day. In *Project Dove,* for example, drones that look and fly like birds are used for surveillance. But Project Dove is not fiction—it is an actual government project. The robots are so convincing that real pigeons flock with them. Hi-tech drones that

---

24 John Hartley, "Pathetic earthlings! Who can save you now?'" "Science fiction, planetary crisis and the globalisation of Chinese culture," *Global Media and China* (2021) 7, 1.

look and move like real birds have already flown over the restive Xinjiang region.[25]

Government-backed surveillance projects are deploying brain-reading technology to detect changes in emotional states in employees on the production line, the military, and at the helm of high-speed trains. Many factory workers, train drivers and soldiers must now wear devices that scan their brainwaves for signs of anger, depression, or loss of concentration. The devices are monitored by artificial intelligence programs that can recommend workers be retrained or reassigned if their emotions are not consistent with productivity goals.[26]

Domestic and foreign policies feed each other. China's rulers have always worried about their borderlands—home now to many of the China's fifty-five ethnic minorities. Xi has tried to settle the problem by redefining what it means to be Chinese. Xi's harshest controls have been imposed on Turkic-language speakers in Xinjiang. More than a million Uyghurs were locked into reeducation centers where they were pressured to learn Mandarin and forgo their culture and religion. Blanket electronic surveillance aims to spot changes in individual behavior that indicates potential extremist thoughts, like giving up smoking or drinking, or spending more time in prayer.

The government in Beijing now wants Han women to have three babies while Uyghurs should have none. Faced with an uncertain future, young couples in China are putting off having children: the number of births in 2021 was the lowest in modern history, barely exceeding the number of deaths.

---

25 Stephen Chen, "China takes surveillance to new heights with flock of robotic Doves, but do they come in peace?" *South China Morning Post*, June 24, 2018.

26 Stephen Chen, "'Forget the Facebook leak': China is mining data directly from workers' brains on an industrial scale," *South China Morning Post*, April 29, 2018. But here is a caveat: Over-the-skin brain scanning through EEG is still very limited in what it can detect, and the relationship between those signals and human emotion is not yet clear. Being able to gather enough information to somehow get a two-billion-yuan ($315 million) boost in profits—which is what State Grid Zhejiang Electric Power claims in the piece—is quite doubtful. Erin Winick, "With brain-scanning hats, China signals it has no interest in workers' privacy." *Technology Review*, April 30, 2018.

The putative great BENEFACTOR Xi Jinping is called "the chairman of everything." Xi personally signs off on corruption investigations, drafts urban blueprints and decides on ecological matters such as the management of lakes. He gives instructions on how to improve public toilets. On a macro scale, he attacks capitalist excesses and the housing bubble. He takes on the country's billionaire class and its movie stars.[27]

Meanwhile the Single State of Xi Jinping is trying to take over the South China Sea—even the waters adjoining the Philippines and other littoral states, while expanding China's reach into disputed border regions of India, Bhutan, and Nepal. China is mobilizing its huge financial and technological assets to build projects that increase Chinese influence from Djibouti to Serbia and from Sri Lanka to South America. If a Chinese spaceship reached another planet, it would surely carry Xi Jinping Thought to ETs there.

No country—including China—is all utopia or dystopia. Despite heavy odds, some Chinese struggle for human rights. Harassed by Chinese authorities, the artist Ai Weiwei linked his own predicament with the struggles of political prisoners elsewhere. Even when barred from foreign travel, he designed installations at the former federal prison on Alcatraz Island in San Francisco Bay honoring political prisoners under confinement around the world.[28]

No need to spell out the details, but we know that other Communist states such as North Korea, Cuba, and Vietnam also embody many of the practices anticipated in *WE*.

WE WARNS THE WEST

However strong the omens of *WE* in the United States, the country's individualism and political culture make it profoundly different from Russia and China. As Barack Obama put it: "Whether it's Whitman or Emerson or Ellison or Kerouac, there is this sense of

---

[27] Andrew Browne, "Xi's 'Great Rejuvenation' Runs into China's 'Great Exhaustion,'" *New Economy Newsletter*, Bloomberg, January 22, 2022, at https://www.bloomberg.com/news/newsletters/2022-01-22/china-s-great-exhaustion-may-confound-xi-jinping-new-economy-saturday

[28] Ai Weiwei, *1000 Years of Joys and Sorrows: A Memoir* (New York: Crown, 2021), p. 346.

self-invention and embrace of contradiction. I think it's in our DNA, from the start, because we come from everywhere, and we contain multitudes. And that has always been the promise of America, and what makes America sometimes so contentious." On the other hand, as Alexis de Tocqueville anticipated, much of common expectations and values—the glue holding Americans together—has frayed. 'Atomization and loneliness and the loss of community" have made American democracy vulnerable.[29]

America's utopian and dystopian writers have moved in many directions. Edward Bellamy's *Looking Backward* (1888) and Jack London's *Iron Heel* (1908) anticipated a sort of welfare state utopia in the United States. Ayn Rand, on the other hand, saw any restraints on free enterprise as evil. Her *Atlas Shrugged* (1957) tells how a few enlightened individuals fight the oppressive regulations of big government. A very different book, *The Turner Diaries* by William Luther Pierce (1978), became a handbook for America's racist right, extolling victory for white supremacists in a genocidal war.

Granted that the realization of *WE* in the United States is far more remote than in Russia or China, the danger signs grow stronger. Many Americans are ready and anxious to believe whatever they hear from certain politicians and their fellow-travelers in the media. Many Republicans and some Democrats agree that violence is warranted to make America great again. Guns sales climb constantly along with rates of homicide.

Republicans embrace the Hobbesian model of dystopia—an individualism that pushes us to a war of all against all, where life is nasty, brutish, and short. Many Americans are influenced by the murderous outcomes glorified in the *Hunger Games* trilogy by Suzanne Collins published by Scholastic Books [!!!] in 2008-2010.[30] The even more violent *Squid Game* became a popular favorite on Netflix. That "game" depicts a competition in which the winner can become rich while the loser is killed. As one critic argues, the Netflix series poses the question: "Can humans retain their souls and

---

29 Interview with Michiko Kakutani, "Self-Portrait of a Storyteller And a President," *The New York Times*, October 9, 2020.

30 By the time the film adaptation was released in 2012, the publisher reported over 26 million *Hunger Games* trilogy books in print.

decency and still compete in the ruthless and merciless environment that capitalism has created for itself?"[31]

Many of Donald Trump's aspiring Guardians have labored to change voting procedures so their great BENEFACTOR will triumph at the polls even if he loses the popular vote. Should foxes guard the henhouse? Nonpartisan election watchdogs are alarmed as election deniers seek state posts to certify votes.[32] Many of Trump's Guardians strive to exclude Blacks and other minorities from positions of power and influence.[33]

Seeing education as a wedge vote getter, some Guardians seek to deputize parents to police what goes on in the classroom. Many want laws to restrict what can be read or discussed regarding issues of gender, sexual orientation, and race. Some school committee members do not want pupils to learn the facts of racism and antisemitism.[34]

Besides the destructive influence of Big Lies and racism, media support for what futurist Herman Kahn called "hedonism" weakens the United States and other Western societies and makes it easier for totalitarians to dominate the world.

For Americans and other readers, Zamyatin and the other dystopians cited here seem to have forecast present realities more accurately than, say, Walt Whitman or Jack London.

The warnings embodied in *WE* may be more salient in the 2020s than when they were first posted in the 1920s. Reading Zamyatin's book should push people everywhere to ponder the forces shaping their futures, such as AI (Artificial Intelligence), and how to channel them in positive directions.

An open letter signed by more than 1,000 technology leaders and researchers warned: "*Advanced AI could represent a profound*

---

31 Kyung Hyun Kim, "Child's Play," *Foreign Policy* (Winter 2022): 80-83.
32 Front-page story *The New York Times*, January 31, 2022.
33 See essays in Julian E. Zelizer, ed., *The Presidency of Donald J. Trump: A First Historical Assessment* (Princeton NJ: Princeton University Press, 2022); also Clemens, *The Republican War on America*.
34 See Michael Cavna, "Art Spiegelman sees the new ban of his book '*Maus*' as a 'red alert," *The Washington Post*, January 28, 2022.

change in the history of life on Earth, and should be planned for and managed with commensurate care and resources. Unfortunately, this level of planning and management is not happening. Instead, AI labs are locked in an out-of-control race to develop and deploy ever more powerful digital minds that no one – not even their creators – can understand, predict, or reliably control."[35]

Some experts are concerned about near-term dangers, including the spread of disinformation and the risk that people would rely on these systems for inaccurate or harmful medical and emotional advice. But other critics are part of a vast and influential online community called rationalists or effective altruists, who believe that AI could eventually destroy humanity. For now, the letter says, there is no agreed plan to mitigate these risks.

The letter said that "AI research and development should be refocused on making today's powerful, state-of-the-art systems more accurate, safe, interpretable, transparent, robust, aligned, trustworthy and loyal." Developers should work with policymakers to create new AI governance systems and oversight bodies. The signatories called on governments to intervene in the development of AI systems if major players don't agree to an immediate public, verifiable pause.[36]

From what we know about Zamyatin, it seems likely he would have agreed with those who signed the letter.

---

35 Text dated 3/22/23 at https://futureoflife.org/open-letter/pause-giant-ai-experiments/

36 Calls to pause the development of artificial intelligence will not "solve the challenges" ahead, Microsoft co-founder Bill Gates told Reuters on April 4, 2023. For the pos and cons of AI, see Cade Metz, "What's the Future for A.I.? *The New York Tines*, 4/8/23: B7

CHAPTER 12
REQUIEM FOR RUSSIA? FOR YIN AND YANG?
A PERSONAL NOTE WITH ACKNOWLEDGMENTS

A professor in Russia agrees with most of this book's analysis but adds, in sorrow, that it amounts to a requiem for his homeland. The book, for me, is written in sorrow, I have been hoping and working for a more constructive relationship between Russia and the West ever since 1952 when, while I studied art in Vienna, Soviet troops, occupying parts of Austria, nearly shot me due to our mutual misunderstandings. Having decided to learn the Russian language, I experienced more misunderstandings as I translated for six Soviet journalists in 1958 while they toured the United States meeting students, factory workers, professors, and political figures such as Eleanor Roosevelt and Adlai Stevenson. That autumn I took part in the first official exchange of U.S. and Soviet graduate students. Researching Lenin's disarmament policies at Moscow State University, mutual misunderstandings multiplied. Political repression was so heavy that several other U.S. students and I agreed that *if*—as historians—we had to choose between being "Red or dead," we would prefer being "dead." Still, negative feelings dissipated when I went every week to the theatre, skied in the countryside, and enjoyed the company of Soviet friends—warm to and curious about Americans. Still, one never knew whom one could trust.

My interests in China and North Korea also date from that year at Moscow State University. In 1958, there were still many Chinese students in Russia. Every morning groups of six to ten Chinese would form circles and do graceful exercises. Preparing for a possible war over Taiwan, they also practiced throwing wooden hand grenades and attended long political indoctrination meetings. I tried to start a conversation with one Chinese student. But he refused to talk with an American until the Taiwan problem was resolved. Applying my lifelong hobby, I performed three American Indian dances (with bells and feathers) for an assembly honoring the founding of Communist China, but no one said thanks. As for the North Koreans, they forced the university to remove the Christmas tree set up by the Americans—a vestige of their un-Marxist superstitions.

I completed my case study of Soviet disarmament policy at Stanford's Hoover Institution and Columbia University in 1960–1961 and went on to study other facets of Soviet affairs and Russian life. I moved from California to Massachusetts in 1963 to work as the principal researcher on a government contract to study Soviet interests in arms control. In 1966, the M.I.T. Press published our *Khrushchev and the Arms Race*. My work at the M.I.T. Center for International Studies benefited greatly from the guidance and examples of professors Lincoln P. Bloomfield and William E. Griffith.

In the 1960s, Mao Zedong's China vehemently criticized the Soviet Union, giving me and other students of Communist affairs a serious reason to read Chinese as well as Soviet materials. My book *The Arms Race and Sino-Soviet Relations* appeared in 1968.

As a sophomore in college, I had observed up close in Berlin the East German uprising crushed by Soviet tanks in 1953. In 1968 I went to Czechoslovakia to watch efforts to construct "Socialism with a Human Face." Soviet tanks again ended hopes for reform, and I escaped via Poland. I then followed the Red Flag around the world—from Egypt to China and Korea to Latin America, noting how some leaders and publics were attracted to and/or repelled by what the Soviet Union had to offer. With Boston University students I toured the USSR and neighboring countries several times. In 1989, we could buy gorgeous fur hats and other bits of army uniforms from Soviet officers returned from Afghanistan. In 1990, I attended in Kazakhstan the Nevada-Palatinsk conference of peace activists from as far away as Nevada and French Polynesia seeking to reveal and halt the damage to human lives and the environment from nuclear testing by the Big Five nuclear-weapons states. Many Kazakhs resented the harm done to their lives and land by Soviet nuclear tests and other abuses.

12. Requiem for Russia? For Yin and Yang?

The Mikhail Gorbachev regime clearly saw the need for deep reforms in Soviet policies but who could know the best way to proceed? In 1990 I wrote: *Can Russia Change? The USSR Confronts Global Interdependence*. No one knew the answer. Gorbachev was nearly ousted in a hard-liners' coup in August 1991. In December, the Soviet empire disappeared.

From contacts at Moscow University and a visit to Latvia in 1959, I was deeply aware of resentments in the Baltic republics toward Soviet occupation since the 1940s. Having visited the region several times as Gorbachev tolerated serious reforms, I wrote *Baltic Independence and Russian Empire* in 1991. The nearly peaceful emergence of Estonia, Latvia, and Lithuania and their integration with the rest of Europe are among the most positive developments of recent decades. I tracked some of this process in my follow-on book *The Baltic Transformed* (2021). Already in the early 1990s, as noted here in chapter 2, Russian strategists were plotting to assist "compatriots [*sootechestveniki*]"—Russians in the Baltic and elsewhere in the "near-abroad."

The point of this historical tour is to note how at different times and places I encountered the brutal face of Soviet power. When the USSR shrank into the Russian Federation in 1991–1992, the Cold War appeared to end. Hopes arose that none of the Big Five would again threaten or employ military force. Most of the former Soviet citizens I met in turn-of-the-century Boston were highly educated, Jewish professionals, who moved to the United States when barriers fell. Standing on the shores of Thoreau's Walden Pond, with several of them I exchanged a few remembered verses from Pushkin's *Eugene Onegin*. Meanwhile, Russian forces stayed on in Moldova, pounded the Chechen independence movement, and occupied parts of Georgia and Ukraine.

The most inspiring individual influencing my work has been Andrei D. Sakharov— probably the greatest Russian of all time. His book, *Progress, Coexistence & Intellectual Freedom*, was smuggled from the Soviet Union to New York and published by W.W. Norton, with notes by Harrison E. Salisbury in January 1968. Electrified by his views, I made photocopies of *The New York Times* book reprint and took them that summer to the Socialism-with-a-Human-Face reformers in Prague. They already knew the book's main ideas but were glad to have the text. It turned out that the Brezhnev regime in Moscow did not like the ideas and suppressed the Czechoslovak reformers with Warsaw Pact armies.

Two years later I was lecturing for the U.S. Information Agency in Korea. U.S. diplomats wondered if there was any way to ameliorate tensions between North and South Korea. I suggested we could point out that there exist good as well as evil people in the Communist Soviet Union. This could also be the case in North Korea. So I drafted an article "Sakharov: A Man for Our Times' which the agency published in Korean in its journal *Non Dan* (November-December 1970), which—revised and expanded—appeared in *Bulletin of the Atomic Scientists* (December 1971). Thinking the world needed to know more about Sakharov and to support and honor his work, I wrote "Sakharov: Why He Deserves the Nobel Peace Prize," *Christian Science Monitor* (September 26, 1973) and, a decade after his death, "Sakharov's Legacy, *Christian Science Monitor* (December 19, 1990).

In 1989, Sakharov agreed to meet me at the front door of his apartment building in Moscow, but my driver, friend of a friend, ran out of gas on a rainy night. Sakharov died later that year, but his wife Elena Bonner and daughter managed to take a large collection of his papers from Moscow to form a Sakharov Archive at Brandeis University, later moved to Harvard's Houghton Library.

Sakharov worked both for human rights and peace against brutal dictators. This duality is the fundamental question of this book, as in my *North Korea and The World: Human Rights, Arms Control, and Strategies for Negotiation* (2016).

A second major influence on my work was Jerome B. Wiesner, then Dean of Science and later President of M.I.T., whom President Lyndon B. Johnson asked to head a Citizens Committee on Arms Control and Disarmament for International Cooperation Year 1965. As Executive Secretary for the Committee, I met with Wiesner, the mathematician Jeremy Stone and economist Carl Kaysen on Saturday mornings to draft recommendations that we later proposed to the citizens committee of scientists and retired diplomats, which

12. Requiem for Russia? For Yin and Yang?

I then put into final form for the White House. Defense Secretary Robert McNamara, along with several major newspapers, liked our suggestion for a three-year moratorium on construction of anti-ballistic missile defenses.

What impressed me about Wiesner was his consistent application of scientific knowledge to constructive ends along with his persistent kindness and patience with us lesser mortals. There was also his wide curiosity and sense of humor. Finding ourselves in the same Moscow hotel one evening, Jerry was glad to take in some avant-garde theatre. Escorted by the KGB, Wiesner laughed as we ducked tails by quickly changing trains.

A third major influence was Hermann F. Eilts, U.S. Ambassador to Egypt and an architect of the Camp David accords. Angry that President Jimmy Carter did so little for Palestinians at Camp David, he resigned from the Foreign Service and became Chair of International Relations and, later, of Political Science at Boston University. Several times he took me to lunch and reviewed every page of whatever I was writing.

My work-study assistant at Boston University, Ronald H. Linden went on to chair Russian and European Studies at the University of Pittsburgh. He and I have reviewed each other's work—including this one—for years.

Czech-born University Professor Igor Lukes at Boston University often discussed with me Eastern Europe as well as USSR.

Alexander Motyl, Professor of Political Science at Rutgers University, has both inspired and influenced my writings on the Baltic republics and Ukraine. Professor Emeritus Mel Gurtov at Portland State University has shown me how to balance hopes and ideals against China's reality. Stuart A. Kauffman, Emeritus at the Santa Fe Institute, has been my close friend, partner in mountaineering, and science guru since 1955, when he was a junior in high school.

Harvard's Davis Center for Russian and Eurasian Studies and Belfer Center for Science and International Affairs have provided library resources, ideas, and inspiration for my work. The insights of professors Joseph Nye and Graham Allison have stayed with me over decades.

I have also built on a knowledge base developed at the Kennan Institute in Washington, 1976-77, headed then by S. Frederick Starr who—half a century later--is still a model of how to combine the study of Russia with analysis of its Eurasian context.

Thanks too to the editors of several periodicals where portions of this book first appeared—David Plott at *Global Asia*, Carla Freeman at *Asian Perspective*, Tamer Balci and Chris Miller at *NETSOL,* Francis Harris at *European Edge*, Sandra Tolliver at *The Hill*, and several editors at *National Interest.* Chris Miller helped with ideas as well as editing.

Social psychologist Stephen Advocate, better read than I or most of my professor friends, has made trenchant remarks about all my work. A Ukrainian-Russian-émigré, Igor Burdenko, inventor of the Burdenko Method, has helped keep my typing fingers and mind limber. Dr. Nikolai Popov, whom I first met skiing at Moscow State University in 1958, helps me keep up-to-date on Russia and see things in perspective. My wife Ali Clemens since 1982 has helped frame and balance my thinking and assisted with multiple computer issues, health, and household issues. Our daughter Anna Sophia (born in China) provides another reason to keep plugging away, as do my other daughter Lani and her offspring in California.

Thanks to Michael Joachim for the book cover. Other art work is by street artist Banksy, *Zavtra*, Alexander J. Motyl, and myself.

Most of this personal note concerns Russia. What about China? Having traveled widely in Asia, my Hong Kong-born wife and I also have also had high hopes for the West and China. In 1982, for example, Chinese workers making a modern road in Nepal invited us to share a hot meal with them. Like so much in life, their actions could be seen as positive or bad—as development assistance or imperial scheming. A year later my wife and I studied tai-chi and watercolor painting techniques in Taiwan and—sandwiched between lectures—climbed the 13,000-foot Ushan (or Jade) Mountain with a "Wandervogel" Club of business people and academics. Back in Boston we have contemplated the 13th century painted statue of Guanyin, Bodhisattva of compassion, in the Museum of Fine Arts.

12. Requiem for Russia? For Yin and Yang?

The first day of November 2013 was blustery in Lexington, Massachusetts. Standing by a silvery pond smaller than Walden, but one that 19th century American thinker Henry David Thoreau might admire, I think—as he often did—what Asia contributes to humanity and to our sense of the natural world from which we have evolved.

I think also of the Korean film released in 2003, *Spring, Summer, Fall, Winter ... and Spring*. The film documents all that happens at a pond nestled in a forest. Thinking of the monk who lived by that pond, while standing next to my own, I begin the simplified *tai-chi ch'uan* form that I learned from the son of a former Kuomintang general, Chungliang Al Huang, as well as from a banker in Taiwan. Each move symbolizes one of the four elements. A push forward

12. Requiem for Russia? For Yin and Yang?

means "Fire!" Rising arms scoop from and pour an imaginary stream over my head—"Water!" A sweep sideways and around recalls "Air!" Scooping with each hand the riches of "Earth!" I take in gorgeous trees, spangled in autumn reds and yellows, and the blue-gray, quite solid rocks still covered with moss that surround the pond. Finally, both hands stretch skyward to embrace the "tiger" and tumult of our world before returning to the "mountain" or *dantian* energy center. This routine proceeds in each of the four directions and then, to balance the flow, repeats the sequence but starting from the other foot.

For me all this underscores the miracle of tai-chi movement when—a strong wind blowing, two pairs of ducks cruising the shimmering waters, the trees dropping their leaves until another season arrives—I feel merged with all of nature and its rhythms.

We all owe a great deal to the forces that brought us fire, water, air, and the riches of our planet. We owe a debt to our ancestors who, though they often overused the earth's resources, still left us a fabulous heritage. Do we not then owe something also to our children and all those who come after them? Before the 21st century, Europeans and Americans produced most of the dirt that pollutes our air and water, along with most of the carbon that heats our climate. Their impact is now being surpassed by Chinese and Indians.

Should we each retreat to a niche, like my nearby pond, where we can enjoy what exists before it is too late? This may not be a practical or ethical strategy. Such ponds are hard to find. I am alone here most of the year, but summer is a different story. The pond is threatened by erosion, by fishermen's tangled lines and hooks, by beer cans and cigarette butts. The sound of birds and children's laughter must sometimes compete with cell phones and big box vibes.

Perhaps the east and west winds can enhance each other. Two Chinese gentlemen stroll by the pond and give me a thumbs up after I emerge from a dip in the freezing November waters. Neither knows much English, but they tell me that their children, now professors at M.I.T., live nearby. One takes photos of the pond with loving attention. I hope he will take back to China memories and images of what beauty remains in a Boston suburb.

The world views of Henry Thoreau, Ralph Waldo Emerson, and other Transcendentalists were enriched by Asia. Reversing the flow, Thoreau's ideas on nonviolent action reached Tolstoy, who passed them on to Gandhi, from whom they shot back to Martin Luther King, who passed them on to Solidarity in Poland, whence they rebounded to the "color" revolutions of Ukraine, Kyrgyzstan, Serbia, and Iran.

The West and East winds may still energize each other.

ABOUT THE AUTHOR

WALTER CLEMENS has analyzed the United States and the world for over 50 years. He has taught at Iolani School, the University of California, M.I.T., Salzburg Seminar in American Studies, University of the West Indies, and Boston University, where he is Emeritus Professor of Political Science. Since 1963 he has been Associate, Harvard University Davis Center for Russian and Eurasian Studies. Supported by the Ford Foundation, Rockefeller Foundation, the Fulbright Program, and the U.S. Information Agency, he has lectured on world affairs across the United States, Asia, Europe, Latin America, North Africa, and the Soviet Union. He has conducted research at the University of Vienna, Moscow State University, Hoover Institution, UCLA, and the Wilson Center. Ph.D. and M.A, Columbia University; A, B., *Magna Cum Laude,* Notre Dame University.

Raised in Cincinnati, Clemens now lives near Boston with his wife, daughter, and Shi-Tzu Eddie, featured in two paintings in chapter 12. He has been Book Review Editor, *Asian Perspective* and a regular contributor to *Global Asia* and *New York Journal of Books.* His essays have been published in *The New York Times, The Wall Street Journal, The Washington Post, Financial Times, Christian Science Monitor, Europe's Edge, The Hill, The Times* (London), *Der Standard* (Vienna), and *Sovetskaya Estoniya* (Tallinn).

For details, see https://en.wikipedia.org/wiki/Walter_Clemens and http://www.bu.edu/polisci/people/faculty/clemens/

For his paintings, see waltclemens.art.

ALSO BY THE AUTHOR

The Republican War on America: Dangers of Trump and Trumpism

North Korea and the World: Human Rights, Arms Control, and Strategies for Negotiation

Complexity Science and World Affairs, Foreword, Stuart A. Kauffman.

Ambushed! A Cartoon History of the George W. Bush Administration, with Jim Morin.

Dynamics of International Relations: Conflict and Mutual Gain in an Era of Global Interdependence

Bushed! What Passionate Conservatives Have Done to America and the World, with Jim Morin.

National Security and U.S.-Soviet Relations

The Baltic Transformed: Complexity Theory and European Security, Foreword, Jack F. Matlock, Jr.

America and the World, 1898-2025: Achievements, Failures, Alternative Futures

Baltic Independence and Russian Empire

Can Russia Change?

The USSR and Global Interdependence

The Superpowers and Arms Control

Die Tschechoslowakei unter Husak

The Arms Race and Sino-Soviet Relations

Outer Space and Arms Control

Co-author, *Khrushchev and the Arms Race*

Co-author and editor, *World Perspectives on International Politics*

Co-author and editor, *Toward a Strategy of Peace*, Foreword, Robert F. Kennedy.

Soviet Disarmament Policy, 1917-1963: An Annotated Bibliography of Soviet and Western Sources

INDEX

ABM Treaty, 172
Adenauer, Konrad, 122
Advocate, Stephen, 222
Afghanistan, 115, 169, 183, 218; Soviets invading, 53, 157; World Happiness Index, 95
AI (Artificial Intelligence), 214–15
Ai Weiwei, 212
Aleksandr II, 83–84n25, 137
Aleksandr III, 137
Alexievich, Svetlana, 19, 22, 22n26
Algeria, 93
Allison, Graham, 155, 165, 221
All-Russian Center for Public Opinion Research, 91
American Psychopath (Ellis), 203
Andreev, E.M., 81n21
"Anti-Cockroach Revolution," 202
antisemitism, 76. *See also* Jews/Jewish
Antonov, Anatoly, 46
Aquinas, Thomas, 64
Aristide, Jean-Bertrand, 100
Armageddon, ix
Arms Race and Sino-Soviet Relations, The (Clemens), 218

Army of the Fatherland,1939-1960, 80
art and artists, 71–73
Atlas Shrugged (Rand), 202, 213
Australia, 45, 46, 130, 141, 161; anti-Muslim hatred in, 44
avant-garde narrative techniques, 207
Az i Ya (Suleimenov), 14, 14n9
Azov Battalion, 45–46

Babbitt, Natalie, 204
Babi Yar: A Document in the Form of a Novel (Kuznetsov), 74
Babi Yar (Yevtushenko), 74, 75–76
Baburova, Anastasia, 44
Balagov, Kantemir, 67
Balanchine, George, 68
Balci, Tamer, 222
Ballets Russes, 68–69
Baltic Independence and Russian Empire (Clemens), 219
Baltic Transformed, The (Clemens), 219
Bank of Russia, 113
Banksy (street artist), 86–87, 109–10, 222

Bartholomew, Ecumenical Patriarch of Constantinople, 28

Baryshnikov, Mikhail, 69, 198

"Base, The," 45

Bashkortostan, 90

Bazhan, Mykota, 74

Beckles, Hilary, 100

Belarus, 20, 88, 93; Belovezha Accords, 24; Corruption Perceptions Index, 92; as fragile state, 94; World Happiness Index, 95

Bellamy, Edward, 207n18, 213

Belovezha Accords, 24

Belt and Road Initiative, 140, 149, 155, 159

Bethune, Norman, 125

Bhutan, 93, 212

Bialiatski, Ales, 87, 88

Biden, Joe, 46–47, 165, 174

Big Lie, 142

Biriukova, Anna, 91–92

blacks in United States: reparations for, 101, 101n5

Blanton, Tom, 32–33

Blinken, Anthony, 142, 164

Bloody Sunday of 1905, 134

Bloomfield, Lincoln P., 218

Bolsheviks, 134–35

Bonner, Yelena, 73

BORN (terrorist group), 44

brain drain, 66–70

brain-reading technology, 211

brainwashing, xi

Brandt, Willy, 122

Brenner, Ian, 139

Brezhnev, Leonid, 22, 23, 72, 94, 157, 172, 176, 180, 220

Brodsky, Josef, 73

Brzezinski, Zbigniew, 147, 157

Budapest Memorandum of 1994, 169, 176–77

Bulletin of the Atomic Scientists, 220

Burdenko, Igor, 222

Bush, George H.W., 147

Bush, George W., 180

Cai Xia, 174

Can Russia Change? The USSR Confronts Global Interdependence (Clemens), 219

Carter, Jimmy, 157, 157n13

Catherine the Great, 17

Chan Koonchung, 209

Charles XII, 16

Chechen Wars, 35, 38–40

Chechnya, xiii

Chemezov, Sergei, 91

Chen Quifan, 208

Chernobyl disaster, 22
Chiang Ching-kuo, 185
Chiang Kai-shek, 143, 156
China, 11; atomic bomb test, 156; consultative democracy, 143–44; Corruption Perceptions Index, 93; Covid lockdown, 144; cultural and physical genocide, 122–23, 127–29; Cultural Revolution, 125, 127, 142, 206, 207, 208; ethnic minorities, 145, 148; events and death tolls, 126–27; as fragile state, 94; Freedom House reports on, 94; Global Innovation Index, 94; Great Leap Forward, 126, 142, 207, 207n18; Human Development Index, 93–94; human rights abuse/violations, 122–29, 212; losses in World War II, 82n22; Mandate from Heaven, 123; military coup, 145; Nobel prizes, 96; nuclear development, 156; poverty in, 93; public discontent, 95–96; real dystopia, 210–12; reparations due, 126–29; Russia and, 147–61; subverting human rights system, 129–30; surveillance projects, 211; Tiananmen Square crackdown/massacre, 124, 125, 127, 143, 157–58, 210; Ukraine as trade partner of, 154–55; United States and, 155–65, 172–73, 174–75; utopia and dystopia, 205–12; war on law, 123–24; World Happiness Index, 95

Chinese Academy of Social Sciences (CASS), 7

Chinese Society of International Law, 163

Christian Science Monitor, 220

Christopher, Warren, 35–37

Chubarov, Refat, 29

Chukovsky, Kornei, 201

Chungliang Al Huang, 224

Cirillo, Lanfranco, 114

"City of Silence, The" (Ma Boyong), 209

civilizations, ix, 10–14, 65–66

Civilization: The West and the Rest (Ferguson), 10

civilizational relativism, 130, 131

civil society, 87–88, 184

Clemens, Ali, 220

Clinton, Bill, 34, 35, 36, 37, 39, 40, 135, 164

Coats, Dan, 148

collectivism, 51–52

collectivization: China, 126; Soviet Union, 20, 89

Collins, James, 36, 37

Collins, Suzanne, 213

color revolutions, 26

commerce, 182–83

Commonwealth of Independent States (CIS), 24
Communist-Nationalist civil war of China, 127
Communist Party of China, 93–94
compatriots doctrine and laws, 40–41
complexity science and bibliography, 12n7, 181n13
Connally, John B., Jr., 157n13
consultative democracy, 143–44
Corruption Perceptions Index of Transparency International, 92–93
Cossacks, 10, 16–17, 20
Council of Europe, 84
Covid-19, 124, 126, 137
Crimea, 17n14, 20; Russian annexation/mobilization, 26, 29, 203; Tatars, 12, 16, 20, 29–30, 43, 79, 83, 105; as a tool in Kremlin power struggles, 21
Cuba: Communist rule/dictatorship, 94, 95, 123, 145; Corruption Perceptions Index, 93; one-party system, 145; UN resolution and, 112, 169, 170, 171
cultural identity, 10–11
Cultural Revolution, 125, 127, 142, 206, 207, 208
cultural thaw, 71–72
Cumans, 13–14

Currie, Kelley E., 129
Cyberspace Administration of China, 93–94
Czechoslovakia, 2, 53, 173, 176, 183, 218, 220
Czech Republic, 33, 38

Dagestan, 90, 161
Death's End (Liu Cixin), 208
DeMille, Cecil B., 202
democracy/democratic societies, 185–86
Deng Xiaoping, 143, 165; "24-Character Strategy," 158; United States and, 158
Denmark, 93
Diaghilev, Sergei, 68–69
Donbass, Russian control/occupation of, 26, 27, 29, 65, 80, 138, 175
"Don't Shoot" (song), 67
Dostoyevsky, Fyodor 64
Dudayev, Dzhokhar, 35
Dugin, Aleksandr, 50–51
Dugina, Darya, 50
Dulyan, Hamlet, 192
Duterte, Rodrigo, 163, 164
Dzhelyal, Nariman, 30

East Germany, xiii, 9, 31, 100, 120, 183

"Eight Controversial and Forbidden Books Everyone Should Read, The," 201
Eilts, Hermann, 219
Ellis, Brett Easton, 203
escalation, xi
Esenin, Sergei, 70
Essays [Traktaty] on War and Peace (Malinovsky), 82–83
Estonia, 31, 32, 39, 42, 61, 145; peaceful emergence of, 219; Russian speakers, 41; Western protection from Russia, 33
Eta ya (Limonov), 203
Europe: Russia as part of, 82–85
European Commission, 113
European Recovery Plan. *See* Marshall Plan
European Union (EU), 81, 82
Evangelista, Matthew, 38–39
Evanston, Illinois, 101n5

fake news, 67
The Fat Years (Chan Koonchung), 209
Ferguson, Niall, 10
Finland: Corruption Perceptions Index, 93; as fragile state, 94; NATO and, 46, 47; World Happiness Index, 95
Flowers in the Mirror, 207n17
"Folding Beijing" (Hao Jingfang), 209

Foreign Affairs, 174
foreign aid, 114
foreign companies, exodus from Russia: public opinion on, 90–91
Fountainhead, The (Rand), 202
fragile state, 94
Freedom House reports, 94
Freeman, Carla, 222
Fumio Kishida, 141

Gao Yusheng, 5–7
Gazprom, 116
genocide, 77, 102, 122–23, 127–31
Genocide Convention, 102n6, 128
"geopolitical catastrophe," xi
Georgia, xiii; NATO and, 9, 46; Rose Revolution of, 26; Russia's attacks on, 53, 80, 183, 219
Gerasimov, Valery, 150
Gergiev, Valery, 70
Germany, 68; being democratic, 185; losses in World War II, 82n22; post-World War II reconstruction, 111; wartime leaders, 176
Gessen, Masha, 77
Ginsburg, Ruth Bader, 203
Giver, The (Lowry), 204

Global Innovation Index, 94, 119
Gogol, Nikolai, 17, 19
gold, 119
Gorbachev, Mikhail, 22, 23, 24, 38, 135, 145, 181, 191, 202, 219; arms accords, 172; Bush and, 147, 172; China and, 157, 158; funeral and burial, 49–50n2; NATO expansion, 32–33; Nobel peace prize, 96; Prokhanov denouncing *perestroika* campaign, 55; Reagan and, 157, 172; universal values and, 49, 51
GQ Rossiia, 191, 201–5
Great Britain, 11, 100; third-party arbitration of disputes, 183
Great Leap Forward, 126, 142, 207, 207n18
Griffith, William E., 218
GRIT (Graduated Reciprocation in Tension-Reduction), 172–73
Grozny, Ivan, 60
Guardia di Finanza of Italy, 114
Guanyin, 222–23
Guterres, António, 169

Han Chinese, 99, 122–23, 126–29, 145, 148, 211
Hansas, 184n17
Hao Jingfang, 209
Harriman, W. Averell, 172

Harris, Francis. 222
Harrison, Mark, 81, 81n21
Hartley, John, 210
Harvard University, Belfer Center and Davis Center, 219
Helsinki Accords, 176
Herero people, 102
Hickel, Jason, 101
His Butler's Story (Limonov), 203
Hitler, Adolf, 121, 122, 175–76
Hobbesian dystopia, 213
Hong Kong, 18, 210
House of Rurik, 13
Hu Jintao, xv
Human Development Index (HDI) of United Nations, 93–94, 131, 186, 186n19
human rights, 212
Hunger Games (Collins), 213
Huntington, Samuel, 10
Hussein, Saddam, 102

Igor (Prince), 13–14, 14n9
India, 141, 180n12
Indo-China War, 157
Indonesia, 162
Instagram, 86
Institute of Social Research, 52
International Claims and Reparations Project, 113

International Criminal Court, 54, 121
Iran, 3, 116, 150, 169, 170, 171, 172; nuclear accord, 180; Western sanctions against, 152–53, 180
Iraq's reparations to Kuwait, 102–3, 112
Iron Heel (London), 213
Islam, 57
Islamist terrorism, 39
Ivan III, 136
Ivashov, Leonid Grigoryevich, 1–6
Ivlev, Igor, 78–80, 81n21

Japan: being democratic, 185; losses in World War II, 82n22; Pacific war, 176; wartime leaders, 176
Jews/Jewish, 71–77; Stalin's purge of, 76
Jiang Yanyong, 124–26
Jiang Zemin, 124
Johnson, Boris, 56
Johnson, Lyndon B., 220
Jordan, 46

Kahn, Herman, 214
Kalinkin, Zhenya, 67
Kant, Immanuel, 181–84, 182nn15–16, 184n17

Kapitsa, Petr, 56
Kara-Mursa, Vladimir, 37–38
Kasyan, Daria, 67
Kauffman, Stuart A., 219
Kaysen, Carl, 220–21
Kazakhstan, 41, 61, 169, 205; Budapest Memorandum, 177; Russian speakers, 41; trade with Russia, 117
Kellogg-Briand Peace Pact, 169, 176
Kennan, George F., 33
Kennedy, John F. (JFK), 172, 172n3, 181
KGB, 73
Khasbulatov, Ruslan, 34, 135
Khodaryenok, Mikhail, 6
Khodorkovsky, Mikhail, 137
Khrushchev, Nikita, 20–21, 133, 137, 141, 147, 160, 172, 177; cultural thaw, 71–72; hare-brained policies, 144, 156; Helsinki and, 19n19; on jazz, 71; Mao and, 156; Neizvestny and, 72; power struggles, 20–21; Ukraine and, 20, 21–22, 23
Khrushcheva, Nina, 21–22
Khrushchev and the Arms Race (Bloomfield, Clemens, and Griffith), 218
Khrzhanovsky, Ilya, 77
Kim Il Sung, 137, 156
Kim Jong Un, 173, 174

Kissinger, Henry, 147, 157, 172
Kochubey, Viktor, 83
Kolmanovsky, Ilya, 67, 68
Komi, 90
Kommersant', 52, 53, 56
Koneva, Elena, 91–92
Korean War, 127
Kozyrev, Andrei, 32, 36, 37
Kramer, Mark. "NATO Enlargement," 32n1
Kropotkin, Petr, 181
Krupskaya, Nadezhda, 201
Kupchan, Charles, 139
Kuwait, Iraq's reparations to, 102–3, 112
Kuwait Petroleum Corporation (KPC), 103
Kuznetsov, Anatoly, 71, 74, 198n5
Kuznetsov, Eduard, 73
Kyiv, xii, 13; Mongol invaders, 15; Rus', 14, 15; Viking rule, 14–15; Volodymyr the Great, 14. *See also* Ukraine
Kyslytsya, Sergiy, 112

Latvia, 34, 42, 56, 61, 145; peaceful emergence of, 219; Russian speakers in, 41
Lay of Igor's Host, The, 14, 14n9
League of Nation, 176
Lebanon, 171; World Happiness Index, 95
Lee Teng-hui, 185
Le Guin, Ursula K., 197
Leontiev, Konstantin, 62
Lenin, Vladimir, xv
Leopold II, 127
Liang Qichao, 142–43
liberal peace, xiv, 181–86
Limonov, Eduard, 203
Lin Biao, 145
Linden, Ronald, 141, 219
Lithuania, 16, 16n13, 17, 61, 145, 202; losses in World War II, 82n22; peaceful emergence, 219
Litvinov, Maksim, 76, 176; Litvinov Protocol, 169, 176
Liu Cixin, 205, 209–10
Li Wenliang, 126
Li Yuan, 93–94
Lolita (Nabokov), 202–3
London, Jack, 213
Looking Backward (Bellamy), 213
Lowry, Lois, 204
Lukashenko, Aleksandr, 201, 202'
Lukes, Igor, 219
Luo Guanzhong, 159
Luther, Martin, 64
Luzhkov, Yuri, 36

Lvova-Belova, Maria, 121
Lyceum, 83

Ma Boyong, 209, 210
Macron, Emmanuel, xii, 173
Malenkov, Georgi, 21
Mali, 92
Malinovsky, Vasyli, 82–83, 83n3, 84
Mandate from Heaven, 123
Mao Zedong, xiii, 93, 172, 207, 207nn17–18; "Anti- Rightist" campaign, 143; coup planned against, 145; Khrushchev and, 156; Stalin and, 156
Marcos, Ferdinand, Jr., 164–65
Markelov, Stanislav, 44
Marshall, George C., 114
Marshall Plan, 114–15
Maskhadov, Aslan, 40
Matsuev, Denis, 70
Mattis, James, 155, 177
Matyushin, Aleksandr, 44
Mayakovsky, Vladimir, 70
May Fourth Movement (1919), 143
Mayor's Mailbox, 143–44
Mazepa, Ivan, 16, 23, 31
McFaul, Michael, 46
McNamara, Robert, 221
Medinsky, Vladimir, 80–81, 81n20
Megalē Rosiia, 15
Mephistopheles, 160
Meta, 86
Mikrā Rosiia, 15
military industrial complex, 59, 91
military intervention, 138–39
military values, 53–54
Miller, Chris, 222
Minsk Agreements, 26–27
Modi, Narendra Das, 180n12
Moldova, xiii
Mongolia/Mongolians, xiii, 15, 127, 131, 148, 150, 169, 210
Monnet, Jean, 114
Monster Cockroach, The (Chukovsky), 201–2
moral values. *See* spiritual and moral values
More, Thomas, 119, 207n18
Motyl, Alexander, xii, xiii, 105, 219
Mo Yan, 205
Muratov, Dmitry, x, xi
Muscovy, 10, 15–16, 136. *See also* Russia
Mussolini, Benito, 122
mutiny, xv

Nabokov, Vladimir, 202–3

Nadal, Rafael, 205
Nama people, 102
Namibia: genocide in, 102; Germany's reparations to, 102
Narodnaya Volya, 137
Narodniki, 136–37, 142
National Anti-Corruption Strategy of Ukraine, 93
National Bolshevik Party, 203
National Research University Higher School of Economics of Russia, 103
National Security Strategy: Russia, 49, 51; Ukraine, 46
National Wealth Fund (NWF) of Russia, 119
Native Americans, 127
NATO, 113–14; expansion, 31–33; Georgia and, 9, 46; Indo-Pacific as security interest of, 141; Ukraine and, 46–47
Navalny, Aleksei, 43–44, 91–92
Nazzaro, Rinaldo, 45
near abroad, 40–41
Neizvestny, Ernst, 72
Nepal, 212, 222
Nesselrode, Karl, 63
Nevskii, Aleksandr, 15
New York Times, The, 4–5, 94, 219
Nezavisimaya Gazeta, x
Nicholas I, 63, 83, 83–84n25

Nie Rong Zhen, 156
nihilism, 64
Nineteen Eighty-Four (Orwell), 191, 197, 198, 210
Nixon, Richard, 147, 156–57, 172
Nobel laureates, x, 178–81; harassment of, 87–88
Nobel prizes, distribution of, 96
nonconformists in Russia, 70–73
North Korea, 93, 156, 184; Corruption Perceptions Index, 92; invading South Korea in 1950, 168n1
Norway, 93
Novaya Gazeta, 51–52
nuclear reactors, 116
nuclear weapons, 37, 89, 177
Nureyev, Rudolf, 68, 69
Nye, Joseph, 221

Obama, Barack, 180, 212–13
Objectivism, 202
Office of the High Commissioner for Human Rights (OHCHR), 129
oil and gas, 117–18, 151, 159
On Perpetual Peace (Kant), xiv, 181–86
Orange Revolution, 25–26
Orthodox Christians/Christianity, 10, 28; Ukrainian

population of, 28
Orwell, George, 191
Osgood, Charles, 172
Osipova, Natalya, 69, 198
Overreach, xv
Overreach: How China Derailed Its Peaceful Rise (Shirk, Susan.), xvn9
Oxxxymiron, 77

Paley, Maggie, 203
Paraguay, 92
Partnership for Peace (PFP), 37
Pasternak, Boris, 72
Patriarchate of Russian Orthodoxy, 54–55
Patrushev, Nikolai, x
People's Liberation Army (PLA), 145
People's Republic of China. *See* China
Peskov, Dmitry, 113
Peter I (Peter the Great), 15–16, 31, 60, 68
Philippines, 162, 163–65
Phoenix News Media, 6
Pierce, William Luther, 213
Pin Ho, 7
Plott, David, 222
poets, 70, 72, 73, 74–76
Poland, ix, 14, 16, 17, 21, 25, 31, 34, 38, 56, 61, 66, 115, 176; losses in World War II, 82n22; Western protection, 33
Popov, Nikolai, 222
power, hard and soft, xv
Prigozhin, Yevgeny, xv, 78, 137–38
Prince Igor, 14
Prison Diaries (Kuznetzov), 73
Project Dove, 210–11
Prokhanov, Aleksandr, 54–61, 62
Prokofiev, Sergei, 70
public opinion on Russia-Ukraine war: in Russia, 89–93; in Ukraine, 96–98; in United States, 98
propaganda, xi
Pushkin, Aleksandr, 17, 31, 62, 70, 193, 198, 219
Putin, Vladimir, ix, 25–29; on annexation of Crimea, 9; blunders committed by, 133–34; corruption, 92–93; expanding personal power and realm, 84–85; inauguration speech, 31; Ivashov on, 1, 2; law banning fake news, 67; as mafioso dictator, 68; NATO and, 84; oligarchs and, 137; passivity of Russians, 87; private armies, 78; public opinion on, 90; repression, 66, 94; as risen Christ, 54–56; *siloviki* and, 137; as spin

dictator, 133; ultranationalists and, 54–56; vision of a "Russian world," 12. *See also* Russia

Qatar, 2n2
Qatar-Turkey pipeline, 2
Qianlong, 174
Qing dynasty, 142, 174
Quemoy (Kinmen) islands crisis, 160

Rabin, Oskar, 71–72
Rachinsky, Yan, 87
Rand, Ayn, 202, 203, 213; *Atlas Shrugged*, 213; *The Fountainhead*, 202
Red Army, 19, 20, 53, 82, 105, 205
Reagan, Ronald, 157; election victory, 157n13; Strategic Defense Initiative, 180
religious identity, 27–28. *See also* Orthodox Christians/Christianity
reparations, Chinese, 126–29
reparations to Ukraine, xiii, 99–122; for damaged assets and environment, 105–12; for lives damaged and lost, 103–5; Marshall Plan, 114–15; precedents, 99–103
Republic, The (Plato).119

representative government, 182, 182n15, 184
responsibility to protect, 99
"River Elegy" (documentary), 143
Robinson, George, 84
Romance of the Three Kingdoms (Luo Guanzhong), 159
Romeo and Juliet (Prokofiev), 70
Romney, Mitt, xi, xii, xiii
Rosenberg, Elizabeth, 113
Rosenberg, Steve, 85
Rosenfeld, Bryn, 91
Rose Revolution of Georgia, 26
Rossiskaya, 16
Rostekha, 91
Rostropovich, Mstislav, 73
RT (Kremlin's cable TV), 44, 45–46
Rukh, 23
rules-based maritime order, 162
Rus', 9, 13–14, 15–16
Rushdie, Salman, 205
Russia, 16; categorization, 82–85; censorship of foreign publications, 56; China and, 147–61; as a commodities exporter, 118; Corruption Perceptions Index, 92–93; domestic production, 118–19; economy, 86, 115–20; elections, 135; foreign or

world trade, 116–18; as fragile state, 94; Freedom House reports on, 94; GDP, 115, 118; Global Innovation Index, 94, 119; historical background, 14–18; Human Development Index, 93; masking, 77–82; metaphysics and Realpolitik, 61–64; military expenditure, 119; military industrial complex, 59, 91; National Security Strategy, 49, 51; National Wealth Fund, 119; Nobel prizes, 96; oil and gas, 117–18; Orthodoxy and military values, 53–54; as part of Europe, 82–85; passivity of people, 87; public discontent, 95–96; religious identity, 27–28; self-rule, 136; spiritual and moral values, 49–53; as Third Rome, 61–64; United States and, 155–65, 172–73, 174–75; utopia and dystopia in, 191–205; value of a human life, 103–4; world and, 85–88; World Happiness Index, 95. *See also* reparations to Ukraine; Soviet Union; Tsarist Russia/Russian Empire; Ukraine, Russian invasion of

Russia Hand, The (Talbott), 40

Russian Orthodox Church, 28, 49, 54, 56, 61, 64

Russian World, 12, 30, 49–53, 139

Russkii, 16

Russkii Obraz (RO), 43–44

Rutskoy, Aleksandr, 34, 135

Ryan, Kevin, xi

Sackur, Stephen, 87

Sakharov, Andrei, 57, 73, 168, 178–80, 219–20

Salih, Mazhar Muhammad, 103n7

Salisbury, Harrison E., 219

SARS epidemic, Chinese government's cover-up of, 124–26

Savranskaya, Svetlana, 32–33

School Library Journal, 204

Schuman, Robert, 114

Seleznev, Nikita, 67

Serebrennikov, Kirill, 68

Shayevich, Bela, 191

Shevardnadze, Eduard, 33

Shevchenko, Taras, 18–19

Sholokhov, Mikhail, 72

Shostakovich, Dmitri, 70

Shtein, Boris, 76

Siberia, 83, 155–56

Silver Age, Russia, xiv

Slaughterhouse-Five (Vonnegut), 204, 205

Slavophiles, 62–64

Smyslov, Vadim, 67

Snyder, Timothy, 10, 76

social field, 184
socialist realism, 71
societal fitness, 12
Solius, Maxim, 67
Solovyev, Vladimir, 62
Solzhenitsyn, Aleksandr, 72, 178, 179
Sotoudeh, Nasrin, 88
South China Sea, 123, 130, 212; US and China on, 161–65
South China Sea Arbitral Tribunal, 163
South China Sea Arbitration Awards: A Critical Study, The, 163
Sovetskaya Rossiya, 1n1
Soviet Union: art and artists, 71–72; collectivization, 20, 89; dissolution, 24; empire, xi; formation of, 19; Jews/Jewish in, 71–77; power and influence, 147; Ukraine and, 19–24; union-republics added to, 19. *See also* Gorbachev; Khrushchev; Russia; Stalin
Spaak, Paul-Henri, 114
Special Military Operation (SMO): protests against, 92; public opinion on, 89–90
spirit of trade, 182–83
spiritual and moral values, 49–53
Spring, Summer, Fall, Winter… and Spring, 224

Squid Game, 213–14
Stalin, Iosif, xv, 20, 22, 42, 56, 60–61, 70, 72, 104, 114, 167–68, 172, 176, 198; antisemitism, 76; collectivization, 20, 89; death, 20, 71; Mao and, 156; nationalism and, 11; Soviet Constitution and, 3; union-republics added by, 19; World War II and, 20, 78–82
Stanford University, 45–46
Starr, S.F., 220
START I treaty, 177
Steshin, Dmitri, 44
Stimson Doctrine, 176
Stone, Jeremy, 220–21
Subplot (Walsh), 205–6
Suleimenov, Olzhas, 14, 14n9
Sun Yat-sen, 143
Sweden, 13, 14, 16, 31; Global Innovation Index, 119; NATO and, 46, 47; Nobel prizes, 96
Switzerland, 93
Symphony No. 13 (Shostakovich), 70
Synthesis, 10

tactical nuclear weapons, x
Taiwan, xii, 11, 123, 131, 141, 145, 185, 217–18, 222; Corruption Perceptions Index, 93

Talbott, Strobe, 38, 39–40; *The Russia Hand,* 40

Taoist harmony, xv

Tatars, 12, 16, 20, 29–30, 43, 79, 83, 105. *See also* Crimea

Tchaikovsky, Pyotr Ilyich, ix, 31, 70

technological totalitarianism, 210

Testament (Shevchenko), 18–19

Thomas, Clarence, 123n24

Thoreau, H.D. and Walden, 223-24

Three-Body Problem, The (Liu Cixin), 208

Thucydides, 154, 165, 175

Tiananmen Square crackdown/massacre, 124, 125, 127, 143, 157–58, 210

Tibet/Tibetans, ix, 18, 99, 122, 123, 127, 130, 145, 148, 210

Tikhanovsky, Sergei, 201–2

Tikhonov, Nikita, 44

Tikhonova, Katerina, 67

Tinkov, Oleg, 56

Tocqueville, Alexis de, 213

Tolliver, Sandra, 222

Tolstoy, Lev, 62, 70, 226

Tong Zhao, 7, 153

Toynbee, Arnold, 10

triangular diplomacy, 157

Trigga, Anna, 44

Truman, Harry, 162n20

Trump, Donald, 158–59, 173, 180, 214

Tsai Ing-wen, 185

Tsarist Russia: empire, 12, 15–17, 19, 20, 31, 61, 63; Bloody Sunday, 134; boyars, 136; features, 65–66; Narodniki, 136–37; Zamyatin and, 198. *See also* Russia

Turgenev, Ivan, 64

Turner Diaries, The (Pierce), 213

Tyutchev, Fyodor, 62–64; "Vision," 181

Ukraine: x; citizenship, 24; Corruption Perceptions Index, 92, 93; economy, 97–98; as fragile state, 94; Global Innovation Index, 119; historical background, 14–18; independent, 24–25; issues defining relationship with Russia, 25; Khrushchev and, 20, 21–22, 23; language law, 23; National Anti-Corruption Strategy, 93; national revival, 23; National Security Strategy, 46; NATO and, 46–47; Nazi rule, 42–46; nuclear weapon, 25, 37; Orange Revolution, 25–26; Orthodox population, 28; parliamentary democracy, 23–24; public opinion in, 96–98; religious identity,

27–28; religious revival, 23; self-organized fitness, 12, 28–29; Soviet rule, 19–24; US arms and military assistance, 46–47; as a virtual colony, 18. *See also* Russia

Ukraine, Russian invasion of: ix; damaging assets and environment, 105–12; Gao on, 5–7; Ivashov on, 1–3; justification or reasons for, 9, 31, 42–47; lives damaged and lost, 103–5; reparations for (*See* reparations to Ukraine); UN resolutions, 168–72

Ukrainian Autocephalous Orthodox Church, 23

Ukrainian Orthodox Church, 28

UN Charter Article 51, 3

UN Compensation Commission (UNCC), 102–3, 112, 120

UN General Assembly: resolution deploring Russia's invasion of Ukraine, 170–71; Resolution ES-11/4, 168–69; "Uniting for Peace" Resolution 377 (V), 168, 168n1

United States, 28, 147; Chechen War and, 35, 38–40; China and, 155–65, 172–73, 174–75; Corruption Perceptions Index, 93; as fragile state, 94; Gao on role of, 6–7; interventions and invasions, 183; losses in World War II, 82n22; Marshall Plan, 114–15; policy dilemmas for, 34–38; public opinion on supporting Ukraine, 98; Supreme Court, 123n24; third-party arbitration of disputes, 183; U.S.-Philippines Mutual Defense Treaty of 1951, 164; utopia and dystopia in, 212–14

"Uniting for Peace" Resolution 377 (V), 168, 168n1

universal values, 49, 51

UN Law of the Sea Convention (UNCLOS), 162, 163, 164

utopia and dystopia, 191–214; in China, 205–12; in Russia, 191–205; in United States, 212–14

Uyghurs, xiii, 17–18, 122, 211

values: military, 53–54; spiritual and moral, 49–53; universal, 49, 51

Venezuela, 92

Vietnam, ix, 162, 183, 184

Vikings, 13

Vinogradov, Oleg, 69

Vinokurov, Vladimir, xiin6

"Vision" (Tyutchev), 181

Volodymyr the Great, 14

Vonnegut, Kurt, 204

Wagner Group, xv, 138

Walsh, Megan, 205–6

Wandering Earth, The (Liu Cixin), 208
Wandering Earth (film), 209–10
War Historical Archive, 78
war losses, ix
WeChat, 210
WE (film), 192
Weiss, Jessica Chen, 174
WE (Zamyatin), 54, 191–98, 199, 201
When Will You Ever Learn? (Litvinova), 67
Where Have All the Flowers Gone? (Seeger), 67
Wiesner, Jerome B., 220–21
Wild Lilly, 185
World Happiness Index, 95
World Trade Organization, 131, 158
writers in Soviet Union, 70–73
Wu, Empress of Tang dynasty, 207n17
Wu Jing, 209–10

Xie Yanyi, 123–24
Xi Jinping, ix, 17, 210; Chinese civilization and, 11, 66; civilizational relativism and, 130, 131; economy and, 139; elite displeasure with, 174; Global Security Initiative, 7; Global South and, 7; policies and actions, 139–42; on poverty, 93; Putin and, 89, 147, 148–49, 155, 161; statist and nationalist policy agenda, 139; war on law, 123–24. *See also* China
Xinjiang, 127, 129, 211

Yale School of Management, 118
Yalta Conference, 20
Yanukovych, Viktor, 25, 26
Yeltsin, Boris, 24, 34–42, 55; challenges, 38–42; Chechen War of 1994-1996, 35, 38–40; Clinton and, 34, 35, 36, 37, 39, 40, 135; collapse of the USSR, 3, 34; Collins on, 36; designating Putin as successor, 40, 135; dissolving and attacking parliament in 1993, 34–35, 135; Evangelista on, 38–39; oligarchs and, 137; political rivals, 34; Talbott on, 38, 39–40; Zabushko on, 22. *See also* Russia
Yemen, 94
Yermolenko, Volodymyr, 17
Yevtushenko, Yevgeny, 74, 75–77
Yin and Yang, ix
"Yin and Yang of China's Power" (Shree Jain and Sukalpa Chakrabarti), xvn9
younger generation in Russia, xi
Yushchenko, Viktor, 25–26

Zabushko, Oksana, 22

Zakharov, Andrey, 67–68

Zambia, 93

Zamyatin, Yevgeny, 54, 191

Zaporozhian Cossacks, 16–17

Zavtra, 42, 54, 55–56, 57, 60, 62, 222

Zelenskyy, Volodymyr, xii, 43, 86; on cost to rebuilding Ukraine, 109; measures against pro-Moscow oligarchs, 28; National Security Strategy, 46; on Qatar, 2n2; Xi Jinping and, 154

Zeleny Svit ("Green World"), 23

Zemfira (Russian rock singer), 67

Zemskov, Nikolai, 80

Zemskov, Viktor N., 79–80, 80n18

Zen, Joseph, 88

Zhirinovsky, Vladimir, 55

Zhou Enlai, 172

Zilboorg, Gregory, 191

Related Titles from Westphalia Press

The Limits of Moderation: Jimmy Carter and the Ironies of American Liberalism
by Leo P. Ribuffo

The Limits of Moderation: Jimmy Carter and the Ironies of American Liberalism is not a finished product. Yet, this book is a close and careful history of a short yet transformative period in American political history, when big changes were afoot. and continue to shape our world.

Bunker Diplomacy: An Arab-American in the U.S. Foreign Service
by Nabeel Khoury

After twenty-five years in the Foreign Service, Dr. Nabeel A. Khoury retired from the U.S. Department of State in 2013 with the rank of Minister Counselor. In his last overseas posting, Khoury served as deputy chief of mission at the U.S. embassy in Yemen (2004-2007).

Energy Law and Policy in a Climate-Constrained World
by Victor Byers Flatt, Alfonso López de la Osa Escribano, Aubin Nzaou-Kongo

This book presents reflections on concepts, foreign policy, regional and international cooperation, and the specific role the state is to play when it comes to such thing as energy law and policy.

The Zelensky Method
by Grant Farred

Locating Russian's war within a global context, The Zelensky Method is unsparing in its critique of those nations, who have refused to condemn Russia's invasion and are doing everything they can to prevent economic sanctions from being imposed on the Kremlin.

The Lord of the Desert: A Study of the Papers of the British Officer John B. Glubb in Jordan and Iraq
by Dr. Sa'ad Abudayeh

John Bajot Glubb, a British engineer officer, was sent to Iraq in 1920 to resolve the problems which erupted after the Iraqi revolt. He remained in the area for ten years, working with the Bedouins. In 1930, he moved to Jordan for twenty-six successful years. He invented what Dr. Abudayeh calls the Diplomacy of Desert.

Managing Challenges for the Flint Water Crisis
Edited by Toyna E. Thornton, Andrew D. Williams, Katherine M. Simon, Jennifer F. Sklarew

This edited volume examines several public management and intergovernmental failures, with particular attention on social, political, and financial impacts. Understanding disaster meaning, even causality, is essential to the problem-solving process.

Resistance: Reflections on Survival, Hope and Love
Poetry by William Morris, Photography by Jackie Malden

Resistance is a book of poems with photographs or a book of photographs with poems depending on your perspective. The book is comprised of three sections titled respectively: On Survival, On Hope, and On Love.

Abortion and Informed Common Sense
by Max J. Skidmore

The controversy over a woman's "right to choose," as opposed to the numerous "rights" that abortion opponents decide should be assumed to exist for "unborn children," has always struck me as incomplete. Two missing elements of the argument seems obvious, yet they remain almost completely overlooked.

Geopolitics of Outer Space: Global Security and Development
by Ilayda Aydin

A desire for increased security and rapid development is driving nation-states to engage in an intensifying competition for the unique assets of space. This book analyses the Chinese-American space discourse from the lenses of international relations theory, history and political psychology to explore these questions.

The Athenian Year Primer: Attic Time-Reckoning and the Julian Calendar
by Christopher Planeaux

The ability to translate ancient Athenian calendar references into precise Julian-Gregorian dates will not only assist Ancient Historians and Classicists to date numerous historical events with much greater accuracy but also aid epigraphists in the restorations of numerous Attic inscriptions.

The Politics of Fiscal Responsibility: A Comparative Perspective
by Tonya E. Thornton and F. Stevens Redburn

Fiscal policy challenges following the Great Recession forced members of the Organisation for Economic Co-operation and Development (OECD) to implement a set of economic policies to manage public debt.

China & Europe: The Turning Point
by David Baverez

In creating five fictitious conversations between Xi Jinping and five European experts, David Baverez, who lives and works in Hong Kong, offers up a totally new vision of the relationship between China and Europe.

Issues in Maritime Cyber Security
Edited by Dr. Joe DiRenzo III, Dr. Nicole K. Drumhiller, and Dr. Fred S. Roberts

The complexity of making MTS safe from cyber attack is daunting and the need for all stakeholders in both government (at all levels) and private industry to be involved in cyber security is more significant than ever as the use of the MTS continues to grow.

Freemasonry, Heir to the Enlightenment
by Cécile Révauger

Modern Freemasonry may have mythical roots in Solomon's time but is really the heir to the Enlightenment. Ever since the early eighteenth century freemasons have endeavored to convey the values of the Enlightenment in the cultural, political and religious fields, in Europe, the American colonies and the emerging United States.

Growing Inequality: Bridging Complex Systems, Population Health, and Health Disparities
Editors: George A. Kaplan, Ana V. Diez Roux, Carl P. Simon, and Sandro Galea

Why is America's health is poorer than the health of other wealthy countries and why health inequities persist despite our efforts? In this book, researchers report on groundbreaking insights to simulate how these determinants come together to produce levels of population health and disparities and test new solutions.

Contests of Initiative: Countering China's Gray Zone Strategy in the East and South China Seas
by Dr. Raymond Kuo

China is engaged in a widespread assertion of sovereignty in the South and East China Seas. It employs a "gray zone" strategy: using coercive but sub-conventional military power to drive off challengers and prevent escalation, while simultaneously seizing territory and asserting maritime control.

Brought to Light: The Mysterious George Washington Masonic Cave
by Jason Williams, MD

The George Washington Masonic Cave near Charles Town, West Virginia, contains a signature carving of George Washington dated 1748. Although this inscription appears authentic, it has yet to be verified by historical accounts or scientific inquiry.

Frontline Diplomacy: A Memoir of a Foreign Service Officer in the Middle East
by William A. Rugh

In short vignettes, this book describes how American diplomats working in the Middle East dealt with a variety of challenges over the last decades of the 20th century. Each of the vignettes concludes with an insight about diplomatic practice derived from the experience.

westphaliapress.org

Policy Studies Organization

The Policy Studies Organization (PSO) is a publisher of academic journals and book series, sponsor of conferences, and producer of programs.

Policy Studies Organization publishes dozens of journals on a range of topics, such as European Policy Analysis, Journal of Elder Studies, Indian Politics & Polity, Journal of Critical Infrastructure Policy, and Popular Culture Review.

Additionally, Policy Studies Organization hosts numerous conferences. These conferences include the Middle East Dialogue, Space Education and Strategic Applications Conference, International Criminology Conference, Dupont Summit on Science, Technology and Environmental Policy, World Conference on Fraternalism, Freemasonry and History, and the Internet Policy & Politics Conference.

For more information on these projects, access videos of past events, and upcoming events, please visit us at:

www.ipsonet.org

www.ingramcontent.com/pod-product-compliance
Lightning Source LLC
Chambersburg PA
CBHW051533020426
42333CB00016B/1902